TRANSFARMATION

TRANSFARMATION

THE MOVEMENT TO FREE US FROM FACTORY FARMING

LEAH GARCÉS

BEACON PRESS ◼ BOSTON

BEACON PRESS
Boston, Massachusetts
www.beacon.org

Beacon Press books
are published under the auspices of
the Unitarian Universalist Association of Congregations.

27 26 25 24   8 7 6 5 4 3 2 1

This book is printed on acid-free paper that meets the uncoated paper
ANSI/NISO specifications for permanence as revised in 1992.

Text design and composition by Kim Arney

While the author and publisher have made every effort to ensure the information
in this book is accurate, they make no guarantee of accuracy, adequacy, or
completeness and they disclaim liability for any losses or damages related to any
errors, omissions, inaccuracies, or inconsistencies. This book does not guarantee
any results or outcomes and is not a substitute for the reader's performance of
any and all reasonable due diligence, including consulting independent financial,
legal, medical, agricultural, or other expert advisors.

This book depicts real individuals and events, though some individuals' names and
identifying details have been changed to maintain their privacy. The views, opinions,
and experiences of the individuals depicted herein belong solely to them and
do not necessarily represent those of the author or the publisher.

The Transfarmation Project® is a registered trademark owned by Mercy For Animals,
Inc. As used in this book, the terms "Transfarmation," "Transfarmation project,"
and "Transfarmation program" all refer to the Transfarmation Project®.

Library of Congress Cataloguing-in-Publication
Data is available for this title.
Hardcover ISBN: 978-0-8070-1490-5
E-book ISBN: 978-0-8070-1491-2
Audiobook: 978-0-8070-1710-4

Dedicated to Bo, Henrietta, and Elsie,
and all who suffer at the hands of factory farming.

Better days are coming.

CONTENTS

Introduction   ix

PART ONE: THE FARMERS

CHAPTER ONE   From Chickens to Hemp and Dog Rescue   3

CHAPTER TWO   From Chickens to Mushrooms   20

CHAPTER THREE   From Chickens to Greenhouses   32

CHAPTER FOUR   The Last Pigs   45

PART TWO: THE ANIMALS

CHAPTER FIVE   The Year of Henrietta the Hen   61

CHAPTER SIX   Felix the Pig   79

CHAPTER SEVEN   Norma the Cow   92

PART THREE: THE COMMUNITIES

CHAPTER EIGHT   Eastern North Carolina Communities of Color:
                    Rosemary and René   107

CHAPTER NINE   Immigrants: Sandra, Leticia, Marisol, and Carmen   121

CHAPTER TEN   Refugees: Tom, Mykia, and Maykeu   143

CONCLUSION   Harvesting Change: A Vision Toward a Humane,
                    Sustainable, and Just Food and Farming System   156

                    Acknowledgments   173
                    Notes   175
                    Index   192

INTRODUCTION

IN THE SPRING OF 2014, I found myself sitting across from a man who was by every definition my enemy. His name was Craig Watts and he was a chicken factory farmer, raising chickens for slaughter. My career is devoted to protecting farmed animals and ending factory farming. Until that point, I'd spent my whole life working against everything Craig Watts stood for. Now I was sitting in his living room.

As I sat there, a thousand questions were swirling in my mind. I'd been trying for years to get footage from inside a chicken factory farm at a time in our country when seeing inside a chicken farm was—and still is—nearly impossible. I'd failed every previous attempt.

That day, I'd driven from my home in Atlanta to Craig's home in rural North Carolina. Before I left, I gave my husband the address and told him, "If I don't come back, look for me rotting away in the chicken litter." I was convinced I was heading into an ambush, not knowing my life would soon be changed forever.

Prior to our meeting, Craig Watts had been raising chickens for twenty-two years in factory farms for Perdue, the fourth-largest chicken company in the United States. When Craig was a young adult, he had searched for a way to stay on the land that had been passed down in his family for five generations, in one of the poorest counties in North Carolina. There were very few jobs in the area, so when Perdue came to town and offered him a contract to raise chickens, it sounded like a dream come true. He took out a $200,000 loan from the bank to build the chicken houses while Perdue agreed to pay him for each flock he raised. With that money, he planned to pay off the loan, as you would a mortgage.

But soon the chickens started to get sick—it was a factory farm, after all. Twenty-five thousand chickens were stuffed wall-to-wall in darkened warehouses, living on their own feces, breathing air thick with toxic ammonia. Many of the sick chickens died, and you don't get paid for dead chickens. Craig started to struggle to pay off his loan. His paychecks got smaller, but the bills kept coming. Soon he wanted out, but he'd been trapped. Now he was all but an indentured servant, and if he stopped, he'd risk losing everything.

By the time he and I met, Craig had reached a breaking point. His payments seemed never-ending, and so did the illness, death, and despair of the chickens. He was ready for a change. Through late afternoon conversations, and much soul-searching, I realized that I had overlooked an ally. I learned that chicken factory farmers wanted to see factory farming change about as much as animal rights activists did. We had been overlooking each other all these years.

Throughout the summer of 2014, I came back many times with my filmmaker partner Raegan Hodge to learn from Craig. I walked those warehouses as Craig explained the problems, as he picked up the chickens who had died or had to be killed because they had messed-up legs, trouble breathing, difficulty walking. All of these horrors, all of our conversations, were captured on film.

In the winter of 2014, after months of filming and learning to trust each other, Craig and I did something neither of us expected to do. We decided to release the footage together. This was a huge risk. He feared losing his income, his land, and having his neighbors hate him. But he did it anyway. The *New York Times* broke the story. Within twenty-four hours, a million people had seen our video about the horrors of chicken factory farming. Our story went viral. Suddenly, we had a megaphone. Our unlikely alliance put the truth about factory farming on a global platform.

Too often we become so entrenched in our values, in our fight, that we don't stop to consider what we might have in common with the so-called opposition. We jump straight to the differences. And it is often the tyranny of small differences that holds progress hostage. Craig was the very first chicken factory farmer I ever connected with, but there would be many more.

In the United States, we still hold close an image of a quaint, independent family farm. But what actually exists is industrial animal agriculture, a system that does more harm than good. If you cross the country, no matter what state you are in, you'll find a similar story. There is a person in a poor rural county who is searching for a way to stay on the land that had been passed down in their family for generations, searching for a way to make their living off the land and live out their version of the American dream, one in tune with nature and set to the soundtrack of crickets, cicadas, warblers, and chickadees. With few jobs around, the chicken industry's offer sounds like a dream come true. This farmer often ends up just like Craig.

Meeting Craig would change my trajectory as an activist. We'd become close friends, collaborators, and conspirators in the decade that followed, working to dismantle factory farming piece by piece. We'd see that we'd been fooled. As Craig said: "We were red ants and black ants trapped in a jar. And then someone would shake the jar and we'd start fighting each other. But we'd never stop to question—who's shaking the jar?" And I'd ask, "Why are we trapped in *this* jar?" The years ahead, we'd look to smash the jar and remove the shaker's power. We'd look to reform our food system away from industrial animal agriculture and remove the power of Big Animal Agriculture—the great monopolies with strongholds over our political and economic systems.

If humans tried to design a farming system that was horribly cruel, dirty, and unjust, we could not have come up with anything worse than factory farming. We inflict unquantifiable suffering on billions of sentient beings—many of them proven to be more intelligent than the companion animals we share our homes with. This normalized atrocity is something I've had to come to live with. I don't accept it, but I do endure it out of necessity.

Eighty billion land animals (excluding fish, shrimp, crabs, lobsters, and the like) come to live and die for our palettes and preferences, in the most horrific conditions, those that would result in jail if the same were done to a dog or cat.[1] Yet instead it is simply the way business is done.

That's not just a problem for the animals. Collectively, farmed animals emit more greenhouse gases than the world's planes, trains, and automobiles put together. A third of our precious arable land is used to grow feed for factory-farmed animals rather than food we humans could eat directly. We spray this land with immeasurable amounts of chemicals and cut down ecologically important habitats like rainforests—mostly notably right now with the clearing of the Amazon—all to feed and "house" animals on factory farms. Put simply, industrial animal agriculture is one of the most destructive industries on our planet.

The way things are going, my children will never see a wild polar bear or elephant. In precisely my lifetime, the total number of birds, amphibians, mammals, and reptiles in the world has halved. One of the main culprits? Industrial animal agriculture.

Added to that is the fact that this food system keeps farmers in soul-crushing debt, communities sick and workers living in fear with little freedom. It truly is the most horrific system we could have come up with to deliver our calories.

But one can't just smash a jar before thinking about solutions. What happens when you smash the jar? Where do we go from here? How do we rebuild a world of our own design? Craig and I had an idea, and we weren't the only ones. Around the country, fed-up farmers were starting to ask: What else? What else can we do with this land, these structures, our lives?

Mike Weaver in West Virginia was another one of the first farmers I met. Fed up with the debt, death and despair of factory farming, in 2018, he gave up the business of raising chickens for good and made the transition to repurpose his warehouses to grow industrial hemp. In doing so, he employed far more people (adding jobs to the struggling local economy), used a fraction of the water and energy, provided a healing rather than harmful product to consumers, made a lot more money, and, of course, caused no animal suffering. It was an experience like no other to see this transformation taking place before my eyes. I had worked with Mike to expose what was happening on his chicken farm a couple of years earlier, and now he was on the other side, actively building an alternative, blazing a new path, and serving as a model for what the future could look like for factory farmers all over the world.

As I started to travel the country looking for solutions to end factory farming, I met farmers rolling up their sleeves, as they always do, ready to innovate, create and work hard. I heard their stories of hardship, but also hope. And farmers weren't the only ones I met who were affected by the destructive path of factory farming and looking for a way forward. I met the communities who were also affected but had no say in the surrounding farms' construction or ongoing existence. I observed the conflict this created between farmers and communities—another case of red ant versus black ant in a shaken jar. I also saw the animals. The animals who suffered. I looked into their eyes while they were clearly in pain. I even met those who through some cosmic grace escaped and now enjoyed their freedom in homes or sanctuaries.

Then the most unexpected of events accelerated our development of a solution: a global pandemic. The pandemic shone a spotlight on factory farming, exposing it as a fragile and cruel system in desperate need of an overhaul.

THE NEXT PANDEMIC

In the new year of 2020, my spouse, an epidemiologist who works on viruses, sent me a disturbing article. He and his colleagues were tracking a novel virus in China, seemingly emerging from wet markets in the city of Wuhan. On January 17, I wrote a blog that asked the question, "Are We on the Cusp of a Pandemic Flu?"[2] At the time it was meant to be a provocative title, drawing attention to how humans' treatment of other animals puts our health at risk. Never did I expect the answer to my question to be an earth-shattering yes.

While our lives became suspended by a virus, my work became busier than ever, albeit now it was conducted from my basement and over Zoom. The virus thrust a mirror in front of society, exposing industrial animal agriculture, the system through which 99 percent of meat, eggs, and dairy products are produced in America. We saw how this food system stood on a house of cards.

For years, global health experts have pointed to the livestock sector as the most likely origin of a pathogen that could spark a pandemic. The Food and Agriculture Organization of the United Nations has even stated that in terms of infectious diseases, "livestock health is the weakest link in our global health chain."[3] In fact, an FAO report found that 70 percent of diseases that have emerged in humans in recent decades are "in part, directly related to the human quest for more animal-sourced food."[4]

We may never know exactly where the virus that causes COVID-19 originated. But we've long known that the way we farm animals for food today—crammed indoors by the thousands, sickened by their filthy surroundings, stressed beyond belief, mutilated as common practice, and constantly drugged at low doses—creates *the perfect* incubator for new diseases like COVID-19 to emerge, spread, strengthen, and leap to human hosts. Similarly, the destruction of habitat to make way for animal factories raises the risk that a virus will jump from an animal raised for food to wildlife or to humans.

It's happened again and again, and it'll happen in the future. It's not a question of *if*, but when. Because big farms lead to big flu.[5]

Indeed, public health experts have sounded the alarm for decades about the risk of a pandemic. Bill Gates called the COVID-19 pandemic a once-in-a-century event.[6] While it's true that the last devastating pandemic happened around one hundred years ago, the chance of another is unaffected by the one we are having now. It's like a game of dice: rolling "snake eyes" doesn't bear on whether you'll roll ones again. We're rolling the dice faster than ever, and now we know what happens when our luck runs out.

COVID-19 has taken an extraordinary toll on human health and the economy. This fact should be reason enough to reimagine our global food system. Combine pandemic risk with the multitude of other harms that industrial animal agriculture inflicts on our health and the environment—chronic disease epidemics,[7] antibiotic resistance,[8] climate change,[9] and deforestation[10]—and we've got what amounts to the most pressing public health and ecological crisis of this century.

The United Nations sums up "the world's most urgent problem" in one word: "meat."[11]

With meatpacking workers standing shoulder to shoulder while the rest of the nation stood six feet apart, it was no surprise that slaughterhouses became COVID-19 hot spots. The first story to hit the headlines came from a Smithfield slaughterhouse in South Dakota early in the pandemic. This plant became one of the nation's largest hotspots for COVID-19. Within months, every major poultry company was reporting processing problems owing to worker outbreaks and related worker shortages.[12] The higher rates of COVID among slaughterhouse workers (many of whom are people of color or recent immigrants) spotlighted the compounding effects of racial inequity—how living on the margins exposes someone to greater harm from illnesses like this. Tragically, few populations are more vulnerable than these workers and their families.

When it comes to the meat, dairy, and eggs we eat, the price at the grocery store or restaurant is never a fair reflection of the true cost. In factory farming, risks and liability are mostly externalized by the industry, and most often to the most vulnerable among us. This damage, this harm, is borne by many—from the workers to the animals to the farmers. The industry makes extraordinary profits off this harm by externalizing risk and liability. Externalities are the root of the business model, and they've driven the spectacular success, power, and wealth of this industry. But because these costs are hidden from those who purchase the products, consumers don't affirmatively consent to the harm caused by eating animals and their products.

The workforce in slaughterhouses, the communities living around factory farming, and, in recent years, refugee communities who've been brought in as the next generation of farming communities are some of the most affected. These vulnerable communities lack political and social capital, and they have few choices and little ability to fight against the harm that factory farming imposes upon them.

In slaughterhouses, some immigrant workers have documentation and some don't, but regardless of their situation, if they complain they take risks. When people die on the job, the federal agencies don't respond 85 percent of the time, according to Civil Eats.[13] Agricultural work is some of the most dangerous work in the country, ranking third among all occupations in fatal injuries together with forestry, fishing, and hunting. According to Civil Eats, animal confinement workers are subject to long-term lung and acute respiratory injuries from their work environments and are exposed to asphyxiating gases from manure.

Black communities in the South, many of whom are descendants of enslaved people, are also disproportionately affected by factory farms. Maps of North Carolina clearly show higher clusters of factory farms surrounding historically Black and low-income rural communities. Studies indicate that in some communities in North Carolina, for example, there are ten times more concentrated animal feeding operations (CAFOs) in low-income and Black and Brown neighborhoods than in higher income, whiter areas.[14] This is a clear example of environmental racism, a form of institutional racism where environmental hazards and harms are disproportionately distributed in and around communities of color. Where once these communities enjoyed the land that meant so much to their families' freedom and history, that enjoyment is now ruined. Now they are surrounded by hog and chicken farms, unable to even leave their homes without suffering the smells, flies, and even spray from the farm's waste.

As the pool of people willing to take on the perils of working in factory farms and slaughterhouses diminishes, the industry has begun to recruit a new, unsuspecting crop of factory farmers: refugees fleeing persecution in war-torn countries. From Burma to Cambodia to Laos, families looking for opportunity and escape come to the US and take on factory farming, only to find themselves trapped and unexpectedly in danger again.

Though farmers, workers, and animals have been suffering for decades, the system responsible for their collective oppression was thrust into the public eye during the pandemic. The attention it received was unprecedented, as was the desire for change.

TRANSFARMATION

During this time of great loss and uncertainty, the people closest to factory farming—farmers, slaughterhouse workers, and communities living next to factory farms—who had already begun to build a new way, accelerated their efforts. They were tired of feeling vulnerable to the fragility and oppression of factory farming.

In late 2019, Mercy For Animals, the organization I lead, launched a new project. We called it the "Transfarmation Project," and it aimed to be a platform where we could support farmers wanting to make the transition from animal agriculture to plants. It built on the work Craig and I started all those years earlier. But it ended up being so much more. In the years that followed, I would continue my curious journey through rural America, meeting farmers and together rolling up our sleeves to set out a road map for a new rural economy—everything from hemp to mushrooms to lettuce and whatever other innovations we could dream up.

It turns out that hundreds of farmers, maybe even thousands, want out of this model of despair. We rolled out our Transfarmation website, saying we would help farmers who were sick and tired of factory farming and wanted a way out, and even though there was no advertising campaign, hundreds of farmers immediately wrote to us. We had no idea the interest would be that high.

It wasn't just chicken farmers, either—pig and dairy farmers came to us as well. And while this book does not detail laying hens or cows raised for beef, the system is also broken there. This book and the Transfarmation Project have focused on pigs and chickens for a couple of reasons. First, the majority of pig and broiler chicken farmers, in particular, overwhelmingly work under contract rather than as independent farmers. The highest disproportionate rate of contract farming is in the broiler chicken sector, at 99 percent.[15] Trends indicate that hog farming is heading that way too. In 2015, 69 percent of pig farmers were under contract with a company. In some states it is more extreme. In North Carolina, for example, 91 percent of hog farmers were reported to be under contract by 2017.[16] Farmers under contract have little freedom and are the most saddled in terms of the debt and risk associated with raising animals for food. They thus tend to be the farmers that are the most eager for a way out. They are often stuck in cycles of debt, despair, and disillusionment, and lack control over how their own farms function.

Politicians have also woken up to the need for change. For example, in December 2019, Senator Cory Booker introduced the Farm System Reform Act.[17] It proposed monumental legislation to essentially ban factory farming as we know it. It proposed an immediate moratorium on the construction of new confined animal feeding operations and a plan to phase out the largest existing CAFOs by 2040. It would also create a $100 billion fund to help farmers transition out of factory farming, and impose liabilities and costs onto the industry, rather than workers and independent farmers, for all of the damage that factory farming creates—from pollution to injuries and illness.

Booker, a longtime vegan, visited farms and came to a realization about the debt and despair so many farmers suffered. In a *Vox* interview with Ezra Klein, he said: "We can't vilify each other. If we can't have compassion for people in these broken systems, then we're not going to have the compassion or coalitions to end these systems themselves."[18]

As the pandemic unfolded, and the industry's lack of accountability came into sharp focus, other leading politicians joined Booker's efforts. By

June 2020, Senators Elizabeth Warren and, by July, Bernie Sanders were cosponsors of the bill, putting ending factory farming on the agenda. In addition, Congress came to focus on the need to overhaul slaughterhouses. In July 2020, Representatives Marcia L. Fudge of Ohio, Rosa DeLauro of Connecticut, and Bennie Thompson of Mississippi introduced the Safe Line Speeds in COVID-19 Act to protect worker, food, and animal safety at meatpacking plants during the COVID-19 pandemic. Booker introduced companion legislation in the Senate.

When the government proposed to give bailout money to the animal farming industry for more mass on-farm slaughter, it was met with new resistance and a call for change.

Fueling this call for change is resistance to a business model that relies on keeping farmers and slaughterhouse workers in positions of debt and vulnerability, and animals in continual suffering. That commonly held image of the happy and independent farmer is part of an agenda, a "manufacturing of consent."[19] While most people assume that the burgers, nuggets, milk, eggs, and bacon they purchase in supermarkets comes from local family farms, the reality is 99 percent of all the animal products are derived from factory farms where animals, workers, and farmers are exploited for profit.[20]

This is a food system that prioritizes above all else maximizing profits for highly centralized companies and externalizes risks, costs, and harm wherever possible. Someone else is forced to take on the risks, the damage, and the debt. The cheapness of things rarely is just that.[21] Someone, somewhere else, is paying the price. As the United Nations Environment Programme recently said about industrial farming: "It's not quite the bargain it seems."[22]

The unending debt saddling America's chicken farmers, for example, is ingrained in the very success of how cheap chicken gets to our plates. In total, US individual chicken farmers and their families stomach $5.2 billion in debt for the task of delivering America's nuggets, tenders, and wings.[23] While the industry paints a picture of happy family farms, nothing could be further from the truth.

While these may seem like the hopeless circumstances of a deeply unjust system, in the past few years, with pressure on our food system increasing during COVID and the climate crisis, cracks have formed in the foundation. There are those who have managed to find an escape through those cracks, where light is shining through. They are, against all odds, building a new way. What follows are their inspiring journeys from hardship to hope.

This book is about more than individual farmers going through a career transition. It is about how we transition away entirely from factory farming. Many times, when people are tackling systemic challenges, they write about either the problem or the solution. But a gulf is left in the middle—the complexity of how. This book peers deeply into that gulf, at the transitional moment, and shows how it might be done, through the experience of those who are already doing it. It is told in three parts from the perspective of those closest to factory farming: farmers, the animals, and vulnerable communities working in or near factory farms or slaughterhouses.

This book is about smashing the jar and changing the common narrative that this food and farming system is serving us well. It is about rebuilding our food systems so that we are not trapped in a container, controlled by a monopoly causing us harm. Instead, we are in a collaborative, community-built network that honors all animals and nature, unlocks our highest potential, and empowers everyone to thrive.

TRANSFARMATION

PART ONE

THE FARMERS

CHAPTER ONE

FROM CHICKENS TO HEMP
AND DOG RESCUE

EVEN AFTER DECADES OF CHICKEN FARMING, Devvie Deany's family, the Halley family, in Cookville, Texas, owed $130,000. Now they were being asked by the mega-chicken company they were contracting with, Pilgrim's, to take out even more loans to upgrade their warehouses in order to meet the latest standards. The company wouldn't give them any more chickens unless they did. So now they were faced with a decision: take out more debt, which would tie them to raising chickens for even longer, or find a way out.

Devvie had seen the damage the chicken business had done to her twin brothers, her mother, and her late father. She had moved away from it all, to California, hoping to leave that life behind. She wanted nothing to do with the chicken farm. She'd turned vegan and rescued dogs. She never thought she'd find her true calling right back where she'd started—in rural northeast Texas.

But when the upgrade request came, Devvie and her partner, Evan, had to step in. Enough, she thought. She convinced her mother to stop chicken farming. Devvie and Evan had been doing research on the internet and came across a video that struck them. It shared the story of another ex-chicken farmer, Mike Weaver, in West Virginia. Just like them, he was tired of being under the thumb of mega-chicken and fed up with the death and despair the practice entailed. He was transitioning from growing chickens to growing hemp. He'd converted his chicken warehouses from the dingy, dark, and smelly caverns that once stuffed tens of thousands of chickens wall-to-wall, to warm, glowing grow lights and rows of hemp seedlings. His story, featured by the Transfarmation Project, showcased a new movement of farmers getting out of their debt and their hardships and finding a way to repurpose their animal warehouses for growing plants. Devvie and Evan couldn't believe there were other farmers like them, who also wanted to get out. Mike's story gave them hope. They thought maybe this was their way out.

In March of 2020, as the world shut down, my team that is working on the Transfarmation Project got a call from Devvie. After a few months of phone calls and building trust, Devvie and Evan agreed to have us come out and take a look at their warehouses and discuss plans for a transition.

It's not necessarily easy for farmers to just quit. Many are saddled with debt and their rural economies offer them few options. Devvie's family was no different. In order to get out of debt, they decided to sell off a portion of their land and use the money to pay off the rest of their debt. Now they had thirteen chicken warehouses sitting on their property, and they wanted to make something good of them, make a living that didn't involve killing chickens.

I didn't hesitate. Armed with my PPE, I prepared to leave my neighborhood for the first time in months. With the kids still in their beds, a dew of sweat on their heads on a hot August day, I kissed each one and slipped out of their bedrooms. The house was warm, too warm for an early summer morning. Ben stood in the doorway, steaming coffee in hand, and regarded me head cocked to the side. He was accustomed after twenty years of marriage to seeing me go forward without a precise plan, without the certainty of any outcome. I had packed the car with a set of materials that felt foreign at the time, but by now are all too familiar: face masks, nitrile gloves, hand sanitizer, alcohol wipes, and food and drink to last me for a week, including water and coffee, so that I didn't have to stop anywhere. I also packed the more familiar things like farm boots, an extra phone battery, headlamp, sunscreen, bug spray, and clothes I didn't mind destroying—that can absorb sweat, blood, feces, and dirt.

I headed out with the hope to meet Devvie, hatch plans with her family, and film their story, with Shawn Bannon, a talented video producer at Mercy For Animals—and a talented filmmaker in his own right—meeting me in Texas. After six months of being stuck in my house, and not being exposed firsthand to factory farming, I could almost believe factory farming was a myth, that it didn't exist, that it was a bad dream. I knew it would take just one breath inside an ammonia-laden house, one eyeful of suffering animals, to remind me of my purpose and my responsibility to change this unjust and broken food system. This trip would shake that rather comforting illusion.

Lost in thought, I reached Alabama only an hour or so from my home. The roads were strangely without traffic or obstacles, and I had been warned by my husband, who lived for a decade in Texas, that the road west from Atlanta is one of the most boring in the world and to brace myself for monotony. But at the time, I could think of nothing more thrilling.

Once outside Atlanta, the landscape relaxed, shifting from intense buildings and suburban communities to lines of tall pines, kudzu vines, and bushes with an untamable spirit. Deep summer green filled my peripheral view. As I passed through Mississippi's state capital, Jackson, I spotted glimpses of long metal warehouses that I knew to be factory farms. The tires across the rough road made a soothing rhythmic beat. The kudzu vines were so overgrown that at times it felt as if they might swallow up the road, giving a green tunnel illusion to the path ahead.

About two hours from my destination, I turned off the highway and began winding through rural parts of first Louisiana and then into East Texas. The landscape changed dramatically, filled with cows, fields, swamps, and lakes with forests of cypress trees growing in the middle of them. There were Texas flags and no real landmarks to speak of, except for the odd casino—Magic Money—and a scattering of Baptist churches. I slowed down for a raccoon who, in an unhurried fashion, crossed the road.

Shawn and I met that evening at our Airbnb and prepared for the day ahead. The next morning, we started the day with a little history lesson. We drove to the nearby city of Pittsburg. Remarkably, this was the origin city of Pilgrim's Pride, the second largest chicken company in the world. Bo and Aubrey Pilgrim, two brothers, came back from World War II and decided to start a chicken company. They bought a feed mill. Then they started contacting chicken farmers to sell their feed to.

Something similar had already happened in rural Georgia, where a man named Jesse Jewel had created an enterprise selling feed to chicken farmers. Once he made enough money from that, he started to hire the farmers to raise chickens, too, collecting the chickens at the end and bringing them to slaughter, cutting the farmers a check for the job of raising the birds. Eventually he also made enough to own his own slaughterhouse, thereby creating a closed loop where he could control every aspect up and down the production—known today as "vertical integration." It was the beginning of factory farming in the United States.

We visited the local heritage museum, where we got a tour from a man named Jim who told us the history of the town, which included a train depot that once had "colored" and "white" waiting rooms. They were pictures of Bo and Aubrey Pilgrim. There was a taxidermied chicken in a glass display. Jim told us that Bo brought this chicken everywhere with him. Her name was Henrietta. There's a cutout of Bo with Henrietta under his arm that once appeared in Pilgrim's Pride advertisements. Jim told us that the actual Henrietta was right there in the glass display. The stuffed bird had plastic eyes and plastic feet, but Jim insisted that was actually her. I was bewildered at this idea that Bo Pilgrim cared about Henrietta yet created a system for billions like her to live tortured lives. It showed the bizarre complexity of the people in charge of this industry, of people in general, how we can hold two competing, even conflicting, values at the same time.

Devvie's family started farming chickens thirty years ago, when poultry factory farming in the area was just getting started. Her father started as a farmer working for Bo Pilgrim himself. Initially, it was exciting for the area. It was a very small town, rural, and, before the poultry industry, there wasn't much by way of jobs. The opportunities for employment with the chicken industry and for families to make a better way of life seemed promising. Yet over time many families, including Devvie's, started seeing that the cost far outweighed the benefit. But by the time they realized that, it was too late.

Farmers started noticing the discrepancy between the poor struggling farmers and the well-off executives. The owners of Pilgrim's were doing just fine. They were able to employ a board and their CEO and executives, all of whom did quite well, with beautiful homes and places of business to show for it. But the farmers were struggling. Pieces of equipment couldn't be maintained. Pastures couldn't be groomed. It was difficult to keep cars running. Life just became tough.

When Devvie was growing up, there were moments when she would see her dad holding his head in his hands. He was a very proud person and so he didn't speak about how he was feeling, but she knew that he was worried. He had always been such a great provider for the family, but it felt fragile.

It was her twin brothers she worried about most. They were trapped, they couldn't leave the farm. There was always so much work to do, and there was no one else who could help with the farm because they didn't have the money to pay any extra people. The twins made a measly salary because the family couldn't afford to pay them.

Devvie's father passed away in 2003 of congestive heart failure, and her mom, who worked in the hospital, had to take over the farm as a second job. But they were a hardworking family. They kept plugging away at that debt and kept reaching for a time when they would not be anchored to raising chickens. By 2007, the Halley family had paid off their original loan. But then, just when they finally thought they were out of the cycle of debt, Pilgrim's told Devvie's mom she had to upgrade the poultry houses or else it was going to drop their contract, and they would no longer be able to be chicken farmers.

This is a typical story for a chicken farmer. They get close to paying off their debt, close to a day when their paycheck is all their own. But by then it's been ten or fifteen or twenty years since they built their warehouses, and standards, technology, and equipment have changed. The mega-chicken company says that if they want to keep raising chickens, they have to upgrade. If they don't, then no more chickens. For Devvie's family, it would cost close to a million dollars of additional debt to upgrade. They felt they had no choice but to take on that loan.

Over a decade later, still $130,000 in debt on that second loan, the company again required upgrades. This time Devvie put her foot down. Enough was enough. When Devvie told her mom she was making the decision for the family and they were getting out of the chicken industry, her mom's response was simple: "Great. It's about time."

Where once chicken was eaten only on occasion as a Sunday roast, it has now become the most popular meat in the US, surpassing all other animals. Americans today on average eat nearly 100 pounds of chicken per year; in 1960, they ate 28 pounds per year.[1] With this incredible increase in demand came incredible pressure on both the animals and the farmers.

For the farmers, it meant a loss of freedom. The days of being an independent farmer have all but disappeared as Big Animal Agriculture has consolidated the industry. While a few farmers are able to maintain independence, most do not. To raise animals and sell their meat and other products to the great American consumer, you have to operate within the network of, or be contracted by, one of the big companies such as Tyson, JBS (of which Pilgrim's is a subsidiary), Perdue, or Sanderson, which together control more than 50 percent of the market.[2] Those choices are instead made at the corporate level, by executives whose priority is mostly focused on maximizing profits.

It was not always so, of course. The United States once had independent small family farms raising its chickens. In 1950 there were some 1.6 million farms raising chickens. But by 2007, 98 percent of those farms were gone, despite a 1,400 percent increase in production. The industry had consolidated. It had got bigger, more efficient, and more profitable through cheaper products. With that came a big price to pay for farmers and chickens.[3] For a time, there were efforts to deconsolidate the industry. In 1921, the Packers and Stockyards Act was signed by President Warren Harding. For the first time, legislation established standards to hold meatpacking companies and stockyards accountable and attempted to ban unfair and discriminatory conduct in the market. For farmers it meant first-time protections, as it prevented companies from paying farmers below the market value for products or from pitting farmers against each other. The result was a de-consolidation of the market between 1918 and 1976, where the five largest meatpacking companies in the country went from controlling 55 percent to 25 percent.[4] But there was an opposing force happening simultaneously: policies attempting to force consolidation. Ultimately, consolidation won.

Tyson describes contract farming as follows: "We supply the birds and feed, and provide technical advice, while the poultry farmer provides the labor, housing and utilities. This cooperation between Tyson Foods and family farms increases efficiency and quality, while maintaining affordable prices for consumers."[5] But contract farmers will tell you this arrangement just makes them a simple number in the grand calculations of a cold, far-away company. It forces dependency.

The industry argued that the contracting system would stabilize prices, and farmers and companies would only benefit through stable income. It took off as a system. Where in 1950 almost all poultry farms were independent, by 1958, 90 percent were under contract. It didn't take long for the hog and cattle industry to follow suit.[6] Farmers raised concerns. One farmer at a Des Moines meeting asked in 1958: "Will we be able to control our own farming?" It would turn out to be a very valid concern.[7] Today we have all but a total monopoly, one that multiple US administrations have taken a closer look at—some with concern, but with little action or impact; others accepted it with outright enthusiasm.

But in the 1980s, the Reagan administration and a group of economists out of the Chicago School made a new interpretation of antitrust laws. Up until then, these laws were interpreted to ensure increased competition by protecting people's welfare. In 1981, the Reagan administration and the Department of Justice newly interpreted this to mean that the goal of antitrust laws was increased efficiency and consumer access to cheap products. The result was a significant and rapid transformation of the industry. It gave way to a series of mergers and acquisitions that set off a wave of consolidation in the meat and poultry industry. For example, where in 1980 the four biggest beef companies controlled 36 percent of the market, a decade later they controlled 72 percent.[8] And today they control 85 percent.[9]

In January of 2022, the White House put out a statement regarding unfair competition in the industry, stating, "The meat and poultry processing sector is a textbook example, with lack of competition hurting consumers, producers, and our economy." The White House announced it would start working on an action plan for a fairer, more competitive, and more resilient meat and poultry supply chain. COVID had revealed just how fragile the system was. The press statement continued: "[When] too few companies control such a large portion of the market, our food supply chains are susceptible to shocks. When COVID-19 or other disasters such as fires or cyberattacks shutter a plant, many ranchers have no other place to take their animals. Our overreliance on just a handful of giant processors leaves us all vulnerable, with any disruptions at these bottlenecks rippling throughout our food system."[10]

This is not the first time a president has tried to push for a fairer system in the meat and poultry industry. The Obama administration made an attempt a decade earlier to no avail. Secretary of Agriculture Tom Vilsack and Department of Justice officials toured the country, visiting with farmers and activists trying to get a handle on the problem. The Department of Justice held a hearing in 2010 in Normal, Alabama, inviting farmers to give testimony and share their experience. But little change occurred following these testimonies.

The Halley farm is located in Cookville, Texas, nestled in northeast Texas. It is mostly agricultural, mostly hay fields or cattle ranches—and many chicken houses, because right here, just fifteen minutes down the road in Mount Pleasant, is the slaughterhouse for Pilgrim's Pride. Most of the surrounding farmers are in the chicken industry.

Typically, the slaughterhouse is the first thing to be established when the industry comes to town. Then they solicit around two hundred chicken farmers to contract with them within a thirty-mile radius or so of the slaughterhouse. Building chicken warehouse units from scratch is far from cheap, with a house averaging $200,000 to $280,000.[11] Most farmers have multiple houses, with the average farm having between three and five houses.[12] This number is expected to rise over the next decade as the industry further consolidates. New mega-farms are moving in, with as many as fifty warehouses on a single property.

Chicken farmers are an aging group, with 80 percent of the population forty years old or older. While the industry suggests that this is an indication "that live chicken production is dominated by experienced live chicken producer owner-operators," many of the farmers will tell you it's because they don't want their kids anywhere near these farms.[13]

The chicken industry contacts farmers within that small radius of their slaughterhouse to create a constant daily stream of trucks, full of chickens arriving at one end and exiting the other to go pick up chickens from more farms. Typically, one slaughterhouse kills over a hundred thousand birds per day. Tyson, for example, kills 37 million birds per week in just fifty slaughterhouses.[14] That's 740,000 birds per slaughterhouse per week, week after week after week. This system of relentless supply surrounding a slaughterhouse is what is known in the industry as a "complex"—the slaughterhouse and two hundred farmers are one unit in the corporate calculation of supply to the ever-growing American demand for chicken. It is a completely integrated unit that provides maximum efficiency. Farmers are on a precise schedule, dictated by market demand and corporate calculations as to when they will receive chicken, how long they are allowed to keep them and when they will be sent to slaughter.

Shawn and I pass farm after farm, each with neat rows of metal warehouses, until we turn down a pothole-ridden road. We pass through a white gate and enter what looks like a scene from a zombie film. There are three rows—twelve total—of long metal barns with weeds growing all around them, derelict with the front doors wide open. Cobwebs, rust, and disrepair hang off the houses like a reminder of the past, as if the family has always just been hanging on by a thread. These are the warehouses in which the Halley family once grew millions of chickens for Pilgrim's.

The farm consists of a thousand acres, unusually big for a chicken farming family. It's summer, so it is lush and green with giant oak trees hanging shade on the meadows and an old horse living his own life meandering the pasture.

Evan, Devvie's partner, is the first to greet us in jeans, Converse, and a forest green T-shirt. He's a San Diego transplant, and with a cool California toss of his long hair, he extends a firm handshake. Devvie is not ready yet, he explains. She's tending to the dogs—Evan says she'll be along after she's done feeding and walking them. She's taken a fifth of the land to open a dog rescue shelter. There are about twenty or so dogs at any time that she takes from kill shelters, where they'd otherwise be put down because no one else will have them. They are building a house that can hold the unwanted dogs, where they can rehabilitate and rehome them. That is part of the big dream to change this land from something that once did harm to something that heals.

Devvie's father was once a pillar of the community. He would treat people's animals as a veterinarian, so it feels like Devvie, by taking in these dogs, is maintaining the thread. When members of the community couldn't pay her father, he would trade his services for baskets of vegetables.

Devvie is fiercely protective of her younger twin brothers. Bo and Sam started working in the chicken houses when they were fourteen. They were in their twenties when their father died, and the boys all but took over the farming, while their mom handled the numbers. Bo, now forty-seven, is working out in the field in the blazing hot sun. He's got a hoe and he's picking away at the weeds around hemp seedlings that they've just got going. He enjoys this work—the labor, the sweat, the simplicity of it.

Bo wears a patch over one eye and has a limp. He and Sam have had their fair share of hospital stays and accidents, all directly or indirectly related to the chicken business. He lost his eye in a chain accident. It broke and smacked him in the eye and pulled it right out. Then there's the missing fingertip. He had a simple paper cut on his finger and it got infected while he was in the chicken warehouses, which are riddled with bacteria. The infection got worse and he ended up in the hospital. The only solution the doctors could come up with, after extensive antibiotics and surgery to scrape the inside of the finger, was to chop off the tip. It probably saved his life. It was the kind of infection that could have just kept spreading. He also had an infection in his nose that became drug-resistant. "The doctor told me if I had waited two or three more days, it would probably have killed me," he said. The years of difficulty led to his substance abuse, which led to an ATV accident, from which he got his limp. His body is a daily reminder to him of the hardships he suffered from farming chickens. It's a job where a small cut can turn into a life-threatening illness.

Devvie thinks that her brothers just never got a fair shot at life. From age fourteen they were working in the chicken warehouses, wading through thousands of suffering chickens day-to-day. It took its toll on all aspects of their lives. Both ended up divorced. "I think the only time they ever even went anywhere with their spouses was for their honeymoons, because one person couldn't do the work alone," Devvie lamented. These were demons Bo could not shake and would eventually drive him to the darkest of places.

When I ask why they're doing this, why they're making such a big change and moving over to hemp, I'm told again and again they're doing it for Bo, so he can live off this land again, so that he can truly live again. Bo stands by, nodding.

Evan only spent a summer working in the chicken houses with Devvie's brothers, and that was enough. He helped them do maintenance. He didn't work in the houses or pick up dead chickens. He refused to do that. But he did try to help them get things prepared and ready for when they were going to bring chickens in or out. This was during a time when the houses were really struggling, the finances were *really* struggling, and they were trying to see whether or not the farm had a financially viable future.

Evan's most vivid memory of working that summer was when the water lines leaked. "Even as a slow leak, it creates a mud puddle and the chickens will fall into that mud puddle and can't get out," he said. "They'll be basically neck deep and sometimes just drown right there. Once they go in, you can't save them and they just have to be picked up and killed. Seeing something as simple as not having all your water lines tight, how destructive it was to the chickens, it just turned my stomach. It was ridiculous."

Coming from California, having lived there his whole life, Evan found East Texas to be a different world. Despite having different political views, he felt a closeness and admiration for the people here. He found them to be good people, caring people, willing to help a neighbor out.

The Halleys had long talked about growing something out here before hemp became legal and before they opted out of the contract with Pilgrim's Pride. Although Devvie made the final call, it was a group decision. Bo was the one who wanted it the most. Evan, after all, had a business in San Diego he could go back to, but this was Bo's opportunity to stay on the land and build a future. Without this opportunity, Bo might not be able to make a living off the land anymore. And that would crush him.

Bo's days as a chicken farmer nearly crushed him. The barns were full of ammonia wafting off the feces. Over time, it filled his lungs. His main job, like that of most chicken farmers, was to comb the warehouses looking for dead, dying, or ill chickens. He would pick up the dead ones and toss them in a bucket. And the ones that weren't doing well, he'd kill them by hand. Then he'd carry the dead birds out to a cold storage unit until they could be disposed of. While the debt was always the same, the monthly payments consistent, the flock performance never was. They'd raise six flocks of chickens per year. Sometimes they'd bring in $60,000 off a flock, and sometimes, because of an unusually high number of sickly birds, $50,000 or $48,000, which wouldn't be enough to cover the bills. And when a flock got sick or something else had gone wrong, they sunk further in debt.

Bo was ten years old when his dad built the first two chicken houses in 1983. Then his dad built three more in 1986, and the last six in 1991. At fourteen, Bo was in those houses every day with Sam, hunched over, picking up the dead chickens and checking the feed and water lines. Sometimes the number of birds would get so big he'd struggle to walk through them. It was a lot of work. But there simply weren't many prospects for him, not much other work, so he tucked into life as a chicken farmer even before he'd finished high school. This is what he did, day in and day out, hardly ever taking a break, unless you count the hospital stays, right up until his family decided to call it quits, over three decades later.

When it became obvious that the chicken business was not something that made financial sense, they decided to bite the bullet, eat the debt by selling off some of the land, shut down the chicken houses, and look for a different way for the farm to make money. Most importantly, they wanted to find a long-term, viable business for Bo and Sam.

"This is all they've known," remarks Evan. "They grew up on this ranch, they grew up doing chicken farming, they grew up working the land. For either of them, the idea of having to go get a desk job just doesn't make sense. It's not in their DNA. So, we reached out, or we started doing research: What can we do with empty chicken houses?" That's when they came across the Mercy For Animals video depicting an ex-chicken farmer who had transitioned his chicken houses to hemp.

They are five weeks into the first growth of hemp plants. Nobody's grown hemp like this in Texas in a hundred years. It's a gamble, for sure. They don't know what bugs might do to the plants, or if the weather will work for them. So they decided just to do an acre to try it out. But after the first five weeks, the plants are doing wonderfully. "They seem to really like the East Texas, Northeast Texas weather. It looks like it's going to be a successful crop," Evan explains.

The hemp fields are spotlit in the morning summer sun. The smell is refreshing and energizing in comparison to the chicken warehouses. The morning dew evaporates off the plants, filling the air with a fragrance of basil, other herbs, fresh air, and maybe optimism. For about an acre, there are neat rows of knee-high hemp bushes. With the blazing sun, the stifling humidity, and the regular rainfall, Texas seems to be the perfect place for hemp, even though it leaves the humans in a heap of sweat.

In 2019, House Bill 1325 authorized the production, manufacture, and sale of hemp-related products. In 2020, the USDA approved Texas's hemp cultivation plan. On March 16, 2020, the Texas Department of Agriculture opened applications for hemp licenses and permits.[15] The Halleys were one of the first to apply. They decided to just start with an acre and calculate out how much they could make per acre, and if it went well, they would keep expanding. This first batch seemed very promising.

Under an old oak tree by the house, the family began talking passionately about a future they all dream of, a replicable model, not just getting farmers out of their debt but really looking for solutions that will last and can be implemented anywhere. The cicadas erupt in chorus and a lone armadillo is nosing the dirt. As the sun was setting, I walked through one of the Halley family's thirteen chicken warehouses to assess how they might be repurposed for drying the hemp once it is harvested. The smell of the old chicken feces, though the chickens are long gone, is still pungent.

I walk silently. I know what's gone on here, what made this smell. In the dark corners of the impossibly long warehouse, I sense the ghosts of the hundreds of thousands of tortured souls who have passed through these doors. I left Texas trusting that in a few months' time, I would return and those ghosts would be put to rest, replaced by a bloom of hemp and hope.

HEMP HARVEST

In October of 2020, the Halley family made ready for their first ever harvest. According to federal regulations on hemp farming, the threshold for THC (the psychoactive element of cannabis) is 0.3 percent.[16] It can be tough for farmers, especially first-time ones, to guess when that threshold will be crossed. If they go over, the crop is lost. The Halley hemp will be processed for CBD, and they have no intention of going over that limit.

In the first week of October, a USDA inspector comes out to the Halley farm and measures the buds on the plant to ensure the threshold isn't being surpassed. The Halley family wait on the edge of their seats for the results to return from the lab. Finally, they are in: 0.26 percent THC—about as close as any farmer wants to get to that threshold—and 9.5 percent CBD. They all breathe a sigh of relief. The time is right to pull the plants out of the ground. It's a little sooner than they expected. They had thought it might be late October. But nature is unpredictable, and a warm, wet summer made for faster growth.

The plants went in the ground July 11, and on October 7, the Halley family prepared to harvest their first crop of hemp. Corn earworms, and armyworms have been a big concern during the growing. Big fat cartoon-like worms roam the hemp plants, wreaking havoc, especially on the buds. Given another month, they might have done too much damage for the farm to yield a decent crop. So the family is grateful for the early harvest. Evan predicts it will take up to four days to pull all the plants out of the ground. The edge is off the summer heat now, so maybe it will take less time, especially with a few extra hands. Shawn and I join the harvest.

The autumn sky is rippled with gray cotton clouds outlined by silver. "Silver lining" is what I'm thinking as I look up that morning, standing in the middle of the hemp field. The Halley family has gathered back together after decades of hardship. At the center of that hardship was the chicken industry. But here, at this moment, that is all in the past. And today begins a new future, the silver lining they have been waiting for.

Devvie's daughter Morgan, age twenty-five, has moved back from San Diego to be part of this new family endeavor. She embodies all that is young, fresh, and strong. Evan owned a bar in San Diego, which he continued to run remotely from Texas. Morgan had been bartending at Evan's bar but left when she heard what was happening here. She remembers coming here as a kid, going into those chicken houses, and feeling sick for their chickens. As an adult, she's curious and kind, joyful in the act of getting her hands in the soil, in the natural world. She shows me a reishi mushroom she found in the forest, and a wild boar's tusks she also found, which she plans to make earrings out of. She tells me she wants to have a greenhouse, grow tropical plants and medicinal mushrooms. She's here to stay now, to fix this farm and heal this soil.

Evan's fifteen-year-old son, Ashby, is standing in the field too. He's wearing Converse, an '80s punk band T-shirt, ripped jeans, and shoulder-length hair. He's quiet, but he's here to work too. I ask him if he remembers the chicken houses. He says simply, "Yes, they were disgusting." He gets excited and distracted when he finds a poisonous hairy brown caterpillar, showing how young he still is at heart. Evan throws a comment toward Ashby, "This isn't a field trip," and motions for him to get back to work.

Sam has also returned. He moved away, but with the promise of the farm up and running again with the hemp, he is back for good. He is an identical twin to Bo, though heavier, and seemingly has seen an easier life than Bo, who is thin, quiet, and withdrawn.

As the family works the field together, the moment is all the more moving considering the difficulties they have endured. They have come from different places, in every possible sense—politically, geographically, mentally—to reunite and rebuild as a family. There is this desire to be a single unit, to build on the land together, with pride. They think of their father as they toil in the autumn sun. They think he would be happy to see them together working the land. They're motivated by more than monetary gain or another kind of success. The Halleys work as one—the kids, the uncles, the parents—all together to pull the hemp from the soil.

It can take two or three tugs from Morgan before the hemp plant comes loose from the soil. Evan clips the roots off each plant, as Morgan holds one on each arm, each one a heavy lift at four feet in height. Then they throw the whole plant in the back of the pickup truck.

The metal longhouse stands off in the distance. To go from death and destruction—the chicken houses—to growth and creation—the hemp—creates a simple feeling of fulfillment the family has not felt before. Once the pile is high enough, they drive the truck the short distance to the old chicken barn, where a wire lines each side of the long warehouses. Here we hang the plants upside down, where they will be left to dry out, protected from the elements. The scent of ammonia from the chicken feces is fading as we hang the hemp plants. Soon there is no scent, no sign, that the chickens were once here. Slowly, the hemp is putting to rest the ghost of the past held inside these warehouses. There is only an aroma of hemp filling the air, filling our pores, oil sticky on our hands and clothes.

"Growing something just changes your heart, compared to killing something," reflects Evan as he's finishing up his first day of the harvest. "This whole process has transformed our whole family that was really in despair for a very long time. And it's transformed it into something that is now thriving and is connected and close."

We work all day until our backs are sore and hands are black from the soil and hemp oil. I have dirt in my socks, ant bites around my ankles, and hives on my arms from brushing up against the leaves and pollen. But I could not feel more content. I am sweaty and tired but fulfilled to see this farm fully leave behind a dark past for a bright future. We are buzzing, euphoric with hope—and possibly from absorbing so much hemp oil. This is the story of the family coming back together, working the land together and healing.

Months later, I returned again to sit with Devvie in the warehouse to take the now-dried buds off the plants. This will be what they use to make CBD oil. She is quietly content as she does this. Devvie speaks of her plan to process the CBD oil and use it to relieve companion animals of their pain and anxiety. Who knew her dreams could come true right here, right in this warehouse, where there had been so much despair? As time went on, the hemp wouldn't end up being a total solution for them, but it was a critical stepping stone into a new way of life.

In the spring of 2021, Shawn and I got a call from Evan. Bo Halley, at the age of forty-eight, has died by suicide on April 12. Despite all the hope in front of him, letting go of the past proved too difficult.

I remember Bo that first day I met him, picking weeds on the land, making way for the new growth, his quiet disposition hiding so much pain and loss. The Halley family go inward. We don't hear from them for many months, and I can only imagine the pain they are going through. They were so close to the next chapter of their lives, one Bo now will never see.

For farmers, death by suicide is tragically common. According to a 2020 report by the Centers for Disease Control and Prevention, in comparison with rates in the total study population, suicide rates were significantly higher in five major industry groups—farmers were chief among them.[17]

It takes many months, but Devvie and Evan let us know they aren't giving up. They are determined to go on, in memory of Bo, and for all the others out there like Bo, who think there isn't another way. They built the shelter, a clean and safe place where homeless dogs can rest their paws. They buy a van, air-conditioned and kitted out for maximum comfort, for transporting dogs to their forever families all over the country. They process hemp buds, and with the CBD oil they heal the dogs of their aches and pains. They lean into healing animals, healing themselves, and expanding their dog rescue facility. They make plans to turn more of the chicken houses into shelters for homeless dogs. They even establish a donkey sanctuary.

The cycle of abuse has ended, but the scars on the Halley family remain. The Halleys' story makes the case all the more compellingly that we must stop the harm factory farming does to farmers before it even starts. Even though some will succeed in their fight for freedom and a new way, not all will be able to.

CHAPTER TWO

FROM CHICKENS TO MUSHROOMS

ON THE OTHER SIDE OF THE COUNTRY, on the border of North Carolina and South
Carolina, Craig Watts adjusted the humidity and temperature in his
shed. A fogger sprayed a warm mist into the air. An exhaust fan pumped
stale air out and new air in. Conditions had to be just right. Twenty logs
in the shed had been inoculated with a potion, a fragile magic that would
give way to life.

The dome-shaped plastic tent looked more like the quarantine scene
from the movie *E.T.* than a farming trial. But this was Craig's first attempt
at growing mushrooms. The growing dome was warm, humid, and smelled
of dirt, like a cave. There was no sign of suffering, just earthy goodness.
Craig had placed twenty logs, bought from Carolina Mushroom for $3 a
log, inside the dome. In his previous life as a chicken farmer, he'd make
$0.05 per pound of flesh. Now, Craig would make, by a conservative esti-
mate, $6 per pound for shiitake mushrooms by the end of his experiment.

Those logs, the size of loaves of bread, had been inoculated with shiitake
mushroom spores and placed on metal racks. Craig had waited patiently.
Now, from each log emerged a dozen or so full-grown shiitake mushrooms.
Not as much as he'd hoped for, but it was his first time, and it would get
better.

Craig wasn't afraid of risk or trying things he didn't yet know anything about. He was a nonconformist. Sometimes it took a little while,
but he always landed on his feet. He was outspoken against his former
employer—the chicken industry—and its hold on rural America. He'd

been interviewed by diverse media outlets, from the *New York Times* to *Al Jazeera*. He knew firsthand what raising factory-farmed chickens felt like and was dedicating his life now to ensuring no one else ever did. It had never been his plan to become an advocate for farmers or stand up to one of the biggest companies in the country. "My plan all along was just to raise chickens and raise a family and die. Some stuff got in the way," he chuckles. His principles got in the way.

Years before, in the summer of 2014, I had found myself sitting in Craig Watts's living room. At the time, he was my sworn enemy. But that changed.

I learned how Craig's suffering as a poultry farmer, like the Halleys', is the story of thousands of farmers across the country. Experts estimate that approximately three-quarters of all contract poultry farmers live below the poverty line, living flock to flock, relying on fragile payments from big poultry companies.[1] If these payments stop, even for one flock, a farmer teeters on the brink of losing everything: their farm, their land, their home, and their dignity. Craig and his cohort of American contract poultry farmers collectively owe $5.2 billion worth of debt.[2]

With the collective debt at such dizzying heights, solutions for change cannot be left to individual choice or the willingness of the corporations making record profits. This broken system is the result of an unchecked corporate monopoly over the market and government subsidies encouraging overproduction. These combined factors result in the squashing of individual farmers' freedom to grow what they want, when they want, and how they want, as well as squashing their liberty to sell it in a free and fair market. Solving the $5 billion crisis that farmers face will require government funding and corrective policy to help farmers transition to viable alternatives. Half the battle is coming up with viable alternatives, which the Transfarmation Project is working to model. The other half involves shifting power so that the government is required to help rural economies and farming communities get out of the trap of factory farming and transition to economies and businesses they actually want to be in.

One such effort was introduced by Senator Cory Booker in July of 2021: the Farm System Reform Act. This historic bill, backed by Senator Elizabeth Warren and Senator Bernie Sanders, proposed to provide grants to farmers to permanently transition them from operating an industrial animal farm to carrying out any other activities on the property where the industrial animal farm was once located. Along with putting a moratorium on industrial animal farming, the bill would partially or fully pay off any outstanding debt that farmers had incurred to construct and operate an industrial animal farm, and it would cover the cost of a transition, allowing a former factory farm property "to be used for alternative agriculture activities, such as raising pasture-based livestock, growing specialty crops, or organic commodity production."[3] The bill proposed setting aside $10 billion for this transition and debt relief.

That may sound like a lot of money, but $10 billion is not a huge amount for the government to foot for food, farming, and rural development. By comparison, the US government spends $38 billion *each year* to subsidize the meat, fish, egg, and dairy industries in their entirety (including crop subsidies that benefit industrial animal farming).[4]

The Farm System Reform Act was largely symbolic in nature and did not get further than being introduced. But it was an important first step. Much previously symbolic legislation has moved into the realm of "politically feasible," such as that advancing women's suffrage, after continual effort. First proposed in Congress in 1878, the Nineteenth Amendment, which gave most white women the right to vote, only became law in 1920.[5] In the case of the Farm System Reform Act, it started the conversation at the policy level and introduced an idea that needs more champions: that factory farmers want to do anything but factory farming, given the choice and the opportunity to transition from it.

What does this say about our current farming system, which literally has to trap farmers, not to mention animals, in order to function? We cannot call this a free market. It's truly the opposite: a captive one, with captive workers and animals alike. This bill, for the first time, set out a viable policy path to transition farmers out of debt and despair, and reduce the inherently inhumane treatment of animals raised for food.

THE SEARCH FOR ALTERNATIVES

The Halley family were unusual in that they had land to sell off to cover their debt. Most factory farmers don't have that option. Craig wanted out of chicken farming but had to find a new way to pay off the debt he'd incurred from building his chicken houses. Despite having some debt still to be paid off, he decided he'd had enough and quit chicken farming two years after the release of our video, in 2016. He became a farmer-activist for the Socially Responsible Agriculture Project (SRAP), touring the country and talking to farmers about the industry not being what it seems, about the debt and destruction it can cause. But on the side, he started dreaming up a way to transition the four empty chicken warehouses that sit a mile down the road from his home. He had rented them out to another farmer to store hay. But one day, when someone said they were tired of raising chickens, he wanted to be able to show them how to get out.

After a few years as a farmer-activist, Craig had gotten the itch to farm again, to grow and create. He was still paying off the debt from his chicken houses through his SRAP salary. He got in touch with the Transfarmation Project.

Then in its second year, the Transfarmation Project had completed its first experiment with the Halleys and commissioned the consulting firm Highland Economics to analyze which crops were most likely to succeed. The economists reviewed six possible crops that could be grown in a chicken warehouse: cucumbers, strawberries, tomatoes, hemp, specialty mushrooms, and microgreens. Although the Halley farm had kicked off the Transfarmation Project by transitioning to hemp, deeper research showed that hemp wasn't the best option. There was one crop that, on paper at least, was the most profitable and likely to succeed: specialty mushrooms.

Specialty mushrooms are defined by the United States Department of Agriculture (USDA) as any farmed mushroom that is not of the *Agaricus* genus (which includes the common button and portobello varieties). These include the shiitake, oyster, reishi, and lion's mane varieties, to name a few. In 2021, the USDA estimated there were over 20 million pounds of specialty mushrooms produced in the nation. This was up approximately 8 percent from the 2018–2019 marketing season (July to June).[6] This increase in production in recent years has been the long-term trend in the US and is indicative of the growing interest in and demand for specialty mushrooms generally.

The comparative economic research conducted by Highland Economics and commissioned by the Transfarmation Project looked at a simple question: What were the costs of converting a poultry warehouse into something that could grow a crop, and how profitable would that be? For hemp, the costs could include buying growing lights (if growing indoors), installing drying lines to hand-dry the hemp, and making room for picking the buds. For mushrooms, they would include installing shelves of growing substrate, purchasing lights and humidifiers, and maintaining a controlled atmosphere. And for microgreens, strawberries, tomatoes, and cucumbers, transitioning would require ripping off the roof of the warehouse and creating a greenhouse with an irrigation system.

In the research, mushrooms came out substantially higher in gross profit than any other product, with microgreens in second. Hemp came out last, with a potential for profit loss. Tomatoes, cucumbers, and strawberries were projected to see only moderate profits, yet still yield higher profits than those from chicken farming. (More details on this are featured in chapter 3.) In comparison to chicken, growing specialty mushrooms was like winning the jackpot. Of course, the bar is low when you're comparing any alternative crop to raising chickens. Contract chicken farmers on average make $0.24 for a four-pound bird, which works out to a little over $0.05 per pound.[7] Each chicken gets only about three-quarters of a square foot in a warehouse in normal industry conditions. That adds up to a profit of about $0.32 per square foot for the farmer.

Chicken farmers are particularly hungry for better pay. Between 1990 and 2020, farmers' pay per pound of chicken actually went down by 3 percent, even when adjusted for inflation, according to the trade association that represents chicken companies, the National Chicken Council.[8] At the same time, consumers are paying record prices for chicken. In 2022, consumers saw the highest prices in forty years for food, with the highest increases in meat prices.[9] Chicken prices rose by 13 percent for consumers, while overall prices rose by 9 percent. Farmers are getting paid less money, and consumers are paying more money. The result? Chicken companies' profits are skyrocketing. In the first quarter of 2022, two of the largest poultry companies in the country saw shocking rises in profits. Tyson's profits rose 48 percent, and Pilgrim's Pride, owned by JBS, saw profits rise 124 percent.[10]

Monopolies in the chicken meat market are only getting stronger. In 2022, the USDA approved a historic $4.5 billion merger between Wayne Farms and Sanderson Farms, the sixth- and the third-largest chicken companies in the US, respectively. This merger meant the new company would now control 15 percent of the chicken market. It also meant that the top four poultry companies would control 60 percent of the market, up from 50 percent before the merger.[11]

Joe Maxwell, who heads up the farmers' advocacy group Farm Action and was consulted by the Justice Department over the merger, vehemently disagreed with the move toward more centralized power and with this merger in particular. "These are two global food giants. It's very disturbing," Maxwell said. "The manipulation which can go on within the market on feed costs, knowledge, data, could be used against the other 40%, only causing greater concentration in the future. When you get to these levels of control of a market, it allows for corruption, collusion and price-gouging."[12]

But despite all the power, all the profits and control, there is one thing that companies need more than anything to make their record profits: farmers. And currently farmers are unhappy, underpaid, and ready for change.[13]

Given that mushrooms have a hundred times higher profit margin compared with chickens, and given the chicken industry's history of treating farmers poorly, mushrooms provide a compelling potential exit strategy for farmers. Transitioning more farmers to growing mushrooms would mean pulling the rug out from under the poultry companies who are unwilling to pay farmers fairly and treat animals humanely. No farmers means no chickens.

By the summer of 2022, the trial in the shed was over and Craig was ready to fully transition. Craig was working with the Transfarmation Project to build his family a new kind of farming operation—one that contributes to his community and land instead of exploiting them. He wanted his new operation to be "as removed from the industrial model as it can be," he told me. In the end, Craig just wanted to be a farmer: "It's part of me, in the blood. It's a calling. I like to watch things grow."

After looking at the numbers, with the first shed experiment going well, Craig decided to start a formal shiitake mushroom operation. He decided to consult with Kevin Frasier, a mycologist, who came to visit and help him figure out just how much of a warehouse he wanted to convert. Kevin walked the now-empty chicken warehouses, discussing what it would take, after this trial, to expand the mushroom operation to fill the vast warehouse. Kevin thought the chicken houses might be too big for a first-time mushroom farmer. One house was huge—forty feet wide and fifty feet long. He suggested Craig take a shipping container, where he could control the conditions better, and place it inside the poultry houses, using the insulation of the poultry houses to help with the heating and the cooling. Craig started working over the months on this new idea.

He'd learned a lot about risk from raising chickens. And, unlike signing a contract with a big chicken company, he was well and truly his own boss here. He could decide how much to try growing and when to do it. Finally, he had the freedom that was never afforded to him as a chicken farmer.

He decided to start with a shipping container, 300 square feet, which he purchased through a Transformation Project research grant for $5,000. He'd need to invest in installing an HVAC system, the biggest cost of the project. He'd also have to pay for the inoculated logs, the shelves, the walls, and protective gear. But in the end he'd plan to sell his mushrooms at a conservative $6 per pound, with an annual gross of $17,000 just from the one shipping container. Craig felt satisfied that this was a good first step. If that worked well, he'd keep expanding.

He planned to sell the mushrooms at farmers' markets and farm-to-table restaurants at first. He'd chosen shiitake mushrooms because of how familiar they are to the consumer. But more exotic mushrooms, like lion's mane, could fetch a much higher profit.

The conditions needed for mushrooms were as close to the poultry house as any crop could come. Mushrooms needed a similar temperature, humidity, and lighting levels. They even had a growth cycle of about six weeks, just like the chickens had. But unlike the chickens, mushrooms can't suffer. They don't have to be killed and incinerated when things go wrong. They don't have a beating heart or a pair of eyes that stare right at you. Unlike chicken farming, mushroom farming was something Craig could bring his kids into, something he'd be happy to show anyone.

Over eight years ago, the chicken warehouses were all shackles and shame for Craig. Now they meant change. They meant hope. They proved he was someone who has struggled and overcome, rather than being a place where dignity dies.

The edge of summer had just come off and a cooler breeze cut through the hot morning the day Craig put the shipping container into his old chicken warehouse. He and his grandnephew had spent the last few weeks cleaning up the old warehouses. The sky was bright and cloudless, and below lay the swampy land that surrounded Craig's home. There was a pink crepe myrtle exploding in the front yard and an old oak tree, extending impossibly wide and tall. Its roots were strong.

Craig invited me to come and see the shipping container-turned-mushroom farm, set inside the cavernous poultry warehouse. When I arrived, Craig and I settled in to review the state of affairs in the battle against factory farming, in the same living room where I'd first spoken with him eight years prior.

We discussed big news about Wayne Farms, Sanderson, and Cargill, some of the largest poultry integrators in the country. In an antitrust lawsuit filed by the USDA in cooperation with the Department of Justice against meat giants Cargill, Wayne, and Sanderson, the government alleged that these companies participated in practices that were unfair and in violation of antitrust laws, especially with regard to how they paid and treated slaughterhouse workers and farmers. The suit stated:

> Poultry processing plant workers deserve the benefits of free market competition for their labor. For at least two decades, however, poultry processors that employ more than 90 percent of all poultry processing plant workers in the United States conspired to (i) collaborate with and assist their competitors in making decisions about worker compensation, including wages and benefits; (ii) exchange information about current and future compensation plans; and (iii) facilitate their collaboration and information exchanges through data consultants. This conspiracy distorted the normal bargaining and compensation-setting processes that would have existed in the relevant labor markets, and it harmed a generation of poultry processing plant workers by artificially suppressing their compensation.
>
> Poultry processors have also engaged in deceptive practices associated with the "tournament system." Under this system, growers are penalized if they underperform other growers, but poultry processors control the key inputs (like chicks and seed) that often determine a grower's success.

> Poultry processors often fail to disclose the information that growers
> would need to evaluate and manage their financial risk or compare of-
> fers from competing processors. The United States of America brings
> this civil action under Section 1 of the Sherman Act, 15 U.S.C. § 1, and
> Section 202(a) of the Packers and Stockyards Act, 7 U.S.C. § 192(a), to
> enjoin this unlawful conduct.[14]

These were strong words of reprimand, with the US government actually stating the true nature of the industry and its power over workers and
farmers. It felt like perhaps we were entering a new era, one that might
hold these companies accountable.

The Campaign for Contract Agriculture Reform (CCAR), an alliance
working to provide a voice for farmers and ranchers involved in contract
agriculture, has been fighting the tournament system used in the poultry
industry. They argue that it is specifically designed to benefit the poultry
processing corporation by putting all the financial risk onto the farmer.[15]
That farmer is in the "tournament" with other farmers in their area. Growers don't just get paid on how efficiently (biggest bird for the least feed) they
brought a chicken to slaughter. They also get pitted against each grower
in their area, getting more or less pay depending on how well they do in
comparison to the other growers. A chief injustice, according to CCAR,
is that farmers control hardly any of the inputs; rather, they are controlled
by the corporations, from the breed, to the space given to each bird, to the
feed and the lighting, to the setting of the time when the birds are picked
up. All of these factors can greatly affect the size of the birds and the efficiency of the growing period. None of these are controlled by the farmer,
yet this is exactly what they are judged on and what determines their pay.

Now, through a consent decree, the Department of Justice and USDA
are taking steps to reform this tournament system, at least for two of the
largest poultry companies. A consent decree is an order by a judge, in
this case a federal judge, in a case where no one has admitted guilt, but
all parties have agreed to the order. Consent decrees are often used as a
means to create reform where there are systemic problems. In this case, the
consent decree agreed to by Sanderson and Wayne Farms would reform the
"tournament system" by establishing a base pay for chicken farmers while
allowing for incentives and bonus pay. Cargill Inc., Sanderson Farms Inc.,

and Wayne Farms LLC also agreed to pay $84.8 million in restitution to workers who were harmed by the alleged exchanges of wage data between the companies in violation of antitrust law, which resulted in suppressed wages and benefits for slaughterhouse workers.[16]

When the consent decree was issued, Principal Deputy Assistant Attorney General Doha Mekki of the Justice Department's Antitrust Division said, "Today's action puts companies and individuals on notice: the Antitrust Division will use all of its available legal authorities to address anticompetitive conduct that harms consumers, workers, farmers and other American producers."[17]

While the decree was a step in the right direction, Craig was skeptical. He'd heard the industry was planning an appeal. Would that affect the decree as it was being finalized, and if so, how? While the two companies had been ordered to set a base pay rate, would they actually set a rate that would benefit farmers? Historically, they never had. He imagined that the companies would work out the lowest base pay possible to maintain the companies' same cash flow, would continue to keep farmers in debt and despair, and would continue to use incentives and bonuses as a way to withhold extra income from non-submissive or trouble-making farmers. He worried the companies would ensure that the cash flow was good for them, but not farmers. And what about the rest of the industry? This was only two companies, and the largest of them—for example, Tyson—were not subject to the decree. Finally, what would happen when the administration changed? Would the Justice Department swing back to support industry, and suppress worker and farmer rights?

Craig saw the upside of having transparency established, including the fact that it required greater disclosure regarding grower contracts. And he certainly was happy to see the USDA sue the big meat companies. The proposed consent decree would stop the companies from "penalizing chicken growers by reducing their base payments as a result of relative performance." And it specifically prohibited retaliation when growers spoke up about unfair practices, something that had been established in the past but was reinforced by the decree.

This was progress, aimed at exposing the industry for the true nature of its business, including its habit of outsourcing risk to farmers while paying as little as possible to the farmers taking on those risks. In a system where success relies on maximum efficiency, ignoring fairness, dignity, and the welfare of animals and farmers was part of the equation. To work most efficiently, the meat industry relies on stripping farmers of their power and treating animals like machines. Though Craig welcomed the consent decree's call for transparency and fairness, the government had failed thus far to do anything substantial to actually create a just and fair system. Enforcing and, even more importantly, expanding this decree to the entire industry would be necessary for it to mean anything to the majority of farmers and workers.

Craig wasn't willing to wait to see if that happened. He was fifty-six now and had already seen enough, had relied too long on the industry and government to fix rural America's problems. He'd show his fellow farmers another way, as an insurance policy in case the government's intervention fell through like it has so many times in the past.

On my first visit to Craig's farm, in the spring of 2014, the warehouse was scattered with little yellow puffballs, chicks the size of my fist. Sweet cheeps filled the house, but as I shuffled through the litter, images that would haunt my nightmares came into view. I had intentionally come when the chicks were three to four days old, when I knew mortality spiked. This was when it became clear the birds that were genetically problematic weren't going to make it. For the first days after they hatch, chickens live off the nutrients from the egg yolk. But after that, they have to be able to reach the water and feed lines to survive. And the ones that can't slowly begin to die. Craig's job back then was to find those suffering babies and kill them by hand, to put them out of their inevitable misery. I remember birds with crossed beaks, deformed legs, and others that had been mangled in machines after hatching.

By my second visit, the birds of that same flock, in just under forty days, had ballooned up to football size. The warehouse was a sea of white, wall-to-wall birds. Birds were panting, reaching up for air, for space, for peace. Some were barely able to walk, too top-heavy for their musculo-skeletal system to hold them up. Some had their legs splayed out to the side or backward, collapsed under their immense weight. I lifted one up, and her chest was raw, red, from sitting on the hot litter filled with feces from tens of thousands of birds.

But now Craig and I stood together in that same house, and it was a vast blank canvas, waiting to tell a new story. By 2022, Craig was set up to grow and sell mushrooms. He created a new name and logo for his business: Victors' Village Farms. He named it after the Victors' Village in *The Hunger Games*, the wealthy neighborhood in every district where the past victors of various Hunger Games reside. He said that "leaving contract poultry on my own terms was like winning the Hunger Games. Winners from the games were placed in this cool place close to the Victors' Village . . . Voilà! . . . Victors' Village Farms."

Craig's job at one point was just to observe, collect, and kill dead and dying chickens. But after leaving the chicken industry, he began slowly to remember why he'd gotten into farming in the first place. He remembered his love of growing things—how fulfilling it was, and how good he was at it. Craig's front yard now has rows of corn and squash and okra growing high. But it's not just his farm that has transformed—it's his spirit. Instead of waking up day after day to face the daily defeat and despair on the farm, he embodies the name his farm now yields: a victor, a triumphant decider of his fate.

CHAPTER THREE

FROM CHICKENS TO GREENHOUSES

C RAIG DIDN'T KNOW IT, but his story had inspired another farming family to get out: Paula and Dale Boles. In 2014, they had seen the *New York Times* exposé, and it rocked their world. Before that, they thought they were alone. They thought they were doing something wrong. They even felt ashamed. Chickens were dying, they were losing money, and they were so tired, working the hardest they had ever worked in their lives but still hardly making ends meet. When they saw Craig speak up and watched the video describing chicken farmers as indentured servants, Paula and Dale knew it wasn't them who were at fault. It was the system.

Paula and Dale live in Granite Falls, North Carolina, an hour and a half north of Charlotte. As I headed out to meet them, dark gray clouds stretched across the sky in front of the road, while the sun began to set behind them. The Transfarmation Project team and I are meeting Paula after she gets off work, as the day is ending. The clouds drop all the way to the ground—vertical streaks of dramatic rain. Soon the land is engulfed in heavy drops, then rain so thick and violent cars stop on the side of the highway and put their hazards on.

Off the highway, the country road winds. On one side of the road there are fields of corn and on the other side, soy. Tyler Whitley, the Trans-farmation Project director, is at the chicken warehouses already, poking around with Paula and Dale. As I drive down the dirt hill leading to the warehouses, mourning doves part in front of me and steamy green hills roll around us. The Boles' black lab, named Bo, is the first to greet me. Tyler has his measuring tape out. He's here to help the Boleses make further conversions to their chicken warehouses. The aim is to fully convert the warehouses to greenhouses for growing crops year-round.

Paula is warm and full of smiles, with a thick Southern accent. She wears chunky jewelry and sunglasses propped on her wispy dark blond hair. She's eager to show me the warehouse they've already started converting into a greenhouse. The space is already almost unrecognizable. Unlike a chicken warehouse, it feels airy and spacious, and is flooded with natural light. The roof has been ripped off and replaced with opaque plastic. It's a temporary measure that can't withstand too much weather, but it'll do until they can afford a more permanent roof that lets the light in but keeps the elements out.

They have just harvested the fruits of eight hundred cherry tomato plants and the scent hangs in the air. The flesh of the plants is scattered around the floor. They've divided the 20,000-square-foot house into five parts, five microclimates, in which they aim to grow different crops. Paula's real passion is flowers. Outside the warehouse are rows of zinnia in bloom, extending upward toward the sky, against a backdrop of the orange setting sun.

As I scan the warehouse, I see remnants of what it once was. An old refrigerator turned on its side is now being used to germinate seeds. The cool cells that once lined the outside length of the chicken house to cool the environment that thousands of chickens endured are now inside the warehouse at the entrance, repurposed to maintain the temperature for plants, not sentient beings. Water lines that once brought hydration to birds now bring irrigation to plants. It's a world reimagined, repurposed.

Paula tells me that now that the tomatoes are done, she's hoping to start the flowers indoors, followed by other vegetables. She's hoping to increase her flower business, already a rainbow of bright rows off the dirt road. The flower business has been growing. Currently, she just sells what grows off the side of her road and does pretty well considering she hasn't invested much. But she knows she can do better. She tells me her best customer is a local catering company that does weddings and events. Paula once helped the company out with setting up for an event, and one thing led to another. The caterer supports buying from local farmers, and has a diverse menu. "It doesn't matter what I'm growing. He just uses it and turns it into something that's so cool," she says.

This kind of buyer has been transformative for the Boleses. Working with a local business like this has allowed them to have a diverse product—from ghost peppers to microgreens to tomatoes to zinnia flowers. It's allowed flexibility so that when one item fails, it doesn't mean total failure for them. For a farmer like Paula, who emerged out of the industrial animal model, this kind of connection is the ticket.

There are three key elements that will enable the Boleses to successfully convert their farm. The first is finding a reliable and loyal buyer, which they have in the event caterer. The second is finding the right mix of plants to grow. The final factor is the physical conversion of the chicken warehouses into greenhouses. Each of these is critical for creating a viable model, not just for them, but for others to follow.

The Boleses started with cherry tomatoes. Just outside the warehouse, there are short rows of ghost peppers and Carolina Reapers, and zinnias growing further back. This growth outside will be limited to the warm weather. Indoor growth, however, can meet demand year-round.

The United States has a deficit of tomatoes, so it seems a wise choice at first glance. The US imports an average of 3.16 billion pounds of fresh tomatoes and exports just 121 million pounds, so there is room for farmers in the US to expand.[1] Tomatoes are, after all, one of Americans' favorite vegetables, after potatoes.[2] But in order for the Boleses to pull ahead, they'll need a differentiator—an organic certification or some other way to add value. Indoor tomatoes are grown so intensively in the United States that the larger producers (those with more than one acre under glass) have captured economies of scale whereby they can enter the value chain at a much lower price point and still be profitable. Calculations from Highland Economics suggest that the only way a farmer like Paula can turn a profit at the scale of a single poultry house will be to add "certified organic" or another distinguishable product feature that will allow for a price premium. Assuming a $2 per pound price point, which they could achieve through this added-value characteristic, they might expect an annual profit of $55,294 from converting about 16,000 square feet of a poultry house, or a profit of $0.49 per pound.[3]

Other crops prove more lucrative under the glass of a greenhouse. Microgreens in particular are a promising option. Microgreens are shoots of vegetables that are picked just after the first true leaves have developed. The market for microgreens is typically driven by restaurants closely located to the producer, but emerging personal consumption and cosmetic lines are also expected to be important segments for future growth of microgreens in the near term.

There are several different methods for producing microgreens, and production is highly scalable, which makes for easy entry for producers. Microgreens are a fast-cycle, high-value crop option within the horticultural industry. They can be harvested in as little as two weeks. Microgreens are still a small part of the US market, found on only 2 percent of restaurant menus. But that figure has grown by 79 percent from 2016 to 2020.[4] The local culinary industry continues to grow and adapt its menus to include more intricate flavors and complex plate design, and the demand for products like microgreens is expected to increase. For the microgreens, the Boleses might expect, according to Highland Economics calculations, an annual profit of $284,578 for 16,000 square feet in a greenhouse selling at around $7.83 per pound.[5] Apart from specialty mushrooms, this makes microgreens one of the most profitable plants farmers like the Boleses could choose.

They've also considered strawberries and cucumbers. For cucumbers, for 16,000 square feet of greenhouse, with a price point of around $1 per pound, the net profit is expected to be over $26,046.[6] For strawberries, after converting a poultry house into an 16,000-square-foot greenhouse, with a price point of $2.72 per pound, the expected profit is $52,944.[7] For tomatoes, after converting a poultry house into a 16,000-square-foot warehouse, with a price point of $1.51 per pound, the expected profit is $55,294.[8]

The Transfarmation Project crop market analysis shows potential profitability for farmers. Of the six crops analyzed (hemp, mushrooms, microgreens, strawberries, cucumbers, and tomatoes), five indicated the potential to match or exceed profit from factory farming. Hemp did not show profitability. The potential profits from the five crops that could be produced in converted greenhouses are listed below. Specialty mushrooms brought in the highest profit, at $890,000, from 16,000 square feet with a price point around $8 per pound wholesale and $16 per pound retail.[9]

The profit calculated here was based on one-third of mushrooms being sold at the retail price and two-thirds being sold at the wholesale price.[10]

Projected Annual Profit from Four Greenhouse Crops According to Transfarmation Crop Market Analyses for 16,000 Square Feet of Converted Warehouse

CROP	PROJECTED ANNUAL PROFIT	SELLING POINT PER POUND
Microgreens	$284,578	$7.83
Cucumbers	$26,046	$1.85
Strawberries	$52,944	$2.72
Tomatoes	$55,294	$1.51
Mushrooms	$890,000	$8 wholesale, $16 retail

It is worth putting these greenhouse crops side by side for comparison. It is also worth noting that mushrooms are unlikely to be grown in a 16,000-square-foot area. Most farmers would agree that that's just too much space and that sufficient amounts of mushrooms can be grown in much smaller areas. Therefore, given the high profitability, farmers have the option to grow in much smaller areas—such as within a shipping container. They would not need to source external labor and could still manage a good profit.

The Boleses have two houses, each 20,000 square feet, to play with. Like Craig, they want to start one step at a time. Like Craig, they were never allowed that option while raising chickens. Now they can limit their risk. Their initial experiment converting one-fifth of the house for raising tomatoes was successful, thanks to their relationship with the caterer. Now they are ready to convert more space. Tyler and I have come to discuss the options.

As we pass from one warehouse to another that once held tens of thousands of chickens, hundreds of crickets jump around us with each step, fireworks in the grass. Bo spots Gabriel the cat and chases him up a tree, a routine they've perfected, Paula tells me.

The second house has hemp hanging in it, drying. "Hemp was a bust," she says. They aren't doing that again. But that failure didn't deter her. And with diverse options, and a consistent local buyer, failing on one item didn't mean failing altogether. This is a choice they didn't have when they raised chickens. If chickens failed, they failed entirely. And there was no option to stop and try something else.

We settle onto some lawn chairs just outside the houses. Dale is chewing tobacco as he talks, spitting out a brown liquid in between sentences. He tells me he's hard of hearing and I repeat myself now and again. He's had COVID and a heart attack in the last year, but when I drop my pen, he jumps to pick it up, the reflex of a Southern gentleman. The sun is setting behind the second warehouse, rays extending into the gray sky. A rooster crows, calling in the evening. Crickets chirp the asynchronous rhythms of a summer chorus. As we sit in front of the warehouse, I absorb this beauty that we are able to enjoy, a beauty that would have been hidden and distorted in years past by the smell and sight of suffering chickens. As our conversation extends into the evening, the moon rises in the sky and gets brighter, fuller, more beautiful. I study a ghost pepper, red and expectant, hanging off its stem, the moonlight and sunlight both fighting to shine down upon this place of new growth.

FROM TOBACCO TO CHICKEN

The Boleses' story is like so many others, from Kentucky to North Carolina. A generation ago, Dale's parents were growing tobacco. Tobacco was once king. When the impact on health became widely known in the 1990s, and government support shifted away from tobacco farming, poultry saw its opportunity and moved in.[11] It was a familiar replacement, supported and subsidized by the government much in the same way tobacco once was.

Social and economic pressures, specifically the link between tobacco and cancer, played a role in shaping changes for tobacco farming. In 1998, forty-six states reached an agreement with tobacco companies called the Tobacco Master Settlement Agreement, the result of lawsuits seeking to recover money these states paid to Medicaid for treatment of tobacco-related illnesses.[12] As the economic and social cost became clear, the government withdrew its support for tobacco farming.

"For about seven decades, dating back to the Great Depression, the government imposed production limits on individual tobacco farms but guaranteed an artificially high price for the crop. The policy maintained order in the tobacco growing business for years and kept many small farmers alive," Nathan Bomey wrote in an article published in *USA Today*, just after the government interventions to support tobacco ended in 2015.[13] Will McKitterick, a senior analyst for the research firm IBISWorld who was quoted in the article, said, "A lot of our crops are subsidized by the federal government, but by 2005 it was seen as a little less palatable for the American taxpayer to be subsidizing tobacco."[14]

In 2004, Congress voted to phase out government support for the industry. President George W. Bush signed the Fair and Equitable Tobacco Reform Act, which provided ten years of annual payments to tobacco quota holders (individuals or entities authorized through government regulations and market agreements to grow a specific amount of tobacco). The plan was designed to help these quota holders transition to a less regulated market or other crops. The Tobacco Transition Payment Program, colloquially known as the "Tobacco Buyout," paid out $4.11 billion directly to tobacco growers and $5.85 billion directly to former quota owners over the ten-year transition period between 2004 and 2014.[15] The result was that the number of tobacco farmers declined by 51.5 percent in the year after the legislation took effect in 2005, according to research firm IBISWorld. The numbers of farmers growing tobacco in total dropped from 56,879 in 2002 to only about 4,268 in 2015, when the payments ended.[16] The swift change made it clear that tobacco farming had been largely sustained by government payments.

Farmers throughout North Carolina, like the Boleses and Craig Watts, report that their families transitioned from tobacco to poultry, replacing one government-subsidized farming industry for another. Today, like tobacco, there are growing social and economic concerns for poultry farming (and dairy, egg, and other meats) that should push the government to reconsider its interventions in and support for the industry. In addition to being subsidized, a substantial portion of the cost related to production of meat, dairy, and egg is externalized, in particular to the most vulnerable among us, through environmental, health, and animal welfare costs.

David Robinson Simon, in his book *Meatonomics*, reports, "The total expenses imposed on society—that is, production costs *not* paid by animal food producers—are at least $414 billion. These costs are not reflected in the prices Americans pay at the cash register. Rather, they are exacted in other ways, like higher taxes and health insurance premiums, and decreases in the value of homes and natural resources touched by factory farms."[17] Take, for example, how much meat costs our health. The relatively high levels of meat consumption in high-income countries present significant risks to public health. The World Health Organization has categorized processed meat as carcinogenic and unprocessed red meat as likely carcinogenic. In addition, meat-heavy diets may increase the risk of coronary heart disease, stroke, and type 2 diabetes.[18] Factory farming also creates risks from antimicrobial resistance, food poisoning (chicken is the number one cause of campylobacter-related illness), and zoonotic diseases (the overcrowded and filthy conditions of factory farms are perfect settings for disease outbreaks).

The phasing out of government intervention in tobacco, and the transitioning of farmers away from tobacco previews a potential path for transitioning farmers out of industrial animal agriculture. This time, however, we can demand a transition to something more sustainable, humane, and fair, as stipulated in the Farm System Reform Act introduced by Senator Cory Booker in 2019.

We might take the Bush administration's Fair and Equitable Tobacco Reform Act as a model for transitioning farmers out of poultry, pig, dairy and egg farming—an industry that requires significant financial support in order to stay afloat. Could a buyout program apply to the meat, egg, and dairy industry, allowing farmers to opt to transition to a more sustainable product, supported by government funding?

There are two ways governments tend to shape a market and its industries' success. One is to either add or remove support or intervention, as we saw in the tobacco transition. But the other is through taxing an unwanted product to influence consumer behavior. Take, for example, the soda tax imposed by the city of Berkeley, California, in 2015.[19] The results were clear. According to the *American Journal of Public Health*, when taxes on soda were raised by only a penny per ounce, self-reported rates of consumption of soda dropped by 21 percent. In contrast, when San Francisco rejected a tax, consumption went up by 4 percent. As an activist, I can't help but wonder, what would happen should there be a tax on meat?[20]

We know that price has a huge bearing on how much people consume, which is why government support for keeping meat at artificially low prices is so concerning. We saw this price-consumption relationship play out in the years 2007–14, when meat consumption per capita went down in the US.[21] But just when activists like me were starting to celebrate, in 2015 meat consumption shot back up and has not declined again.

There was a simple reason meat consumption dropped between 2007 and 2014: supplies were tight and prices were higher. Factors causing increased prices included the recession, historically high feed costs, drought in the Great Plains, and domestic disease outbreaks like porcine epidemic diarrhea virus. In the face of those higher costs, Americans cut back on meat. But by 2015, many of these issues driving higher prices had been resolved. By 2015, the retail price of beef had dropped by 22 percent, the price of pork by 7 percent, and the price of chicken by 5 percent.[22] Also during this time, the chicken industry in particular got more efficient and more capable of raising chickens quickly. In some cases, there was even oversupply and a rise in cold storage of meat. The impact was almost immediate and Americans started eating more meat again. This reversal speaks to the importance of price, and how it affects consumption. Would Americans eat so much without government intervention keeping the prices artificially low? These historical trends suggest no.

Chicken production, and all animal production, is heavily supported by government subsidies and does not operate as other businesses do, even within agriculture. For example, in 2011, the US government purchased $40 million worth of chicken from the industry when it overproduced.[23] When the cost of production went up, and consumption went down, there was a glut in the market. Under normal market forces, for any normal business, the result should have been a reduction in production, and therefore in the number of animals being slaughtered. But not in this case. The government purchased the glut and reported it would "donate [the chicken] to federal food assistance programs such as soup kitchens and its national Feeding America programs."

This was not the first time, or the last, that such an intervention helped out the broiler industry. The government made a similar move in 2010, with a $30 million purchase of chicken products, and in 2008, with a $42 million purchase of chicken products, with the intention of stabilizing retail prices. During COVID, the government sent poultry and livestock producers $270 million for "pandemic assistance." It also paid $427 million for the "depopulation" of pigs and chickens, which is a euphemism for mass inhumane slaughter of animals on the farm (usually through shutting down the system's ventilation or suffocating the animals through a type of foam).[24] This occurred because of the low numbers of workers, most of whom were sick with COVID, which caused backups at slaughterhouses.

It can be difficult to calculate the precise subsidies the poultry industry, or any animal industry, receives. Government payouts to agribusiness come from many programs with many different names: direct payments, counter-cyclical payments, new revenue assurance programs, marketing loans, and government-subsidized crop insurance, to name a few. The Environmental Working Group (EWG) reports that since 1995, the Department of Agriculture has spent nearly $50 billion in subsidies for livestock operators. And it is important to note that EWG's analysis did not include a critical part of the equation: funds paid to farmers who grow animal feed like corn and soybeans, which topped $160 billion between 1995 and 2020. The analysis also excluded $670 million in research grants.[25] Another study which attempted to incorporate all of these payment subsidies for meat, fish, eggs, and dairy arrived at a total subsidy figure of nearly $38 billion per year.[26]

But even these calculations don't show us the total cost we pay for cheap meat. First, taxpayers are footing the bill for these subsidies. Second, the most vulnerable among us—people living closest to factory farms—pay untold costs in terms of their health and quality of life. Finally, we all pay the cost of poorer health and higher health care costs. And of course, the animals themselves pay the ultimate price.

A PATH FORWARD

Paula and Dale's family had been through the transition out of tobacco, but they weren't willing to wait for a government transition out of poultry. They were, however, willing to carve out a path for others, to create a model that showed just how a farmer could be successful after being a poultry contract grower, under the thumb of Big Ag and drowning in debt.

They had started with the two warehouses raising chickens in 2000. They had to take out over a quarter of a million dollars in loans to build those houses. They contracted with Tyson. Tyson delivered the chickens, and the Boleses raised those birds on their land. And year after year, they found that with the upgrades Tyson expected, they were losing thousands of dollars. "We were just bleeding and bleeding money," Paula says now. By 2015 their debt had gone from $270,000 to $400,000. And it was only in February 2022, after they had left the chicken business, that they finally found a way to pay off the debt by both working two jobs outside the chicken business.

They tell me stories I've heard from farmers all over the country. They had to face young, fresh-out-of-college service techs from Tyson telling them how to run their farm. They faced disease in their flocks. Sometimes they had a great yield and other times they didn't, with little understanding of why. The Boleses, like so many chicken farmers, had to endure the tournament system, where they competed with the other farmers in their complex for the higher rank based on their efficiency score (tabulated by the least amount of feed for the biggest birds). Those toward the top got slightly more dollars per pound than those at the bottom. But for many of the farmers, where they ranked seemed hardly related to how hard they worked or what they did, since so many of the inputs were entirely controlled by Tyson, from the quality of the chickens that farmers got to the standards they were obligated to raise them in. Sometimes a farmer made the most money and was at the top of the list, and sometimes they made the least money, with no clarity on why, leaving farmers frustrated.

The Boleses had to make upgrades to their barns, required by Tyson, which only put them further in debt. They hated walking the barns, picking up the dead and deformed birds. It was backbreaking work, Paula remembers, picking up seven-pound dead birds and putting five in a bucket at a time, hauling them to the incinerator. Dale says the thing he hated the most was the birds who had heart attacks. Called "flip-over syndrome" in the industry, it is a result of fast-growth genetics that make them grow so big and so fast that their hearts and lungs can't keep up with their enormous bodies' demands.

Paula says not one of her kids wants anything to do with the farm now. But she and Dale feel peaceful as they look to the future. They have grandkids, and their grandson, Eli, can't get enough of shadowing Dale around the farm now that there aren't any chickens, especially when it comes to riding the tractor.

Paula tells me of her vision. Along with continuing to grow cucumbers, tomatoes, peppers, and microgreens, one day she wants this to be a place where families can come and enjoy the land, have events and picnics. She points just beyond the warehouses to the old chicken litter shed. "It'll probably be five or six years before I can retire and leave my full-time job, but I just have a vision. I can visualize that litter shed as a picnic shelter. I can see little lights hanging around it and fans hanging down and a picnic table." She hopes family can come here and enjoy each other, enjoy the land. She points across the field in the opposite direction. "We have two ponds down there and I have this vision of making campsites around the pond where people could just come in with their kids."

They've already had success with the microgreens in their first trial, and that's where they want to lean in. The microgreens are a hot commodity—they have been able to sell them at about $20 per pound. "Right now, we only have capacity to deliver about five pounds per week. With a germination chamber and improved equipment, we can increase the crop and our profits very easily," says Paula. And that's just what she wants to do next. "We have tried a number of things and determined several products that have performed the best for our farm and our particular situation. We have had the most success with microgreens, specialty hot peppers, annual spring/summer flowers, and cut flower farming." A small research grant from the Transfarmation Project to purchase improved equipment could increase productivity, and after that they feel confident that soon enough, Paula can quit her second job and just focus on farming.

They've worked with their main microgreen customer to increase the varieties they offer and plan to experiment with several new hot peppers the event caterer has requested for a retail product he is creating. With the cut flower farming, Paula is working with a local florist who is interested in purchasing local flowers for her business and has offered to work with Paula on various stages of flower farming, such as planning, growing, and marketing.

Paula has also found that when she has the freedom to farm the way she wants, she has more opportunity to connect and heal with others. "Working on the farm can be good therapy," she says. In the spring she employed women who helped in the greenhouse with planting and caring for flowers. Several of the women were elderly (one is eighty-three) and couldn't work long hours but desperately needed to do something and feel valued. Another woman was going through throat cancer and couldn't talk but enjoyed working in the early hours of the day when she felt the most energetic. A young teenage girl who had recently lost her grand-mother enjoyed being around the older ladies and hearing their stories. Another lady just worked for free flowers. "It was a great experience for all of us because I had people who genuinely cared about their work, and I truly appreciated them!" Paula tells me. "Working with the ladies in the greenhouse this spring gave me new inspiration and helped solidify the reason we continue to grow the farm and look for new and better ways to maintain it."

The business plan is sound and will not only get Paula and Dale into the farming they want to be doing; it is also building and strengthening their rural community and economy. It's the opposite of what the chicken indus-try has done for rural America, isolating families and keeping them poor. Paula doesn't pretend that one farm walking away from a billion-dollar industry is really going to disrupt it. "But," she says, "I believe if enough independent farmers like us are able to walk away from them, it will even-tually have an impact on that industry."[27]

It's a beautiful reimagining of this place that once caused them and animals so much despair.

CHAPTER FOUR

THE LAST PIGS

'D BEEN ON THE ROAD FOR TWO WEEKS and was supposed to be going home. But when the call came, I knew I had to go.

The Faaborg family, who had run an Iowa pig farm for over thirty years, had made a decision: they were getting out. They had let Iowa Select know they'd had enough. They had one load out left, and after months of building trust, they'd invited us to witness it.

Why do they always move animals in the middle of the night?

When I told a friend that instead of going home, I was going to a farm at 1 a.m., she said: "Nothing good comes from being at a farm at 1 a.m." It's true. This is the time when the crews heave their bodies through spaces of dust, decay, and despair. It is the time when they work to push unwilling non-human bodies into stacks on metal shelves on trucks waiting in darkness. Sometimes the work is too hard, and the workers grow impatient with the resistant, frightened animals. Sometimes they are rough. But they never really want to be there. No one does.

The sun was setting on Des Moines. An orange panel lined the horizon, topped by a heavy gray mass of clouds. The wind felt angry, picking up dust and slamming it to the ground. We passed the state capital, with its gold dome dull in the gray dusk.

The five of us activists sat around the long farmhouse table at our Airbnb preparing for the night ahead. We got our story straight—we were Tanner's friends, just filming out of a sense of sentimentality, to capture this last load out. We agreed that we could not work on the farm, even if asked. We could not help put the pigs on the truck. We could not be part of sending them to slaughter. Unlike our undercover investigators at Mercy For Animals, we had the luxury to say no and still capture the moment. We'd be there with open permission. Our purpose was to bear witness. We checked our cameras and batteries and discussed lighting and filming vantage points. Where would we position ourselves? What about the truck driver who didn't know our plan? What would they be doing?

Tanner Faaborg stopped by as we deliberated. It was his family's farm and he wanted this moment even more than we did. Fresh-faced, with flopping boyish hair and good looks, he told us his parents were nervous, especially his mother. She was not accustomed to change. But it was time. He told us where we could sit, where we could film. He said we shouldn't go into the warehouses when they were working. It would be dangerous. The pigs would be afraid, and they might bite. Tanner himself had been injured during load outs in the past, slipping on the concrete floor or getting hit with equipment or with the panels that line the chute for loading pigs onto the truck.

By the time we headed to Radcliffe, in Hardin County, where Tanner's farm was located, it was midnight. The night was heavy with darkness, and the wind sliced the air, though it was warmer than it should be in late October. Three loads of 175 pigs and one of 135 would go out in four trucks tonight.

The road had no reflectors on it, not a single streetlamp. Left and right of the road we could feel the vastness of the land, flat and never-ending fields of corn in the middle of America. This corn wasn't intended for humans to eat, but for farmed animals. Once these were prairies that sustained migrating buffalo and a diverse ecosystem. Now it was a monoculture—a desert, as far as nature is concerned. From the air, for miles and miles, this area would look like a sterile grid.

Currently, 50 percent of all habitable land in the world is occupied by agriculture. Of that, 77 percent is just for farmed animals, including grazing and land used for growing animal feed. Yet this 77 percent of land use only provides 18 percent of the world's calories.[1] Conversely, the 23 percent of land used to grow crops for plant-based foods directly for human consumption provides 83 percent of the world's calories.[2] Our current system is a gross misuse of a precious resource: earth. In many ways, it is a simple math problem. We can't keep using the land on which we need to grow food in such a wasteful way. With arable land diminishing and topsoil disappearing at an alarming rate, we will eventually run out of land for growing food if we don't change course.[3] The hope is that we don't wait until it is an emergency, until disaster is upon us.

The American diet is a huge part of the problem. Americans in 2020 consumed, on average, thirty-two animals per person. This is far greater than the consumption levels for similar countries or regions. For example, people in the UK, France, Germany, and Italy, which combined have a similar population size and political and economic status as the US, ate just thirteen animals per person in the same year.[4] Ecologically speaking, it would be impossible for the entire world to eat as Americans eat. We'd need another planet Earth. We'd have to convert all of the remaining habitable land on the planet to agriculture, and still we'd come up 38 percent short.[5]

We turned onto a gravel road, the shadows of the corn stalks falling on each side. In the distance we could see neat rows of lights marking roof lines. These were the Faaborgs' pig warehouses. As my eyes adjusted, I could see these little constellations all over the sea of darkness.

Iowa has one of the highest concentrations of pig farms in the world. Every county in the state has pigs, and 94 percent of counties are listed as having extreme or severe concentrations of pig farms, according to Food & Water Watch.[6] Iowa is the number one producer of pigs in the US, with one-third of the nation's pigs raised here. The state raises and slaughters nearly 50 million pigs per year.[7] After tonight, there will be at least eight thousand fewer every year.

The first truck arrived at midnight, and the loading began. The sky had no moon and was blanketed with stars. Fierce gusts of 35-mile-per-hour wind whipped at our faces. The lagoon of pig waste just off the hill threw a putrid smell in the air and, no doubt, particles into our noses and lungs. We sat just above the warehouses, some hundred feet away in the darkness, to watch the loading of the pigs.

It was hard to separate the man, Tanner, I saw down there heaving pigs, from the man I just had dinner with earlier that night. In truth they were not separate people, though we humans are experts at seeing things in neat categories. We want things to fit into neat boxes. But everything spills into other boxes over and over again. Tanner illustrates well the complexity of dismantling factory farming, which is at heart the complexity of the human spirit, the ability to hold two conflicting truths at once. This was a man who loved his community, his land, and his history. Yet he had been a part of its decay. For so long, factory farming has been this agent of unwilling degradation. Now Tanner was reconsidering his agency, searching for his power.

When he was three years old, his family moved from a small Iowa town called Nevada, with a population of seven thousand, to the even smaller town of Radcliffe, with a population of just five hundred. His ancestors had been in Iowa for years. His grandparents were hog farmers, and then his parents were. "And then I guess I was a hog farmer, growing up, until I left the farm." Tanner says this out loud as if to admit it for the first time. He was pretty young, seven or eight maybe, when he started working all-nighters on the pig farm, sending pigs to slaughter in trucks, next to his dad, and then off to school the next day. To a city slicker this might sound shocking. But it was just the way it was, and still is, for many farming families.

With warm clarity Tanner recalls the day he moved to this new home, marveling at all the space, the freedom to run in any direction, to explore. His parents wanted a place with wide open spaces where their four kids could run around, and they stumbled upon a house. Nobody had lived in it for several years. It had been resold through an auction, and somebody bought it as an investment for the land. The buildings were in disrepair. There were gigantic piles of corncobs everywhere. Weeds were high. But Tammy and Rand Faaborg were young and thought it would be fun to get it all cleaned up. They dreamed of sitting on their porch and shooing their kids outside. And the price was right for a couple with four kids and little money to spare. "So we moved up here with four little kids, and I think $300, a car and a pickup that didn't have a reverse. It was quite an adventure," Rand laughs. "It became just kind of a lifetime of fixing buildings and fixing things," he recalls, "mowing several acres of grass and whatnot. I don't think I knew what we were getting into when we got up here."

Rand said that raising livestock was a complete afterthought. Tammy's father had been a lifelong farmer and had raised pigs from the time he was ten years old until he couldn't anymore at eighty-five. He raised pigs "farrow to finish," as it's called. So he had the sows, then little pigs, and then raised those pigs all the way up to slaughter. Each sow would usually give birth to eight to ten piglets. One time he had four little pigs that were way behind schedule compared with all the others. So he told Rand he could have them. Rand recalls his father-in-law telling him he could just put the piglets in an unused building and raise them until slaughter to feed his own family. "It seemed like a good idea," Rand says. "I was working as a welder at that time, probably making $12,000 a year back in those days. So free meat sounded pretty good. So we got the little pigs, and we raised them up."

Those four piglets happened to all be female. So after a while Rand's father-in-law came back and said, "You know, I could bring one of my boars up here if you would like, and you could breed them." And so it began, the multiplication of beings, one after another, each herd a little bigger than the last. A casual decision, an afterthought. Like so many farmers I meet around the country, Rand never made a conscious decision to start factory farming. He just made choice after choice in search of a lifestyle that offered room to roam, fresh air, freedom, and a connection to the past—and ended up in a trap.

Growing up, Tanner helped take care of the pigs. He did all the things country kids do—he joined 4-H and raised a few calves, pigs, and chickens. He loved waking up to go and get the eggs, reaching into the warm nests to find these treasures. He and his siblings played a lot of football and "barn ball"—that is, basketball in the barn. "It was a lot of fun," he says now. "It was a good way to grow up."

But when he was still a kid, his parents decided to make what they thought would be a bigger investment in their family's future. "Things kind of escalated and we got more and more pigs," Tanner recalls.

Rand saw an ad in the paper one day for a company called Murphy's of Iowa. (Murphy's would later grow to become Smithfield Foods, the largest pork producer in the world.) Murphy's was based out of North Carolina at the time, but was branching into Iowa, and the company wanted growers. Its model of production would change the face of America, especially in rural areas (more on this in chapter 8). It would provide the pigs and would pay growers guaranteed sums per pig.

Rand called the number, and a company representative came out to check out the farm. With so many buildings, he saw the potential. He talked about the upgrades they'd need to make to the warehouses to handle the major increase and higher concentration of pigs, as well as the increased cash flow. At that stage, Rand's day job was swinging a three-pound hammer, running a grinder, and fabricating large tanks and large steel units. For only $12,000 a year, it was hard work—all day, every day. Murphy's offer sounded like a dream come true. Rand recalls his disbelief: "Is he saying what I think he's saying? For four months of raising hogs, I could make more, substantially more than I could swinging a three-pound hammer every day, all year long."

Murphy's offered to help them get a loan to build the modern confinement buildings. The family started with two buildings, for raising 2,200 pigs. They worked day and night getting ready. "Then the pigs came in, and they were vastly more work than what I anticipated," Rand laments. That was the beginning of over thirty years of intense work raising pigs in close confinement. "And now all these years later, we just think enough's enough. Let's do something different and not raise hogs anymore," Rand says. Tammy agrees: "Let's move on and do something a little healthier." She says her knees are shot from the years of hard labor, and they want something better for their lungs as well.

They were one of the first pig farms in their county to get big. The trend eventually changed the landscape of the state. Iowa is also one of the biggest corn producers in the country. And with all that corn depleting the soil of nutrients, the demand for fertilizer was high.

Pigs make a lot of waste, waste that can be used for fertilizer. In theory, corn and pig seemed like a hand-in-glove situation. But, in reality, the hog waste far exceeded the amount of fertilizer needed in the state. And soon the cesspools that held the hog waste were overflowing, with nowhere to go. Farmers sprayed the waste on fields with corn, but also on any fields. Fields next to homes. Fields that ran off into rivers. "The result was that once the rain came, you'd just have so much nitrate runoff into the water system," Tanner laments. "We have terrible water quality in Iowa, but it's not just Iowa, it's downstream too, all of those contaminates flowing down south, all the way to the Dead Zone."

According to the Sierra Club, Iowa is a major contributor to what is known as the Dead Zone. Although the Dead Zone is located in the Gulf of Mexico, the damage starts far upstream, as Tanner notes.[8] There the land is saturated with nutrients, nitrogen and phosphorus in particular. When it rains, these nutrients overflow into watersheds that flow into the Mississippi River, then down into the Gulf of Mexico. These excess nutrients make the environment ripe for algae growth and decomposition processes that steal the oxygen from the water. Once a haven for animal and plant life, the water has become hypoxic, starved of oxygen. Marine animals cannot live in it.[9] Today the Dead Zone is the size of New Jersey and growing.[10] It is an ecological desert in the ocean.

Tanner, the son of pig farmers, in his heart of hearts is an environmentalist. He is the main catalyst for the change the family is making. In his spare time, he plants trees and throws networking events to get people together to solve local environmental problems. "I think the number one problem we face is climate change," he says. "I think it's very real. I think it's happening now. And I think if we don't make more drastic changes, it's only gonna get worse."

Tanner has an entrepreneurial spark. He could have picked up and left, headed to the big city, and never looked back. He had initiative and brains and charm—he'd have done well.

He did leave, for a few years. He traveled around the world, and it was just what he needed to open his eyes. Through his travels he saw all the endless ways humans thrive, invent, collaborate, and build. His travels taught him that things could be different. His home didn't have to be the way it was. He saw the opportunity, and it thrilled him. When he got back, he started to experiment. Something rooted him to this place and called him to do the work to make a change.

First, he proposed solar panels. "I wasn't quite sure if my parents would go for it, but they did," he says. Nobody else had solar panels. They created a lot of buzz, a lot of excitement, and a lot of interest from neighbors. People started calling, asking questions. They'd drive in and want to take a look at them with their own eyes. Soon Tanner and his family saw people actually going through with it and putting up solar panels themselves. Tanner's biggest surprise was when his dad showed up one day with an electric car he had purchased for himself. It just made sense, his dad told him, to use the solar panels to fuel his own car.

After that, other dreams seemed more realistic. Tanner began to plant a seed: What if we stopped pig farming and transitioned to mushrooms? Through some research, he found the Transformation Project and got in touch with Tyler Whitley, the program director, eating up whatever information and advice he could get his hands on. He began the work to lead his family to a final day of pig farming. "If you build something and show people that you can create a different business model, convert a factory farm into a more sustainable agricultural system, I think more people will do it. And I think we could diversify this economy. I think it'll be good for rural America and good for the environment," Tanner says.

Rural America is starting to shift in surprising ways. More and more people today want to live in rural areas. This has not just been an outcome of COVID-19. Even before 2020, people were interested in moving to the country. For a long time, there was a trend where college-educated rural young folks moved away into urban areas for higher-paying jobs and better opportunities, including more open-minded lifestyles. This was known as the "brain drain." Programs have even been established to get young people to stay in rural areas. Recent signals are indicating that there may be a small, but promising, return to the land. While 80 percent of Americans live in urban areas, a pre-pandemic poll showed that many wanted to be in rural areas.[11] In the wake of the pandemic, the increase in remote work has seen more and more people moving out of big cities. This trend goes beyond people like Tanner—that is, predominantly white sons of farmers. It's environmentally minded young people. It's entrepreneurs. It's also the LGBTQ+ community, hoping to find acceptance now in their hometowns. It's Black women reconnecting to their homes in the rural South. It's the young sons and daughters of immigrants from Central and South America, whose parents are now slaughterhouse workers.[12] All seek to belong, hoping to find a place in their small rural hometowns, in places that offer wide open space and cheaper living. They seek to create an economy they can contribute to, and social connections that allow them to feel at home and accepted.

This rural renewal trend is still in the early stages, but it poses interesting questions: How could we rebuild the rural communities that suffered an exodus in past decades? What attracts young, bright, and ambitious creators, thinkers, and builders to return, or move for the first time, to rural America?

As I've traveled across the country, meeting with farmers wanting to transition out of factory farming, I've noticed that many are making this change for their children—who might come back if the farm were different. They talk about how their kids don't want to inherit the despair, debt, and difficulties that factory farming can bring.

We live in a vast and beautiful country, and many people feel a deep calling to be stewards of this land. For many it is the connection to that land that calls them, and the history of their ancestors, whether they be white settlers, Indigenous people, or those who were once enslaved.

GET BIG OR GET OUT

A thousand miles away in North Carolina, another family was facing the same crossroads as the Faaborgs. Tom Butler's family first came to this area of North Carolina over one hundred years ago. A "centennial farm" is what they call it. Before it came into the hands of his family, it was worked by enslaved people, and before that, it was stewarded by the Tuscarora and Saura Native Americans before they were colonized by Scottish settlers in the early eighteenth century. There is a history of opposing forces here: Stewardship and degradation. Self-determination and oppression. Today, in Harnett County, where the farm sits, this thread from the past is carried forward. The residents bear the burdens of hundreds of years of not yet finding answers about how to live at ease with the environment and each other. Tom Butler's story is a continuation of this centuries-old effort for resolution and healing.

In the central part of the state where Tom's farm sits, just south of Raleigh, the coastal plain has always been ready for growth. Shaded ravines and meandering rivers cut through the landscape, lined by maple, beech, and serviceberry. Tobacco, cotton, soybeans, and wheat have been staples of the agricultural catalog for as long as Tom's family has been in the area. Pigs came along later, taking a terrible toll on the environment and the communities but generating a lot of wealth—for some.

While pigs have been a part of North Carolina agriculture for decades, it was only in the 1990s that the industry grew exponentially. It was in 1992 that Smithfield Foods Inc., then the world's largest pig producer (now the third largest after two Chinese companies, Muyuan Foodstuff Co., Ltd., and Wens Group), built what was then the world's largest pig slaughter and processing facility, in Tar Heel, North Carolina.[13] Hog farming grew 89 percent between 1992 and 2002. This growth set the stage for North Carolina to become what it is today: the third-largest pig producing state, after Iowa and Minnesota. North Carolina fell from number two to number three only in recent years, largely owing to slowed growth as a result of a 1997 moratorium on building new hog cesspools (known as lagoons) to store hog urine and feces. The moratorium became permanent in 2007. As a result, no new hog farms have been built in North Carolina since.

This has made the existing farms all the more central to the industry and the state. While the number of pigs went up in the 1990s, the number of farms went down. Between 1986 and 2006, the number of farms with at least one head of hogs dropped from 15,000 to just 2,300. "Get big or get out" became the motto.

The house where Tom grew up was built in 1922. Like most in the area, Tom's family ran a tobacco farm initially, with twenty or so people working the land. In 1967, when Tom was in his thirties, his father passed away at the age of fifty-eight, and the farm was passed on to him and his brother. But it wasn't until 1995 that Tom would take on pigs, thanks to the explosive growth in hog farming in the state and the dwindling tobacco industry.

Once the moratorium was in place, Tom Butler's farm would become critical for the area's hog production. The pressure and push to produce more and more was relentless. Tom's farm went from a small operation to what it is today—ten warehouses, each keeping around eight hundred "feeder" pigs in one of the several stages of production. The property contains eight thousand pigs at any one time, plus all of their constant feces and urine.

The first stage begins with a pregnant pig. She is kept in a gestation crate, surrounded by metal bars, for the entirety of her pregnancy and even after giving birth. Sows are deeply driven to make a nest when giving birth, but pigs in factory farms are denied the ability to carry out this natural behavior. A sow is kept on a concrete slatted floor, unable to root in the ground the way she normally would. Pigs kept in crates like this exhibit "stereotypic behavior," where they pointlessly and repeatedly gnaw on bars and sway, a sign of psychological damage. When a sow gives birth, she's moved into a farrowing crate, which again means enclosing her in metal bars while her babies move in and out of the bars. Piglets are then taken from their mother and sent to farms like Tom's, where they are kept for fattening until their final days. Here they are kept crowded together, again on concrete slatted floors.

Pigs are very social animals and rely on hierarchies for herd balance. They prefer to remain in small groups for extended periods so they know where they stand socially. But on factory farms, they're repeatedly thrown into new groups of unfamiliar pigs. This constant mixing causes them stress and anxiety, along with their overcrowded, poorly lit, and feces-filled living environments.

Despite their reputation, pigs enjoy being clean. But in the setting of a factory farm, they cannot escape the spray of urine and puddles of feces from their unfortunate companions. Instead of providing the animals with the space and environment they want and need, farmers cut their tails off and clip their teeth to prevent them from biting each other's tails or otherwise hurting each other in these cramped and stressful environments. We know these procedures are both painful and distressing for pigs, who will vocalize, tremble, and shake afterward.

Tom remembers growing pigs that went only up to 60 to 65 pounds, but today's pigs grow to be 300 pounds. Like chickens, pigs have been genetically designed and fed to grow bigger, faster, cheaper. In addition, there has been a push for pigs to be leaner, with less fat. The consequences for their bodies and welfare have been tremendous.

Like broiler chickens, pigs now suffer the unintended consequences of selective breeding, including increased behavior and health problems. From the farmer's perspective, this selective breeding for a bigger but leaner pig has led to a more excitable and reactive pig, who is much harder to manage. Today's pigs are attracted to and at the same time fearful of novel situations and are reactive to even a light touch, including by their pen mates.

Just like chickens, the majority of pigs are raised by contract farmers like Tom. "I'm a puppet," Tom explains, "a foolish puppet that should have known better than to sign that contract. They take the profit and leave me with the dead hogs and the manure. The pig belongs to them until it dies, unless it dies [prematurely]. Then it belongs to me."

It wasn't long after Tom had taken on the hog contract with Prestage Farms, then a major player in the hog industry, that he realized he'd made a mistake. Tom recalls a moment in around 2000 when he first realized the impact his operation had on his community. A neighbor complained to his brother's wife about the smell and the flies. "We realized that we had bit off more than we could chew," Tom says. "And we had a large impact on our community and our neighbors that we had grown up with, and that wasn't fair." But by this time, Tom and his family owed too much money to stop. Like so many other farmers, they'd taken out loans to build the structures required to raise pigs. "We were trapped," Tom says. And now, in 2022, twenty-seven years after starting the operation, he adds, "We're still trapped."

Like the Faaborgs, the Butlers were searching for a way out, a way to move into the future and bring the next generation and the community with them. Tom's son Will, like Tanner, was not looking to inherit a pig farm. He was determined that the cycle would stop with him. Factory farming was causing too much damage to the environment and the community. He had his two daughters to think of. He had his own values to uphold. Like Tanner, Will was an environmentalist at heart, and even beyond that, a vegan. Hog farming was inherently incongruent with who he was.

So, Will started looking for another way to use the farm. The search led him to the Transfarmation Project, and he started hatching a plan. The Butlers were a little behind the Faaborg family in their transition away from hog production, with a lot more debt, but they knew which direction they wanted to go—away from pigs and toward mushrooms.

Tom was on board almost immediately. He'd seen so much suffering, so much destruction, stemming from his own farm. It was time to change course. They started by converting a small shed, with all the equipment and insulation necessary for growing mushrooms. They'd see out these final herds, and they hoped that at the end, they'd have the courage to walk away from hog farming forever. Step by step, they started laying down the tracks for a new life, one that Will could take on, and maybe even his girls too, long after his father passed.

THE LAST HERD

Back in Iowa, the Transfarmation Project team—Tyler, Katherine, Jenn, Stephanie, and I—sat on the darkened hill watching the scene below. It seemed like the loading of the pigs onto the metal truck might never end. The light illuminating the scene was swinging in the wind, throwing shadows on the silos and into the darkness. There was a cowboy-like yelping moving the pigs along, emanating from within the warehouse, from Tanner or his brother or father.

One pig was barking. He was fighting one of the men, who turned him around using a rod. The pigs knew that wherever they were being driven to couldn't be good. The sound was horrific—the gurgling of the truck's motor and the screaming of the pigs and the prodding. The pigs inside were agitated. They were scared. They were pushing. The wind was fierce. One pig pushed another and they tried to turn around. A man yelled, "Come on, come on! Go, go! Hey, hey!" The pigs tried to go back to the barn, to no avail.

This was the third truck, and it was now 1:25 a.m. Each truck took 175 pigs, one row on the bottom, one row on the top. The wind made it feel colder. I couldn't imagine what it would be like here in winter, how harsh it must be when the temperature dropped and there was snow on the ground. I took cover in a barn from the wind, smells, and sounds for a moment, but even from there I could still hear the squealing, screaming pigs and the howling wind. And the smell of the pig waste seeped through the cracks in the walls.

The final truck came. It took several attempts to back up to the chute the pigs would travel down. The truck was lit up from within, looking distinctly like a prison. I took a moment to look away, to steady myself. Above the smells and the noise, the sky was full of stars.

The team began loading the very last pigs, yelling, "Hey, hey, come on now!" Prodding them, pushing them to their destination. The pigs were squealing. They ran on the truck. One pig ran around inside like she'd gone mad. One by one, the pigs were driven to one end of the truck, running in circles around this unfamiliar space. Suddenly the last truck with the last pigs drove away, into the darkness.

The family stood there, frozen, like a portrait. Tammy with her hands on her hips, the others by her side, watching under the light, like a spotlight on a stage, as the last pigs went. Then they turned to us and beckoned for us to come down. We descended the hill, gingerly on the darkened path. We were tired, cold, and emotionally worn out from watching all that suffering.

As we entered the now-empty warehouses, Tanner, Tammy, and Rand's faces were lit up. They were all smiles. It was jarring. It was disorienting, their brightness, after what we had witnessed.

Rand was smiling ear to ear: "Feels good. I think it'll take a while to sink in, but it just really feels good. It's time. It's probably past time. This is the last one." He kept repeating that over and over again: "That's the last one."

And now I understood their smiles. It was over. Now they could let down their guard. Now they could celebrate and look forward. They were done. We scanned the warehouse, walking down the aisle. Left and right were the concrete pens that would never again enclose pigs, slats that would never again let feces run into lagoons and the neighboring water or air. The warehouse was empty, except for the ghosts.

The family excitedly began talking about transforming the barn. It was the end of October and they already had a site visit planned with a mushroom expert for early November. They were working on a design and talked about construction, and what it would take to begin their new lives as mushroom farmers.

PART TWO

THE ANIMALS

CHAPTER FIVE

THE YEAR OF HENRIETTA THE HEN

DROVE EAST ON I-20, down the long, monotonous highway for a whole day to reach my destination in Texas. A chicken factory farmer named Frank,[1] not far from the Halleys, was interested in learning more about our Transfarmation Project. The farmers of rural America don't complain, but they are often flattered and surprised that anyone would take an interest in their hardship. They are used to having to go it alone. But a key priority of the Transfarmation Project is to acknowledge how hard it is for farmers to just quit.

I had been to a chicken factory farm before. I had trudged across the sinking floor, moist with feces and feathers. I had waded through the thousands of birds, like an ice skater fanning out one leg and then the other, attempting not to startle or step on any beings. I've seen this kind of suffering many times now, and it never gets any easier to handle. No matter how hard it is to witness these birds' pain, the one thing I never do on these visits is take any of the animals home. While they belong to a big poultry company, the harder truth for me to face is that there are just too many of them. I could fill my house with birds and there would still be billions left to save. However, this visit would wind up differently.

When we arrived at Frank's farm, a throng of dogs and cats came to greet us, but no humans. I texted him to let him know we were here. He texted back immediately asking us to come down to the warehouses, where he was starting his work for the day.

We spent that first day following Frank as he did his chicken farmer duties. We scooted through the house, filled wall-to-wall with chickens spread across the floor, a sea of suffering. I tried to hear his story, but the chickens' suffering pulled my attention away. The ones with splayed legs that couldn't bear their weight. The ones limping, using their wings as crutches to hop around. The ones I could see were ill, heads hanging low, beaks resting resigned in the dirt—which was really just feces—eyes half open, breathing heavy. I'd be listening to Frank say how he couldn't stand it anymore, how he wanted out but didn't know how to make a change. Then I'd look to the chicken who was too weak to move away from me, who had settled next to my boot.

After many months of really trying, Frank said that, in the end, he couldn't make the leap to quit chicken farming and transition to hemp. The risk was too high, the cost of failing too severe. His family depended on him, and he couldn't put them in danger of losing their home or their land.

COVID had hit slaughterhouse workers hard. While most of us stood six feet apart, slaughterhouse workers stood shoulder to shoulder, mandated by the president to continue producing. So tens of thousands of workers got COVID and hundreds died.[2] The slaughterhouse didn't have enough workers to kill the chickens, and this caused a backup at the slaughter-house. Because of this, the week we were with Frank, the catch crew didn't show up when they were scheduled—and they didn't tell Frank until a few hours beforehand.

All the preparation he'd done during the day had to be undone. Back down came the water lines, down came the feed line. Except now, when he turned the machines back on, only dust came out from the bottom of the feed containers. He tried to get more feed, but the company said he had to make do. It was the height of summer, the middle of a heat wave, temperatures in the triple digits. These fragile baby giants could not handle the heat. Heart attacks were common. Frank would not get paid for dead birds. The catch crew would not take birds that looked too poorly. He turned the lights low to keep the birds still, hoping they might just sleep until the trucks could come. There wasn't much he could do except pray.

In the end, the company took two additional days to come back and get the birds, and by then the birds were in bad shape. As I prepared to say my goodbyes, he let me know the catch crew had left behind about twenty of the chickens, deemed unworthy even for slaughter—too sick or small. "What happens to those that are left behind?" I asked. "Who do they belong to now?" Frank said he'd have to hand-kill them and then they'd just be thrown out.

Five years earlier, my son's kindergarten class decided to raise crayfish, as part of a unit on understanding life cycles. Each day my son would come home excited about how this alien being was changing, how she went from one form to the other, like magic. But I knew exactly where this was headed. At the end of the lesson cycle, I asked the teacher what she would do with the crayfish when the lesson was over. She turned to me with her mouth half covered and said: "I stick them in the freezer, and they just slow down and die. Don't tell the kids." She didn't know who I was. We soon had all five crayfish in a tank in our living room.

So when I asked Frank what would happen to the chickens left behind, I knew exactly what I was asking.

The day before, Shawn and I had stood with Frank in the middle of fifteen thousand birds packed wall-to-wall in a dark warehouse, the air thick with dust and ammonia. To the left of the house lay three more houses, meaning there were sixty thousand birds on Frank's small property. A fog of debris and dust floated in the air, making it difficult to see from one end to the other of the football-field-length warehouse.

When we drove up that morning, it was raining and the warehouse doors were open, the smell rolling out. We walked around, and everywhere I looked, I saw the remnants of the carnage: the remaining chickens were just barely alive, like blinking corpses. A few were on their feet, running in the now-huge expanse of the barn. Without the tens of thousands of chickens, it was a dark cavern. You could see it for what it was: a tomb.

When I asked Frank again what would happen to the birds left behind, he turned and said, "If I have to hand-kill even a few less, that would be just fine with me." And he left me standing in that warehouse.

There were about twenty chickens left. How could I even begin to choose one or two birds to save? I believed myself to be far more practical than that, a big-picture problem solver. I directed an organization that focused on pragmatic, institutional change. We couldn't let ourselves pause to consider what it was really like for an individual to live like this. The pain might stop us entirely.

Most of these birds were not going to make it no matter what I did. They lay near-motionless except for their blinking eyes in the steamy litter. One, spinning in the litter in a panic despite my slow and careful approach, was using her wings to maneuver herself. She was otherwise completely unable to stand up. Her suffering would soon be over.

But a few were upright, alert. Ready. So I told myself: three. I chose the number arbitrarily. Three out of twenty.

One bird caught my eye as I roamed the barn. She was small and hunched over. Someone had pecked her neck to reveal raw angry flesh, caked with dirt and seeping blood. I picked her up and held her limp body for a moment. She seemed resigned, and I thought this would be her last day. I carried her over to a puddle that had formed from the dripping roof. She immediately started guzzling water. She was so thirsty, clearly dehydrated. How long had it been since she'd had water? She was so small, she probably couldn't reach the water lines in the last few days.

Her spirit captivated me. She was not healthy; she would not survive. And yet, she was still fighting for her life. I couldn't let her go. Her desperate efforts to take in more and more water told me all I needed to know: she wanted to live, for however long she could.

A second chicken watched me from the corner of the barn. She was standing upright, head cocked to one side, then the other. She seemed more alert than the others, more discerning. She was taking me in, and I was taking her in. I walked over to her slowly, but she darted just out of reach. It took me a minute, but I caught her. When I picked her up, she was surprisingly strong. Her wings pressed hard against my hands.

A third one, larger than all the rest, was the last one I caught. I thought because he was big, he might survive. But his size would actually be his demise.

Shawn helped me load the three chickens into a big black tub, which I filled with litter, water, and food. It was clear I was doing this on my own, outside of my job, outside of any direction. I watched Shawn in the rearview mirror, standing in the rain on the dirt road, considering me as I drove away.

I'd never taken care of chickens before, though I've fought for their rights my whole adulthood. One of them, the one who had guzzled water, I was sure would not make it. Still, she sang that whole long drive to Georgia. Her voice, her sweet chirping, seemed to celebrate. I can still hear the sound. She wanted to sing, to express something, to be heard. At least, I thought, her last hours would be better spent in the car, cuddling with the other two, rather than in that terrible warehouse.

It was water they were desperate for at first, and as I drove home I had to keep stopping to refill the water container. They were so thirsty. They drank and drank. Within a couple of hours, the one that I thought for sure wouldn't even make it home had started to perk up. But they were far from healthy. They had diarrhea—just yellow liquid—one of them kept twitching from time to time, and they made truly horrible smells. They were plagued with gut problems and dirty feathers. They were so tired, nodding off again and again.

I loved them immediately.

On the drive home I tried not to think about where their flock mates were at that moment, but I kept being reminded. I passed Chick-fil-A, KFC, Popeyes. It felt obscene. My birds' flock mates would be in the mouths of people that very week. But there they were, nestled up against each other, hopefully slowly letting the memory of where they'd come from drift away.

I arrived home at 2 a.m. My house was dark and quiet, the three kids and Ben dreaming and settled. I headed in through the basement with its spare bed and bathroom so as not to disturb them. We would settle there for the night. Also, the cats Sumo and Honey might be a problem—one I had not thought of until the moment I heard them scratching at the door and meowing to come into the basement. Better to leave that introduction for another day. The three birds were sleeping, one's neck nestled on the back of the other's, huddling together in a circle. They had made it here.

Despite my shattering exhaustion, I had to shower. I'd been in the warehouse, crawled around in that death, dust, and feces, then driven half across the country with access only to some wipes and hand sanitizer. I had made the poor choice of eating an Impossible Whopper, with the chickens looking curiously on, and what I'd guess were not the cleanest of hands. I'd pay severely for that trip, get acutely sick, the sickest I've ever been. Not from COVID, but from the disease that comes from keeping chickens crammed together in the tens of thousands living in their own feces and filth.

I turned on the shower, stripped myself of my clothing. I considered my clothes. I didn't even want them in my washing machine, where my children's T-shirts and socks would also go. I stepped into the shower and watched the steam rise and the water fall off me. I don't recall getting into bed. I drifted in and out of sleep, awakened only a few hours later as the sun was rising by my children, big smiles, eyes sparkling. "Where are the chickens? Where are they?"

So it began, my family's work to heal three chickens, only one of whom would survive the week. Most people in the world would call this the year of COVID. But we would look back and call it the year of Henrietta.

SETTLING IN

We let each child name one chicken. Andrea named the smallest one Shakira after the Colombian singer, because she's fancy, has fluffy feathers, and sings nonstop. Asher named the medium-sized one Henrietta. It was my suggestion, and a reference to her origins—the same name as Bo Pilgrim's mascot chicken. Ruben named the last one Bruno.

We filled up the sink with warm water and placed Shakira into the warm bath. We washed her with Dr. Bronner's almond hemp soap, which felt so healing. There was no doubt in my mind that Shakira and the two other chickens enjoyed their bath. I imagine the warm water took the weight off their legs and soothed them. Shakira fell asleep in the bath in a state of complete trust and relaxation. The filth and crusted-on dirt broke away from her in the tenderness of my hands and the warm water. The bath turned a brown color, washing away the past. I took an antiseptic wipe and gently scrubbed the wounds on Shakira's neck.

Then came the hair dryer. Asher took out the hair dryer and I placed Bruno, Henrietta, and Shakira on the bathroom floor. They puffed and fluffed and turned to face the warm air head on, eventually nodding off. Ruben placed wood shavings in a low cardboard box in the shower, along with food and water. The chickens were chirping away immediately. Shakira was weak and slept a lot. Bruno seemed to have an insatiable appetite. Henrietta was definitely our adventurous, curious spirit, immediately on the edge of the bathroom shower door, looking around, wondering where she'd ended up.

Each day the chickens got stronger. They took their first dirt bath underneath my pepper plants. Their joy was palpable as they flung dirt over their backs and shoveled their heads into the dust and fluffed and danced together. They explored the grass for the first time. They perched for the first time. They seemed to not really know how to be chickens, so I had to teach them. I placed them on edges to help them figure out what perching was. I scattered food in the grass to encourage foraging. They began to figure out exploring for themselves—Henrietta being the biggest adventurer, often leading the other two under bushes, into flower patches, marching through the grass. I loved that they followed me. I loved that if I sat in a chair in the yard, they would sit under me.

It was hard to find a vet that would treat chickens. I ended up driving forty minutes away to a vet in Duluth—an all-species vet who had photos of monkeys on his website, which made me hesitant. We weren't actually sure if the chickens were males or females, and when I asked the vet, he said it was too soon to tell. This was another red flag, since I know chicks are sexed as soon as they hatch. His assessment proved useless. I decided to look for a better vet.

In the days that followed, Bruno's right leg began to balloon out at the joints. He limped and rested on his left side, so as to not put pressure on his pain. His right wing appeared to be losing strength. He couldn't walk far anymore, just five steps or so before he'd plop down. I could see his breathing was labored. I thought a warm bath might comfort him. I filled the sink and set him in it, but that only appeared to cause him distress, and we abandoned the idea immediately. Instead, I wrapped him in a towel and held him on my lap. He appeared to purr and settled into a deep slumber while I typed away at my computer. I did several calls like this, with my secret rescued friend on my lap.

Although Shakira's feathers began to fill in, her breathing was labored. She sneezed and coughed. Her breath sounded raspy. I could see the beginnings of a leg disorder and swelling in her left hock, an ailment that mirrored Bruno's own and had already become debilitating for him.

Henrietta was smaller, so her weight caused less problems, for now. But I feared what was coming for her. The hunger that drives these chickens to eat and eat also drives them to destroy themselves. For these two, I knew I would at some point have to make the hard decision of whether or not to prolong their life, when their suffering became too much. For now, they seemed to very much enjoy exploring the grass and snuggling with each other or me. It made me consider and reconsider what makes a life worth living.

Henrietta was the most adventurous and healthy lady. About one week after being with me, she firmly decided one day during one of her outings that she was not going to come out of the bushes. I'd only let them out for supervised outdoor time so far, waiting until they were strong and healthy enough to be outside entirely. While the others remained squatting on the grass, Henrietta took it upon herself to disappear under the foliage. I felt proud and also concerned—what if a hawk or cat came by? Like the mother I am, I was unable to leave her there for long, and soon found myself on hands and knees, in the rain, wrestling with cobwebs and vines to get her out and back to safety. Of the three, Henrietta was the only one who seemed healthy in terms of her musculoskeletal system, and even she had a respiratory infection.

I'd sent out feelers on neighborhood lists and friends, asking for a good chicken vet. But in the meantime, with no vet to guide me, I went down a rabbit hole researching leg disorders in broiler chickens. There was an abundance of literature. It's not like the industry or scientists don't know this is a problem. But the literature had no solutions, other than changing breeds. Nothing that would help my chickens.

I knew it was coming. I'd seen the signs. Right when I brought them home, I could see something was wrong with Bruno's leg and Shakira's overall health. As the days went on, Bruno would almost exclusively lie on his right side with his left leg splayed out to the side. What started as just a resting position became a limp and eventually difficulty in moving at all. These are the same leg problems, lameness, and swollen joints I saw on Frank's farm. This is the curse of the fast-growing breed.

Shakira barely got up. She'd still chirp and chirp, but she stopped trying to forage or explore. She slept most of the time, breathing more heavily than her small body should have needed. She didn't seem to have much of a comb, and what she did have was pale. Soon, she also began to limp. Henrietta grew stronger while the other two seemed to fade.

I tried desperately to help them. I read about their issues and continued my search for a vet that specialized in chickens. I posted on my neighborhood Nextdoor because I knew several neighbors had backyard birds. I tried to give the chickens comfort. A warm bath for Bruno to soothe the leg pain. A cuddle for Shakira. They still weren't robust enough to be outside on their own. They probably would never be. But I'd take them for supervised explorations in the front and back garden while I sat and worked on my laptop. Henrietta did all the things chickens are supposed to do, though at a slower speed and with more resting than a typical backyard hen. Bruno and Shakira hardly got up at all.

One thing the three of them couldn't get enough of was their morning dust bath. I'd bring them out before it got too hot, and they'd make their way under the tomato bushes. Then they'd begin the ritual of rolling their heads in the dirt, fluffing out their feathers and throwing dirt on their back with their wings. They could do this for an hour, spinning slowly in the dirt, a ritual dance, until they had created a crater in the ground. It gave me such pleasure to see them do this, to see the joy they experienced, the excitement as they waddled to what was clearly their favorite spot for their bath. It must have felt so good to them, tossing the warm soil in between their feathers on their skin, relieving and comforting them. Billions of birds never get to experience this pleasure. I didn't teach Henrietta, Bruno, and Shakira to do this. They just instinctively knew how. I know each and every one of the birds in factory farms also want this. They also want to forage in the grass, rest in cool spots under bushes, and explore. They never get the chance.

One morning I woke to a response on Nextdoor: there was a chicken vet, For Pet's Sake, not too far away, and they were avian specialists. I immediately called. It was a Saturday morning and they said to bring the chicks in right away. The entire family piled in the car. I don't know why we all chose to go but we did. We arrived at a house, in a parking lot near a mall. We were told to wait in the parking lot because of COVID. Eventually a friendly, round-faced woman with tattooed eyebrows came out and took the three birds inside. They said if we wanted to run an errand to go ahead and do that; they'd give us a call in about thirty minutes.

School was about to start, and even though it was going to be virtual school, we had a lot of items to purchase to get ready. So we headed to Target. I got the call in the checkout line.

The vet said Shakira had a respiratory infection in both lungs. Bruno also was infected. Both Shakira and Bruno had septic joints. She asked me some questions, but it was all a blur. The vet said the septic joints were unsolvable, unless we wanted to attempt invasive antibiotic treatment, which might not work. And anyhow, Shakira was showing signs of chronic illness. Her pale comb was a sign that she was malnourished and had been sick for a very long time.

She told me what I already knew: "The best thing for Shakira and Bruno is to humanely euthanize them. They have very poor prospects."

I asked: "And Henrietta?"

"She's okay," the vet said, but added, "For now. I can give you some vitamins called Rooster Booster to help her. But only time will tell." She asked me what I wanted to do. I asked if they were open tomorrow, hoping for one more night with them. She said they weren't open on Sunday and that I'd have to come back Monday—but the birds were suffering. I said I'd call her back in five minutes.

I stood there in the Target line, powerless. I knew this was the likely outcome of rescuing these birds, but I had not thought this would be the day. I had even been looking at chicken coops, thinking they had months left. Looking back, I can see how in denial I was. I'd become so attached to them in such a short time. I looked down at my daughter, who had named Shakira and was holding onto my right leg, and knew she, too, would face pain now. I called back. "Yes, today. But can you wait? Can we come back to say goodbye, when we come to get Henrietta?"

She agreed, and we dragged ourselves reluctantly back to the car. We pulled up to the vet's office and they brought out Shakira and Bruno, carrying them in their arms. I was overwhelmed by their pain, by their suffering, by this life they were given. My six-year-old daughter started crying immediately, and I had to pull myself together for her. I told her that Bruno and Shakira's spirits would now be free from their terrible bodies that gave them so much pain and suffering. Now they would be free to be and do as they pleased. I kept saying this over and over again to her, to myself, as tears rolled down my cheeks. Bruno and Shakira rested on my legs and we stroked their heads and necks. They breathed deeply, slowly. My oldest son was trying to be an adult. He told me that I did the right thing, that at least they knew kindness, at least they knew grass and bugs and sunshine. At least they didn't have to die in that horrible place. My middle son stood silent, arms hanging limply at his sides, staring at the pavement.

We took Henrietta home without Shakira and Bruno. She kept looking for her companions.

When we got home, we wrapped Henrietta in a towel, and she joined us for a family movie. She sat on my daughter's lap. Andrea stroked her head and Henrietta drifted in and out of sleep. Now began Henrietta's journey alone, with her new family.

———

Currently, there are no federal or state laws to protect chickens during breeding, hatching, transport, rearing, or slaughter. The main laws intended to protect farmed animals—the Humane Methods of Slaughter Act, the Animal Welfare Act, and the Twenty-Eight Hour Law—specifically exclude chickens from these laws' protections. Apart from prohibitions against carrying out abject cruelty, with intent and malice, you can treat chickens as you like. And the industry chooses to treat them like machines. You can stuff them in dark warehouses, push them to their genetic limits to the point where they cannot walk and can hardly breathe, and take them through any slaughter you see as fit for business.

Attempts thus far to protect chickens through the law have failed, though some progress is being made through corporate animal welfare policy. Over two hundred companies have adopted the Better Chicken Commitment—a science-based chicken welfare policy that addresses housing, stocking density, slaughter, and issues related to breeding for fast growth and high yield. There is hope, but change is slow, and the speed is controlled by the very industry that stands to lose money from implementing methods that treat animals with more dignity. It is only through consumer demand and hard work by animal activists that these companies are moving in a more ethical direction.

By the Tuesday after Shakira and Bruno's death, I started to feel something was not right—this time with myself. First I lost my appetite, and knots rolled through my stomach occasionally, causing me to pause, even double over. By the end of Thursday I was weak, having had diarrhea twenty times in the day, and then further throughout the night. When blood appeared, I knew I needed to call the doctor.

I suspected my visit to the chicken farm was to blame. There had been no way to wash our hands there. We did use hand sanitizer and wipes. But I had had a lot of contact with the birds. I had been picking them up to see what sores and ailments they had—red, bare chests, sores on their hocks and feet, wounds seeping pus. The birds' feathers, feet, and chests were covered in dried feces, the ground simply a layer of dried and hardened feces, feathers, feed, and other particles. I told the doctor all of this and said I suspected salmonella, campylobacter, or E. coli—three bacteria common in factory-farmed animals that cause food poisoning in humans. Usually, people get these infections by eating chickens, but I explained I was vegan and had been holding live chickens at an industrial farm.

The doctor's diagnosis was dysentery, defined as an "infection of the intestines resulting in severe diarrhea with the presence of blood and mucus in the feces." Bacterial dysentery is caused by infection with bacteria from shigella, campylobacter, salmonella, or enterohemorrhagic E. coli. Now we had to figure out through tests what was causing it. Given the appearance of blood, it was imperative that we started a treatment right away. The doctor took a sample and sent me away with antibiotics to see if they would start to help, as we waited for the tests to come back. Dysentery can be fatal if not treated or if the antibiotics don't work because the bacteria is antibiotic-resistant.

Within twelve hours of starting the antibiotics, I started to feel better, which confirmed that what I'd had was bacterial. Three days later and fifteen pounds lighter, I was relieved that the diarrhea and terrible cramping had finally stopped, and I had some energy back. The tests confirmed that the infection was caused by campylobacter. According to the CDC, the number one cause of campylobacter poisoning is chicken.[3] Most often it's a result of eating raw or undercooked chickens (or something that has touched that raw or undercooked chicken), the meat of which is contaminated by fecal matter during slaughter.

Campylobacter is considered the most common bacterial cause of human gastroenteritis in the world and is one of the four key global causes of diarrheal diseases.[4] The bacteria can be transmitted directly or indirectly between animals and humans. With over 246,000 human cases annually, it is the most frequently reported cause of foodborne illness in the European Union.[5] The actual number of cases, however, is believed to be closer to 9 million each year.[6] The most common bacterial cause of diarrheal illness in the United States, campylobacter infections affect 1.5 million US residents every year, according to CDC estimates.[7] Symptoms include diarrhea (often bloody), fever, stomach cramps, nausea, and vomiting.[8] Like other bacteria, some strains of campylobacter are becoming resistant to antibiotics commonly used to treat infection.[9] Luckily, mine was not.

Campylobacter can be carried in the intestines, liver, and other organs of animals and transferred to other body parts during slaughter. In 2015, National Antimicrobial Resistance Monitoring System (NARMS) tests found campylobacter on 24 percent of raw chicken bought from retailers.[10] In fact, the likely causes of most campylobacteriosis cases in humans are handling, preparing, or consuming tainted chicken meat.[11] I had escaped this bacteria's clutches, but I shuddered to think how prevalent this devil was in chickens that people eat every day.

SUMMER

Henrietta's voice began to change. She surprised herself when one of her baby cheeps suddenly turned into an out-of-control clucking noise. Like a teenager, she was maturing into an adult. She preened her snowy feathers with care and pride. She puffed and shook dust into the air. She lived for her dust baths and took delight in flapping her wings and doing short dashes across the grass. Henrietta loved mirrors, any chance to see her reflection. She would turn her head one way and then the other, peck a few times, and chirp to the bird in the mirror. She liked to rest on the windowsill against the green foliage and sleep facing the mirror.

She discovered the Roomba, our robot vacuum, quite by accident. She jumped onto the Roomba and sat down on the CLEAN button. She spun one way, then the other. She rode down the hallway, into the mudroom, until she stepped on the button and turned it off again. We pressed it for her a second time and she stood up, looking like a surfer on a board, riding down the hallway. All the while, the cats were wide-eyed, following her intently, and my kids were laughing.

Henrietta enriched our lives in ways I didn't know were missing. COVID had made us insular, inward, and small. Henrietta forced us all, all five of us, to get out again. She sparked joy in our house, after months of us trying just to survive this restrictive new world. We still couldn't go many places, but Henrietta opened up a whole new world of curiosity for us. We wondered if she liked cats, a black bean, a particular color, a video game, a YouTube video of clucking noises. She was an endless source of wonder to us.

One weekend in early September, after weeks of her healing inside the house, I decided it was time for her to try living outdoors. I am not a builder. I am not handy. When Ben came home to find me with coop instructions sprawled across the lawn, pieces of a kit in disarray, he prepared to intervene. But I raised a hand, halting him. Andrea and I built her a home with Olympic focus and speed. Henrietta's new palace, ordered online from Tractor Supply Co., can fit six chickens—plenty of space for her to stretch her wings.

We put Henrietta to bed on her first night in the coop, telling her we loved her and to be brave. That night, I was nervous having her so far away. But I imagined that she liked the breeze and the sound of the leaves rustling. I imagined her dozing off to the crickets chirping. I imagined the stars in the night sky shining in through cracks in the beams of her coop.

When the bugs had diminished and the cooler air held in the morning, my daughter and I started having breakfast with Henrietta in the backyard. Sometimes my daughter made a trail of her favorite treats—dandelion leaves—down the driveway. Sometimes Andrea carried Henrietta around the garden on her hip, just telling her about her day. Sometimes Andrea just sang to her.

Seven months after her rescue, I began to stop worrying if she had pain, if she would survive the day, the week. I used to ask myself whether I was just prolonging her pain. But in this first half year, she'd become strong, motivated, and assertive. She walked without slipping too much on the hardwood floors. She hardly sat at all now, which she used to do most of the day. She walked with confidence. She also discovered junk food, preferring spaghetti and pancakes over kale and beets. When I offered her salad, she knocked it out of my hand, offended.

The real change came for Henrietta when she started laying eggs. I had convinced myself that she wouldn't be able to do that. I assumed it was too metabolically taxing and her body would not allow it. But I was wrong. One day, five and a half months after I brought Henrietta home, Asher rushed in to say he'd found two brown eggs in the rosemary bushes. This was also a surprise. Because she's white, I thought the eggs would be white. I remember standing over the eggs in disbelief, with Henrietta a few feet away plucking the grass. She laid eggs in the kitty litter, under the porch stairs, in the bushes. Once we found an egg after unrolling an old yoga mat stowed under the porch. Andrea built Henrietta an "egg fort" in her room, made of her robe and her doll crib. Henrietta found it very appealing for egg laying.

Occasionally we didn't find the eggs, just shells. One early morning I found a raccoon on our porch stairs and realized she'd been eating some of Henrietta's eggs. The laying of eggs seemed to give her purpose. Every other day we found them. She became more mobile after this, searching and exploring more, more vocal, and more motivated to exercise.

As winter approached, I declared it too cold, too lonely, for Henrietta to sleep outside alone. So each evening, I called her, and she called back, waddling her way to me before I scooped her up, carrying her on my right hip, as I did my human babies, and bringing her inside. She slept in the mudroom at first, but eventually ended up—in fact demanded to be—in my daughter's room, in the large black bin filled with wood shavings, the one I brought her, Bruno, and Shakira home in. I slept easy too.

Each night, and into the next morning, she was inside our home, our household. She waddled around the hardwood floors, exploring closets and bedrooms. She loved the kitchen, the center of life in my house, not to mention a place of many crumbs. She often left droppings, which I tried to pick up as fast as they dropped. I would say my husband, a public health doctor, tolerated this but did not embrace it. He knew better than to fight it.

I was on a trip when my husband called. "We have a problem with your chicken."

"What?!" I immediately thought the worst.

"She is a free bird. She walked down the driveway, down the sidewalk, and into the next-door neighbor's driveway."

She did it again the next day. I wondered what she was thinking. Was she just becoming her adventurous, confident true self? Was she cold and looking for the front door, but blocked by a fence? I suggested they open the gate at the front garden and see what happened the next day.

The next day my husband sent me a photo of Henrietta through the gate, standing at the front door. She wanted to come in the house—through the front door, like everyone else did in our family. "You have the brain of a chicken, and that is a compliment," he wrote. Truly, nothing would feel more like a compliment than that to me—being able to understand and know what she wanted.

It was a Sunday like any other. The human members of the family were inside making lunch. Henrietta was just outside the kitchen window, looking at her family from the driveway. She looked glorious, shining white in the late autumn sunlight. Her white feathers were all fluffed up, an elegant queen's dress for a ball. She was exquisite, not just in her current state, but because of how she had transformed over the past year.

Andrea and I wanted to go eat lunch with her but decided against it so as to not torture her with our food.

"We'll only be a few minutes and we'll be out with her," I said to Andrea. "Then we can garden together." This would be the last time I saw Henrietta alive.

Later I'd say, *If only I had gone out five minutes earlier, if only I had just eaten with her, maybe*. But she was always on borrowed time. Each day was always an extra day, a gift.

Andrea and I headed outside, ready for an afternoon of gardening with Henrietta. I thought about how much she'd enjoy the pulling up of the weeds, the digging and clucking she'd do. We called for her. We called and called. Sometimes she went into the bushes, under the house, so we looked there. When I saw the clump of white in the backyard, I prayed it was a plastic bag. But my eyes had chosen initially to delete the hawk that was standing over her. I gasped. I knew immediately that Henrietta was dead. Her legs were up, she was on her back, a sign she had had a heart attack, known as "flip-over syndrome" in industrial chicken farming. That's how common heart attacks are in chickens. I always knew that there would never be enough days with her, that I'd always want more.

I turned to Andrea. She hadn't seen Henrietta yet. Somehow, I had the presence of mind to send her inside. I told her we'll garden later, that she can watch a show. When I knew Andrea was out of sight, I ran down toward the opportunistic hawk standing over Henrietta. The hawk flew to the fence and perched to watch as I collapsed to my knees. I picked up Henrietta, still warm.

Her once-bright red comb and waddle, her eyelids, had faded to pink. She was gone. I never knew that a chicken's face could turn pale, but here she was with life drained from her. I looked over her body and could see no injuries, no blood, no feathers lying around. She had not struggled. So the vet later concluded that she most likely had a heart attack first, followed by the arrival of this opportunistic hawk.

I called Ben and he came out, hands to his head, repeating over and over again, *Oh no oh no oh no.* "How will I tell the kids?" I ask him. "How will I tell Andrea?" I hardened at the thought. I prepared in my head a script for telling the kids the news, thinking about how I would prepare her body, which was already stiffening. I took her light green towel, the one we always used for her baths, and swaddled her, her cheek resting to one side. There she lay, as if simply resting. I placed her in a clear container and tucked her in the open garage.

Ben brought out the boys first. They held each other and me. They wanted to see her. I brought them to her. They, too, commented on her pale face, her lifeless sleep. Andrea came out without being called. "What, what's happening? Where is Henrietta? Did you find her? Was she in the bushes?"

"No, my love," I said. I kneeled down so I was close to her face and said what I had to say.

"But who will play with me?" she cried. "Who will have fun with me? I want Henrietta. I want Henrietta." My daughter collapsed in my arms.

"She's gone," I said. "But we were lucky to have her, we were lucky to know her, and we will always have her love in our hearts." She pushed me away and ran back into the house.

An hour or so later, Andrea emerged from under her covers and moved to gather paper and crayons. She created an altar at our fireplace. I put some of Henrietta's brilliant feathers in a jar. We each wrote a message. We reflected that grief can only come from the gift of love.

FEBRUARY 10, 2022

I had set my alarm for 4:55 a.m. At 5 a.m., the world would see the culmination of all the risks Shawn and I took, and all the psychological, emotional, and physical difficulties we endured during our work in Texas.

At exactly 5 a.m., I sat on my couch, my family asleep, and pulled up the *New York Times* app on my phone. There it was: "See the True Cost of Your Cheap Chicken." Out of a commitment to journalistic integrity, they had not let me see it in advance. I had an idea of what the story would say, but not really. It could have shown anything.

The autoplay image they used made me hold my hand to my heart, as if I might stop the memory of it all crashing down. It was Shakira, as I had found her in the warehouse. I had brought her to a puddle, formed under a leaking roof on that rainy day. And with her oversized beak, and her neck wound, she was fighting for her life, taking sip after sip of water. There she was, in the *New York Times*.

I wasn't prepared for the emotions I'd feel that day. I thought I would be—after all, we'd been ready since the fall for the video to come out. But one hurdle after another had presented itself, and I had pushed away anything I felt about this project, in case it never came to fruition. Now I sat alone, in the dark, in the early winter morning hours, finger hovering over the play button. I pressed play and watched the footage, listened as a narrator explained why chicken is so cheap, how it relies on stripping farmers and chickens of any dignity, of any decency. I was looking for Henrietta. In the sea of white, birds packed wall-to-wall, I looked for her. She was in there somewhere.

Many text messages came through asking how we got this access, remarking on the quality of the film, congratulating us on the amazing partnership with the team at the *New York Times*. But the one that stopped me was from a dear colleague: *Henrietta would be proud.*

CHAPTER SIX

FELIX THE PIG

H URRICANE FLORENCE SURPRISED the residents of Duplin County, North Carolina, the way a predator surprises her prey. She began as a tropical wave off the coast of Africa, but gathered up in her arms the warm sea air and the currents that crossed the ocean. With each nautical mile, she grew into a monster—a Category 4 hurricane sustaining wicked 130-mile-per-hour winds. But then, as she approached the coastal southeast of the United States, she relaxed to a Category 1. This felt manageable.

But one should never underestimate a hurricane, ever. Florence's power was in her slowness, her settling upon the land. She crawled, with her deluge of rain, barely seeming to move. Parts of the southeast that had not been affected by hurricanes before saw what a storm can do. Landlocked Atlanta, a six hours' drive from the nearest eastern coast, lost power for three days from downed trees and floods.

Duplin County, which out of all US counties houses the highest number of pig farms, was among the worst affected. The storm homed in and raged on the county for days. The National Weather Service reported that North Carolina received a torrent of 8.04 trillion gallons of water from the hurricane.[1] The relentless rain caused flash flooding and road washouts. The Northeast Cape Fear River rose too fast, flooding roads and homes both close to and far from the river. People drowned in their cars trying to escape: a sixty-five-year-old man on NC Highway 111 in Goshen Swamp, a seventy-nine-year-old woman on North Williams

Road, and an eighty-one-year-old man on Bowden Road near the Duplin/ Sampson County line.[2] Long stretches of I-40, I-95, and US Route 70 were impassable for a week after the storm had moved on.[3] Duplin County residents could not have predicted that their homes, towns, farms, and roads would see record flooding that would devastate their community—and the animals who were trapped on their farms.

The cesspools that housed the state's pig feces, euphemistically called "lagoons," had been compromised by the flooding and storm. Under normal industrial farming circumstances, pigs kept indoors in close confinement defecate on slatted floors inside their warehouses. Their stomping, laying, and walking pushes that waste through the slats into a system that empties into an outdoor cesspool, which is a mix of water, pig waste, and anaerobic bacteria. The bacteria actually turn the water bubblegum pink as they digest the feces. The state reported that at least 130 such cesspools were compromised, some pouring pig feces and urine into roads, land, and even into people's homes.[4]

North Carolina housed some 9.7 million pigs at the time, producing about 10 billion gallons of waste annually.[5] The majority of that waste comes from two counties: Duplin and Sampson. After the hurricane, the images of the pink lagoons' foam and slurry moving into communities, onto roads and towns, were frightening. Community leaders had learned nothing from 1999, when Hurricane Floyd had flooded the cesspools and caused mass fish deaths. Here they were again, in 2018, in the same situation. Experts warned of a potential health and environmental catastrophe, as groundwater was contaminated with the slurry.[6]

Then came the images of millions of drowned, floating chickens and thousands of bloated pig carcasses.[7] Not one of the pigs trapped in a gestation crate escaped the floods alive. These systems entrap pregnant mother pigs for the duration of their pregnancy, and after they give birth as well, in farrowing crates.

The metal crates squeeze her so tight that she cannot turn around and must face one direction the entirety of her existence. Nor can she lay down easily on her side. She must press against the metal bars, lumbering her pregnant body on the cold, wet concrete floor. A mother pig would, given the opportunity, build an elaborate nest of soft materials anticipating the arrival of her young. But gestation crates rob a mother pig of everything she would naturally want to do—explore, root, socialize, and, yes, build a nest for her coming babies. With intelligence greater than a dog, and about equal to that of a three-year-old human, she experiences a boredom and a frustration that is torture.[8] The result is insanity, referred to as "stereotypic behavior"—the pointless repeated biting of the bars, often resulting in self-harm. One mother pig in particular haunts me. An undercover investigator from Mercy For Animals saw her the morning her babies were taken away. And in her mental and physical anguish, full of milk, without her babies, she had bashed and bloodied her face against the bars.[9]

In the United States, eleven states have passed laws to either ban gestation crates or stipulate space requirements that render crates impossible.[10] While these states only house about 3 percent of the nation's pig herds and there is much further to go, these laws are meaningful steps in the right direction, creating a policy pathway for the rest of the nation to follow.

California's Proposition 12 has been perhaps the most historic initiative to date. This was a 2018 California ballot initiative to prohibit the in-state production or sale of pork from pigs, veal from calves, and eggs from hens raised in cruel confinement. Over 7.5 million Californians (63 percent of registered voters) voted in favor of this law, and the regulations went into effect in January of 2024.[11] The passage of Prop 12, however, got the national pork industry up in arms. This was different from just banning the practice within a state. This also banned the sale of bacon, pulled pork, ribs—any pig product at all—that came from cruel systems that put pregnant pigs in close confinement, even if they were produced outside California. As soon as this historic measure passed, the pork industry began implementing a calculated strategy to undo the progress. Its challenge made it all the way to the highest court in the nation: the Supreme Court of the United States.

Very few cases make it to the Supreme Court—the court only takes up about 100 to 150 of the more than seven thousand cases that it is asked to review each year.[12] On October 11, 2022, the Supreme Court, for the first time in history, discussed the welfare of farmed animals when it heard oral arguments on *National Pork Producers Council v. Ross*. It had scheduled an hour, but the hearing lasted over two. The 157-page court transcript shows that while the pork industry may have thought getting to this Supreme Court was a hopeful sign, there was no clear consensus among the justices, as their questions did not fall along any party lines.[13]

Justice Elena Kagan dug deep into the role morality can play in re-stricting commerce, drawing on the historic example of slavery. The Biden administration, represented by lawyer Edwin S. Kneedler, chose to sup-port the pork industry. Questioning Kneedler, Kagan asked: "I mean, just to take an extreme example of this, Mr. Kneedler, suppose we imagine ourselves back into slavery days. Would it have been impermissible for a state to have said we're not going to traffic in products that have been produced by slavery?"

Mr. Kneedler replied: "I think the logic of our position would say yes, but that was at a much earlier time, both in Commerce Clause and, of course, now we have the Thirteenth Amendment . . . and that conduct is prohibited in the state where it occurs. This is the important thing to recognize."

Justice Kagan responded: "Right. I was presuming—I was imagining ourselves back into a world where it wasn't, but I take the point. How about, you know, you also have said total product bans are permissible. But some total product bans are based on moral feelings or even sort of feelings of disgust, like a ban on horse meat. There's nothing dangerous about eating horse meat. People in Iceland do it all the time. There's a kind of *ick*, disgust factor, a kind of moral factor. So could a state not do a ban on horse meat?"

Justice Kagan kept pushing this line of reasoning. The government's lawyer couldn't seem to say why a ban on horse meat would be permissi-ble, but a ban on certain types of pork wouldn't. Justice Sonia Sotomayor similarly questioned Timothy Bishop, a lawyer representing the National Pork Producers Council. She asked, "California's 13 percent of the market. It's a huge market. But . . . you have to concede there are some people who can sell there. They're already labeling themselves as organic or crate-free or antibiotic-free or something-free. What is the critical difference? How much of the market does [sic] the producers in Iowa have to control? All of it?"

Mr. Bishop tried to reply: "No. No, here's—"

She interrupted: "Or just a small part of it?"

Mr. Bishop tried to reply again: "No, no—"

Justice Sotomayor persisted: "And why does that make a difference? Because no one's forcing them to sell to California. They can sell to any other state that they prefer to sell to." It seemed the pork industry was more interested in controlling the market in its entirety, rather than respecting individual producers' and consumers' right of choice.

During the arguments, Justices Clarence Thomas, Neil Gorsuch, and Sotomayor seemed most receptive to the arguments in favor of upholding California's law, while Justices Samuel Alito, Brett Kavanaugh, and Ketanji Brown Jackson seemed most receptive to pork industry arguments. And Justices Kagan, John Roberts, and Amy Coney Barrett seemed most on the fence. For the first time in our country's history, the morality and validity of keeping animals in such appalling conditions was being seriously considered at the highest levels. Forms of cruel confinement such as gestation crates have been banned in the European Union since 2013 (except for crate use in the first four weeks of pregnancy). It's an outdated and archaic practice, one that many small farmers throughout the US have already moved away from—in fact, many of these small farmers already offer their pigs more space than is required by Prop 12, and they filed amicus briefs in support of Prop 12 being upheld.[14] They support citizens' rights to set standards for their food, to have animals treated more humanely, rather than letting big meat corporations decide.

The National Pork Producers Council argued that California was trying to impose its law on the rest of the country, when really it was just regulating within its own borders. The council's main argument was that the changes were too "burdensome," the benefits "negligible," and that state laws should be deemed unconstitutional if they impose substantial costs on interstate commerce, even if they do not discriminate against out-of-state commerce.

First, the changes were not burdensome. Less than 10 percent of North American pork production would need to convert to crate-free to satisfy California's demand, according to an economic analysis conducted by the University of California, Davis.[15] The actual change required in pork production would be much less significant than the pork industry claimed. Small farmers throughout the country had already started to make these changes. Additionally, the pork industry was not hard up—it saw $28 billion in sales in 2021, a 46 percent increase from 2020.[16] It could and should afford pregnant pigs these basic standards. In the case of Prop 12, the task was even simpler: respect California voters' decision to give pregnant pigs these basic standards.

The court reasoned that companies could simply choose not to sell pork in California, so out-of-state producers were not burdened with any requirement to comply with Prop 12. Plus, out-of-state pork producers were no more burdened by Proposition 12 than in-state pork producers, so Prop 12 did not discriminate against out-of-state producers.

The court unanimously rejected the pork industry's primary claim, noting that "while the Constitution addresses many weighty issues, the type of pork chops California merchants may sell is not on that list."

Of course, for pigs, the change would be anything but negligible. For pregnant pigs it would mean the ability to actually turn around and lay down comfortably, and most Americans would welcome the change. But when Hurricane Florence hit, North Carolina was not one of the eleven states with such laws to protect pregnant pigs, and so thousands of pigs in gestation crates, without any way to escape the rising water, drowned. Most of their babies died also, too new to the world to know a way out. The pigs that were kept in groups for fattening, after being taken from their mothers, had a better chance. Some doors opened, and a few escaped.

Images soon emerged of pigs swimming in the flooded land in pairs, a pig alone standing on top of a submerged car, pigs in groups surprised by freedom they had never known before.[17] We saw similar images after Hurricane Floyd in 1999, when pigs were seen crowded on top of a submerged pig warehouse.[18] By the end of September, the water from Hurricane Florence started to be absorbed back into the earth. But the pigs kept wandering the neighborhoods and roads. They ate what scraps they could find. This is how Sisu Refuge came to be.

A CALL TO HELP

In 2018, Erika Lovato and Joseph Purington were living in Jacksonville, North Carolina. She was a volunteer firefighter, and he was about to retire from active duty in the Marine Corps. As people who had always served their community, after Hurricane Florence hit, they did as anyone would under the circumstances and started checking on neighbors and on the elderly.

As animal lovers, they also were thinking about trying to help dogs and cats that had been displaced. But instead, they started getting calls about pigs. Erika recalls, "People were just seeing pigs, just walking around their neighborhood, causing car accidents." Factory farms had been ripped down by the storm, and the pigs who could walk free did so. The females trapped in the farrowing and gestation crates had drowned, so the majority wandering around were males—the hurricane boys, Erika calls them.

"There were forty-four boys," Erika remembers. "And we obviously didn't know what we were doing. So we started calling sanctuaries, and a couple sanctuaries would take a few pigs here, a few pigs there. And then, at the end of it, we still had sixteen pigs that nobody would take. So we started the sanctuary for them."

They bought up land close to where the pigs' needs were greatest, square in the middle of Duplin County, surrounded by Smithfield pig factory farms. As time went on, it wasn't just the hurricane boys that needed them. There were occasional accidents on the road. In one case, the back door of a truck malfunctioned and opened up, and pigs spilled all over the busy street. Pigs left and right made a run for it. Animal control caught some, but Smithfield didn't want them back.

At the entrance of the refuge Erika and Joseph created is a gate with two ceramic pigs on each side. They call their place Sisu Refuge, and it is a sanctuary for pigs who have escaped from factory farms or been rescued from similar dire situations. When I arrived, to the left were about a dozen white goats standing erect on tires and a play set, staring silently with curiosity. As I parked, two dogs came bounding out from behind the gate to meet me, one a white Great Pyrenees and the other a mixed breed. Erika came to greet us and immediately began spinning off stories of the pigs they'd saved. She was carrying her human baby in a carrier on her chest and pulling a wagon full of red apples. She beckoned me to follow her toward a fence.

The pigs must know the sound of the wagon being pulled, because from out of the bushes and trees they started to emerge and move toward the gate. Some of them trotted, some of them ran, and some of them sauntered toward the fence. They snorted and pushed each other to get to us. They were in a huge expanse, more space than I have ever seen given to pigs.

There were some seventy-five or so pigs in this area. The area right in front of the fence was sandy, and the pigs had made some wallows here and there that had filled with water, where they enjoyed cooling off. In the sanctuary was a forest with tall pines that provided shade, and the pigs were at liberty to come and go as they pleased. Some of them were more extroverted and curious, and others preferred the refuge of the forest. There were also ponds where the pigs swam and cooled off.

Erika threw apples out to expectant mouths and snouts. Five hundred apples were gone in fifteen minutes. It was joyous to see the pigs scooping the apples up and crushing them in their mouths. Erika knew each of their stories. Each had been given a name, each an individual who had escaped a dark fate.

Erika said that apart from the hurricane boys, they also get what she calls "truck jumpers." These were tiny piglets who jumped out of a hole in the side of a truck, making a break for a free life. "All the truck jumpers start in the house because when they're small enough to fit through the porthole, they're what, two weeks old," Erika explains. Felix was their first truck jumper.

"He fell out of a truck and he had brain damage because he hit the pavement so hard. So he's a little slower," says Erika. He was only three pounds when he arrived and had just come from a sow farm. People often imagine pigs living on one farm from birth to slaughter, but that is not the case in commercial farming. Typically, pigs start life on the farm where they are birthed to a mother trapped in a gestation crate, who is then moved to a farrowing crate. Farrowing crates offer a little more space than a gestation crate, just enough so the mother can lie on her side, enclosed by bars. Her piglets move in and out of the bars in a slightly larger concrete, slatted area, but she cannot move to them or away from them. The industry renders her unable to practice basic mothering activities, treating her as little more than a milk machine for the piglets who will become bacon, ribs, or pulled pork.

Farrowing crates are as restrictive as gestation crates. Both deny mother pigs what they are innately driven to do. Just as women have a nesting instinct and will have an overwhelming desire to get their home ready for the coming baby just before labor, so do pigs.[19] For a mother pig, this is a desire to protect her babies from the dangers of predators and the cold. Given the opportunity, she would search for substrates to build a protective nest, a place to keep them safe. The crates deny her this ability, causing clinically defined stress and anxiety.[20] It is beautiful to see a pig make her nest in preparation for her coming babies. Studies show that before giving birth, a pig will leave her herd and move a substantial distance in order to find just the right spot to build a nest.[21] She will root around in the soil, using all that she has available—her snout and forelegs. She will forage for materials to place around the dug-out pit. She might use long grasses, flowers, and ferns, decorating this home for her future young. But such a chance is denied the industrial mother. She gives birth and keeps watch over her young from the confines of a metal crate, lying on cold, wet, slatted floors, facing only one direction. She gives birth to two litters per year, each ten to twelve piglets. The bars, apart from denying her mobility, deny her the chance to get away if she needs to. Piglets do bite sometimes. And instead of giving the mother more space, it is common practice for piglets' teeth to be ground down or clipped, most often without pain relief, to minimize biting injuries to the sow and then later to other pigs, when the grown piglets are kept in overcrowded warehouses and aggression can ensue.[22]

Only a couple of weeks after giving birth, her piglets are taken away, piglets like Felix, who are sent to a so-called nursery—a euphemism, of course. The mother's cycle begins again. She is inseminated, impregnated, and again denied everything she desires. Three years is her life in this world. Three years of maybe six litters, birthed by her and taken from her, before she is sent to slaughter for our lower-grade food products—our soups, ready meals, and dog food.

LIFE WITH FELIX

The day Felix jumped the truck, he had just been taken from his mother, and no doubt jumped in an effort to get back to her. Erika explained: "On the sow farm they are with their mom, then they're loaded up, put on a truck and they go to a nursery. Then they're at the nursery for a few months. And then they go to the finisher—called the 'grower-finisher farm.' So they've got trips in between. So Felix fell off when he was going, right when he left his mom."

Erika and Joseph had never had a pig that young, that small before. The hurricane boys had all been full grown, swaying their weight from side to side, not accustomed to gentle human interactions. But Felix was a baby, malleable still, impressionable. In just two weeks, Erika and Joseph took him not only into their home, but into their hearts. He slept in their bed with them. They swaddled him like a baby. They carried him around in a carrier while they went about their business around the house and farm. It felt natural. And Felix did not object. After all he'd been through, he surrendered to the warmth and security of his new family.

He had a couple bumps and bruises but was in pretty good shape physically. His emotional state was another thing entirely. Erika recalls how depressed he was. He still tried to nurse on whatever—your arm or finger, whatever seemed viable—as he desperately searched for his mom. He missed her. But soon he came to love and find comfort and safety in his human family. Felix would actually fall asleep in Erika's or Joseph's arms. "You can't just pick pigs up like that," Erika says. "You can't just hold a pig, like a little infant. I have pictures and videos of Felix sleeping like a baby, like a newborn baby. He used to sleep in the crook of my arm and I could walk around and do chores with him in my arm."

As Felix grew in confidence and strength, Erika and Joseph felt he was ready to go outside. They have a fenced-in halfway area that they put pigs in before they go out to the larger, freer, forested area. It's right next to their home, so they can keep a close eye on these more vulnerable pigs. Right away, Felix was so social and happy. "He met the potbelly pigs first because they're small," Erika says. They were, in a sense, the welcoming party for new pigs just beginning outdoor life. Felix got used to other pigs in the backyard, before they introduced him to the bigger space.

The pigs at the sanctuary are allowed to make their own families, their own friends, their own groups, and Erika tries not to intervene. Felix's chosen family were four pigs named Zeke, Stewy, Pierre, and Penelope. "They bonded," Erika recalls. "They would sleep together, and they would always hang out together, just swim and wallow in the mud together."

Erika says that Felix remains cautious in his relationships. When Stewy passed away as a result of a health condition, Felix became depressed, and for a time returned to his human family for affection and strength, seeking out extra belly rubs and reassurance. The personalities of pigs can vary, depending on an individual's experiences and their nature. Some of them are shy. Some of them are social. Some of them are mean, never able to let go of the life they started out with.

Pigs naturally form hierarchies and groups when given the chance. They prefer to form stable social groups and maintain harmony through these structures. But the setting of the factory farm hardly allows pigs to choose who to socialize with. And even if they manage to establish harmony, it is short-lived. As pigs are moved—from mother to nursery to feeder farm, into and out of trucks—little regard is paid to their social groups. They are mixed and mixed again with unfamiliar pigs, often leading to what the industry characterizes as aggressive, agonistic behavior.[23] In the wild, this behavior is rare, energy-wasting. Pigs are naturally gregarious animals who create close social bonds.[24]

One scientific meta-study that compiled eighty-three peer-reviewed research articles found that the most common personality traits for pigs are exploration, aggressiveness, reactivity to humans, and fearfulness.[25] Note that only one of these is a positive trait. Animal welfare science has for too long only focused on the negative traits of animals rather than acknowledging their needs and wants. It therefore raised the question: What is our obligation to allow more positive traits to develop? Arguably, after being on a factory farm, any being would show up with the negative "personality traits" of being aggressive (maybe a better term would be "protective"), reactive to humans (a natural, protective reaction), and fearful. The scientific community has done very little to look deeply into who pigs are, though Instagram feels differently, with one account after another joyfully celebrating pig personalities. (My personal favorite is @cutest.pigs, with over half a million followers. I warn you not to go there unless you're prepared to go down the most adorable rabbit hole the internet has to offer.)

As Erika wanders through the expanse of the forest, pigs approach her and nudge her for belly rubs. Felix relaxes in a mud wallow at the edge of a pond. The day is just hot enough to make that experience delightful. What a different experience from the one Felix was destined for—one where he'd have no agency, where he'd be trapped until his final day. And such a different life from his mother's—the mother he risked so much to try to return to.

In the spring of 2023, the future of pig welfare hung in the balance. Nine months had passed since the Supreme Court had discussed the constitutionality of California's Prop 12. But then the watershed moment came. On May 11, 2023, the court ruled that Proposition 12—the nation's strongest farmed animal welfare law—was constitutional.[26] This was the ruling despite the pork industry's best efforts to prove otherwise. The strongest farmed animal protection law on record, set to free millions of animals from a miserable life of close confinement in crates, was now affirmed by the highest court in the land.

The decision was unprecedented. It was the first time that SCOTUS had ever upheld not just a farmed animal welfare law, but any animal welfare law. But what's more, it was unexpected. At best, the expectation was further deliberations and delay. As Lewis Bollard astutely pointed out in his *Open Philanthropy Farm Animal Welfare Newsletter*: "Since 2007, the Supreme Court has overturned fully 80% of the cases it heard from the liberal Ninth Circuit Court of Appeals, which had previously upheld California's law here. The pork producers had secured the backing of 26 US states, the nation's biggest industry groups, and even the Biden administration. At oral arguments, Justices barraged California's lawyers with hypothetical arguments about the chaos that upholding Prop 12 could unleash."[27]

On the industry's primary claim that Prop 12 interfered with interstate commerce, all nine justices rejected that argument. The industry had a backup claim: Prop 12 placed burdens on "interstate commerce" (in other words, industry profits) that far outweighed its benefits for Californians (never mind the suffering of the pigs). This too was rejected by a 5–4 vote. These votes did not fall along ideological lines, as Bollard pointed out: "The Court's three most conservative members (Justices Barrett, Gorsuch, and Thomas) joined with two of its most liberal (Justices Kagan and Sotomayor) to uphold Prop 12. The Court's three other conservatives joined with Biden appointee Justice Jackson to dissent against the ruling."[28]

States had long had the right to apply morals to what happened within a state. This ruling, however, confirmed that morality can be extended to farmed animals. It was a sign that states, and the citizens of those states, have a right to apply moral parameters on the treatment of animals in the food system. Justice Gorsuch noted that states may enact laws to "promote . . . public morals." And Proposition 12, one could argue, works in just this way—banning from the state of California all whole pork products derived from practices its voters consider "cruel." Justice Barrett, a conservative

Trump appointee, argued that moral consideration cannot be weighted on a scale opposite to profits.[29]

While activists had always held this belief, having the Supreme Court confirm it unlocked a whole new level of confidence and energy in the movement to get animals in our food system out of factory farming. Just when progress feels unbearably slow, it can come all at once.

Decades of activism made this happen. And the decades ahead will unleash even more progress. Decades of uncovering the reality, risking and pushing and insisting that "this is immoral, this has to stop." From door knocking, to giving testimony in the courtroom, to gathering video evidence, the steady march for protection of farmed animals carries on, now with new support and more legitimacy.

CHAPTER SEVEN

NORMA THE COW

RED, ORANGE, AND YELLOW LEAVES fell like confetti on Lake Echo, where I stopped off scenic Route 100 in rural Vermont. I could not resist a breath of the air from the changing seasons, the letting go of summer.

This day was the best of fall, before the ice and snow trap Vermonters at home. The mountains had just started to change, with spots of color on the slopes. Vermont felt like one continuous national park. Billboards are banned. At first, you don't know why you feel so relaxed. And then, you realize it's because your eyes aren't constantly absorbing unwanted messages about what to buy and how to be. The result is a sense of freedom and spaciousness worthy of rural America. Your mind can focus on the changing of the leaves, the glistening river that you can see clearly to the bottom of, even from the road, and the steel-blue sky overhead. It is a world without direction, and your mind has a moment to just pause. The only informational signs are those telling you to look out for potential moose crossings.

The day was unexpectedly bright and clear, despite a prediction of rain. I'd brought boots and a raincoat, not knowing exactly how much of the animal sanctuary I'd get to see, given the forecast of cold, rainy weather. Sanctuaries are a place that hold space for healing, and not just for the animals. Advocates who bear witness to unrelenting violence find solace here. Visiting a sanctuary is a chance to see animals living out their lives with full agency, a glimpse into a different possible world.

An influential paper titled "Farmed Animal Sanctuaries: The Heart of the Movement? A Socio-political Perspective," by Sue Donaldson and Will Kymlicka, describes the importance of sanctuaries to the movement for animal rights: "One of the fundamental challenges for animal rights theory is to imagine the contours of just relations that humans might have with 'farmed animals' once we stop confining and killing them for food. What sorts of social relationships would cows, pigs, chickens, and other animals be able to form with us, and with members of their own and other species?"[1]

Often I am asked, If I end factory farming, what will happen to all the animals, where will they go? Do you want them extinct? It is as if the only choices are for them to exist in extreme suffering or not exist at all.

The life of a farmed animal is brutally short: just six weeks for a meat chicken, 2 years for an egg-laying hen, 1.5 years for a pig raised for meat, and less than 2 years for a meat cow. If we stopped forcibly breeding them, they would all but cease to exist. Even when they do manage to find sanctuary, their pressurized genetics mean that very few farmed animals ever see old age. Their longevity is so rare that Isa Leshko, in her photo book *Allowed to Grow Old*, assembled a collection of portraits of the few who have made it to old age to commemorate their unlikely existence. But underlying this is the question: If we stop eating them, what exactly would our relationship be to these beings? They are not wild. They are domesticated and thus need our care to thrive.

In southern Vermont, I hoped to uncover some of the answers to that question and feel some of that solace. The Transfarmation Project team and I arrived mid-morning, after taking a long dirt-road detour with no cell reception to avoid a collapsed bridge on a country road. The house sat halfway up a steep hill, on the side of the road. Greeting us was pattrice jones (her name is lowercase), an ecofeminist, author, and the founder of VINE Sanctuary (VINE stands for both "Veganism Is the Next Evolution" and "Veganism Is Not Enough"). Dressed in a blue cap emblazoned with the VINE logo, jeans, boots, and a worn blue shirt, she gave me a long, firm hug.

After disinfecting our boots for avian influenza, we were granted passage into another world. Through a latch and a wooden fence, we entered a garden, a place separate from the world where humans intervene and force themselves upon animals.

The first thing I noticed was how pattrice referred to the residents. She called them people, drawing immediate attention to their individuality and their agency. As pattrice began her introductions, my coworker noticed a sick chicken in a fenced area. With a sense of curiosity and compassion, he approached her enclosure to get a closer look, but pattrice, with kindness, told him that here we were not allowed to stare at the injured or sick. That we were large mammals, and staring at this injured person would scare them. She explained this gently, but with clarity and conviction. This was how our tour began at VINE Sanctuary.

Roosters crowed so loudly at times that I could not hear pattrice over them. The only smell was of fresh-cut sweet hay. Patricce's journey began when she and her partner, Miriam, found a chicken by the side of the road within a few weeks of moving to Delmarva Peninsula, spanning Delaware, Maryland and Virginia, not knowing that they had moved to one of the parts of the country where factory farming was most embedded. "Within six months of finding the first bird, we had incorporated a sanctuary for chickens, called Eastern Shore Sanctuary, on about three acres of land, literally surrounded by factory farms," she said. "You couldn't go in any direction without encountering a factory farm."

At first they took in birds that had escaped or jumped from trucks, then they took in refugees from the egg industry, then roosters. Pattrice is known for creating a groundbreaking protocol for rehabilitating cock-fighting roosters, who are intentionally made to be aggressive. Most people presumed that these birds were inherently aggressive—so much so that they were compelled to euthanize the animals after they were confiscated from illegal cockfighting rings. Cockfighting is now illegal in all fifty states, but it still happens. In fact, while we were visiting the sanctuary, they were preparing to take in a hundred confiscated roosters from a bust in Alabama. The idea that cockfighting roosters won't be able to live peacefully in a flock is just rhetoric, pattrice says. Her protocol illustrates exactly how to introduce these roosters back into a flock.

After nine years in Maryland, in 2009 pattrice and Miriam moved to Vermont, for more land and also to give themselves more opportunities to take in survivors of dairying, "which as feminists, we see as a feminist issue," she told me. As longtime social justice activists, Miriam and pattrice saw their work through that lens. For the past twenty years, pattrice has dedicated her life not only to taking care of animals, but also to explain to others that the exploitation and ill-use of other animals is both founded in and exacerbates the various ways that human beings hurt each other.

"I would like you to meet this duck! I would like you to meet Billy Idol," pattrice exclaimed, with arms reaching out toward a Muscovy duck who'd been sitting there unperturbed by our entrance. Billy Idol came to the original sanctuary in 2002 when he was already an adult. He was now at least twenty-one years old.

"Every year, for at least the last five to eight years when fall comes, I think this is it, he's not going to make it through the winter, and then he makes it through the winter," pattrice told us.

She looked on with tender eyes and said she thinks this really may be his last fall. The average lifespan for a Muscovy duck is just eight to ten years. When I asked pattrice how she explains his long life, she answered, "He is irascible as heck!" and burst out laughing.

He came to the sanctuary with his partner. They had ducklings and he had outlived them all. With clouded eyes and worn feathers, he sat in a spot of sunshine. At this point he did not move around a lot. He had to be lifted into his bath, like any old man. I marveled at seeing an elderly farmed animal. It is rare. Most animals on farms do not make it past early adulthood. Billy Idol had been taken to a livestock auction to be sold, even though he and his partner had been raised as pets, but luckily a feral cat rescuer happened to be there and offered to take them to the sanctuary.

A family of chickens waddled by next, a mother and three teenage chicks. She was a survivor who was used to breed roosters for cockfighting. "As feminists, we believe everybody has a right to reproductive freedom, and as animal liberationists we believe that that is true for non-human animals as well," pattrice said. "And that is actually one of the most mean-ingful choices you can make in life, whether to reproduce or not. We entirely understand why things like spaying of dogs and cats are the norm in animal liberation, but we do wish that people would approach that with more sadness and gravity rather than assuming this is just a thing we have a right to do. Rather, it is a tragic necessity. We are robbing them of a whole bunch of potentialities that might have been important to them."

For the mammals at VINE, the caretakers simply cannot allow for pregnancy because of space issues, though pattrice laments that this was a tough choice to make. For the birds, however, they have attempted to respect reproductive freedom. "If someone chose to nest in a safe space and made it clear, 'I'm brooding these eggs,' we were not going to intervene," pattrice said. In the end, the sanctuary sees successful hatchings just once or twice a year. And it is delightful not just for that mother but for the whole flock, who get to experience living in an intergenerational flock, something they'd be denied in an industrial agriculture setting, just like they'd be denied old age. Even if they had not had young themselves, the elders got to experience helping to raise young. "It enlivens everyone," pattrice explained. This was why we are seeing these chicks now. This mother found rafters in the barn to nest on and hatched herself some chicks.

AN INDUSTRY IN CRISIS

I came to VINE Sanctuary not for the stories of the chickens or the ducks—though they were my favorite—but rather of the dairy cows. I was in search of one in particular—Norma. We left the chicken haven and headed up the road to the pastures and large barns where the other residents of the sanctuary community live.

The previous day, at the Vermont Law School, Professor Delcianna Winders, who was running the school's first animal law program, began her class at 8:30 a.m. sharp on a Monday. She held class at this time and day to weed out anyone who isn't serious. Delci doesn't have time to waste. Some of her students were working on legal support and policy to help transition dairy farmers into plant-based farming. One student asked me if I really believed that factory farming will end. With complete composure, I said it will end, and one day we'll look back and feel so ashamed that we once did such a thing. But what I don't know is when it will end, and if I will see it in my lifetime. All we can do is keep working to speed up that transition, and to help enable the change in any way we can.

What is remarkable about the industrial farming system, from chickens to pigs to dairy, is that all these systems are failing businesses that would be all but bankrupt if it were not for government subsidies and other government-supported programs that ensure they survive. It takes multiple interventions by the government, from subsidies to checkoff programs (government-supported "research" that amounts to advertising for dairy, eggs, and meat), to prop up these supposedly crucial businesses. Perhaps no animal industry illustrates this point better than dairy.

A study conducted by the Dairy Farmers of Canada did a deep dive into just how much government support the US dairy industry received. The authors argued that the World Trade Organization and NAFTA, which are supposed to ensure fair and free trade between nations, should be concerned with the way the US government's support distorts trade.[2] Their 588-page study reported that American taxpayers contributed some $22.2 billion for direct and indirect subsidies to the dairy sector in 2015 alone, and that US dairy subsidies equal 73 percent of producer returns. According to this analysis, the American dairy industry should be out of business—it lost money every year from 2005 to 2016.

That's not all. Dairy milk is losing market share to the plant-based milk industry, which is not supported by subsidies, yet is on the rise. By the end of 2020, plant milk made up 15 percent of all retail sales of milk. Experts project that plant-based milk will reach 30 percent of all milk sales by 2026.[3]

Yet, the dairy industry persists. And in Vermont, dairy is more than just an industry. Dairy is what Vermont is known for, Delci told me: "The culture is centered around dairy. They have forgotten that dairy was not always here and that dairy is a white settler-colonial practice." Regardless, dairy is so entrenched in the identity of modern Vermont that Delci treads very carefully when she brings up her efforts to transition dairy farms, even as she's now investigating specific ways through government policy to support dairy farmer transitions. "I'm just trying to proceed very cautiously," she told me. "Because I feel like we get one shot, and if we blow it . . ." She doesn't finish her sentence, but she doesn't have to. With farmers, the government, the industry, you just don't get a second chance to convince them there is something better out there.

They hardly trust people like Delci, who used to work at PETA. She said they call her a "flatlander," which is what Vermonters call out-of-state folks, and shared the story of a threatening note that was left on her car. We have to do a lot to gain trust, and we can't afford to mess up.

While her team was still in the early days of learning how to approach this work, they hoped to pass funding legislation in Vermont to help struggling dairy farmers transition away from dairy into plant-based crops. It's not unlike the idea floated by Senator Cory Booker's federal bill to help transition farmers to "more sustainable farming" using federal money.

Vermont already has a history of laws supporting the transition to farm systems ensuring higher animal welfare. Farmers can apply for the state's Working Lands grant to help cover the costs of transitioning their farm to a higher welfare certification, such as an Animal Welfare Approved or Global Animal Partnership certification.[4] So, a similar model for transitioning to growing plants would not be unprecedented.

Big dairy companies were making record profits even throughout the pandemic. They continue to do so even as farmers are in crisis. Danone, the global maker of yogurts, for example, ended 2021 with its fastest sales growth in seven years.[5] Vermont-based ice cream company Ben & Jerry's surpassed $1 billion in sales in 2021 for the first time, hitting a new peak in revenue.[6] But despite the way government subsidies prop up the dairy industry as a whole, and enable these record profits, dairy farmers are in crisis, especially smaller dairy farms. Randy Roecker, a fifty-six-year-old dairy farmer and mental health advocate, says, "Our investment keeps going up and up and up, and our return goes down and down and down, and there's just no profit in it."[7] Death by suicide has become tragically common among farmers, with rates being three and a half times higher than the general population, according to the National Rural Health Association.[8] Their situation is a recipe for hopelessness—tremendous financial pressure combined with a lack of power.

Subsidies rarely benefit those who need it most, certainly not the majority of rural farmers. The top 10 percent of farms received 78 percent of the subsidies.[9] The whole system preys on the vulnerable, including farmers and, of course, the countless animals trapped on dairy farms. One such animal was the dairy cow Norma, whom I've come to the sanctuary to meet.

NORMA'S STORY

Norma was raised to provide precisely what the industry demanded of her—milk. Norma was born in 2015, and by 2020, based on the average calves birthed per year in the industrial dairy farming system, she had likely given birth to three babies, all of whom were taken away. If they were female, they were taken to become part of the dairy industry—to be impregnated and have their own babies taken away, for the cycle to go on and on. If they were male, they were killed for dog food or for the veal industry.

Even if one could overlook the sheer immorality of taking a baby away over and over again from her mother to create a product for consumption, Norma's day-to-day life was horrific, though not unusual for the majority of dairy cows in America.

In the United States, only 20 percent of lactating cows and 34 percent of dry cows have access to pasture, according to one study.[10] The US is unique in this. In the UK and Ireland, around 95 percent of cows have access to pasture, and in Finland, Norway, and Sweden, full-time housing is banned.[11] Globally, the majority of dairy cows have some access to pasture.[12] The US industry's negligence in giving pasture access to these animals persists, despite many dairy companies featuring idyllic pastures on their milk cartons and ice cream pints.

Norma was tethered for much of the day with a metal chain around her neck, known as a tie stall. This, too, is a common practice, with 39 percent of US dairy farms using tie stalls as their primary housing type.[13] The rest use it at least some of the time, and only offer pasture access for part of the year. Very few never use tie stalls at all in the United States. Even the most progressive of dairy companies in the United States have not banned the practice. New standards by the Global Animal Partnership, an animal welfare standard used by Whole Foods Market, do require farms to phase out the use of tie stalls by 2027.[14] While this is a disappointingly slow timeline, there is hope that in the years ahead, more companies will begin to adopt this standard. Company-wide bans on tie stalls would be a simple yet meaningful act in the day-to-day lives of these animals. Tie stalls restrict movement so that cows can only move a few steps forward and back, and are associated with increased lameness in cows.[15] For the sake of the billions of animals trapped for the foreseeable future in the overlooked caverns of our food system, banning close confinement of any kind—cages, crates, tie stalls—should be a priority policy for the farming industry and the government.

By the time Norma birthed Nina, she had endured so much. Apart from the brutal conditions, this was likely her fourth baby, and Norma couldn't take it anymore. It started off like it had so many times before. Norma was forcibly impregnated, and nine months later, she gave birth to a beautiful calf; this one was named Nina. She did all the things any new parent would do. Norma attempted to nurture and care for Nina with every ounce of her being. But their happiness was short-lived. A farmworker named Oscar[16] entered the barn. He was there to take the calf away only hours after her birth—a standard practice in the dairy industry.

But this time, Norma had enough. She'd already injured a worker the previous year, but this time she fought back like hell. She kicked, and she wailed, and she gave Oscar everything she had. She fought so fiercely that she sent Oscar to the hospital.

But, as a result of her actions, she was sentenced to death. The farmer deemed her too dangerous to live. The only problem was no one could get anywhere near Norma, or her calf. For the first time, there seemed to be hope for Norma. She'd won herself a pause in the relentless cycle of pregnancy, birth, the loss of a child, and milking. For a moment, Norma got to be a mother.

What happened next is not what you'd expect. What most people saw as a wild and violent act, someone else saw in a different light. That someone was the very farmworker who had been injured. Oscar pleaded to the farm owner for mercy for Norma. He argued she was only doing what any mother would do. He did some research and, after making some calls, found a farm sanctuary, VINE, that was willing to take in Norma. Now it came down to convincing the farmer, who had the final say. VINE Sanctuary manager Cheryl Wylie wanted to convince the farmer to not just give up Norma, but also the calf, Nina, that Norma had so fiercely fought to protect.

Cheryl was no stranger to farmers. The daughter of beef farmers, she grew up in Clark County, Ohio, which boasts the largest county fair in the state. As in most rural areas, her school engaged in both Future Farmers of America (FFA) and 4-H. FFA is a formal education program for farmers, sponsored by local schools, and 4-H is an after-school program sponsored by the Extension Service, where kids raise animals and often enter competitions in a county fair. (Think *Charlotte's Web* and Wilbur's county fair.)

Cheryl joined 4-H when she was nine years old and continued until she was eighteen. She hated the fairs.[17] She hated that the pattern was always the same: raise and love the animals, only to have them killed. She felt she had little agency in a culture where that's just what everyone did. It's hard to fight against culture and tradition. No one questioned the system.

But by eighteen, when Cheryl finally aged out of the program, she got out. She ended up in Florida with her partner, Kathy, working as a vet tech. A friend of Kathy's told her about the job at VINE, and in May of 2010 they moved up to Vermont and never looked back. When Cheryl heard about Norma, she knew this was a rare chance to unite a mother and daughter in the dairy industry, and she tried her hardest to convince the farmer. The farmer told Cheryl she was concerned that Norma was going to kill the VINE staff on-site. She was worried Norma had mastitis and would get milk fever. Patiently, Kathy explained that these were all issues VINE staff were used to working through.

Kathy recalled: "So [the farmer] had some care. She did. In her mind [Norma] was a good producer and she was a great mother, but she was a danger to the staff. She didn't necessarily want to see her dead. She just said . . . she kept saying, 'She can never breed again.' I said, 'Well, we don't have any bulls. That's not our purpose. Our purpose is to let them come here and live out their lives as they choose to live it out.' We just kept reiterating that and finally, I said, 'Well, if her calf comes with her, then she shouldn't get mastitis.' And she said, 'Well, I guess that's very true.'"

Somehow, that was the logic that convinced the farmer to let go of Norma and Nina. And mother and daughter were surrendered to VINE Sanctuary. Norma got what she so desperately fought for.

Cheryl was largely responsible for convincing the farmer to let Norma and Nina go free together. No doubt Cheryl's upbringing played an important role. She knew that somewhere in this farmer was a sense of caring—for Norma, for the farm staff, for the sanctuary staff. She knew that because her parents had this same care within them.

I wandered about the sanctuary with pattrice. Over steep, muddy paths, sinking into the mixture of manure and rock, standing over the ridge, peering through the beech trees, we looked for Norma and Nina. There were 105 acres here. I started to realize we might not find her if she did not want to be found.

We found others in our search. There was Autumn, a kind of lifeguard, who sat just back from a pond watching the wild ducks flap and splash and quack, enjoying themselves. Then pattrice told me of the first nights with Autumn. Autumn had been at a small dairy where families went to buy milk and ate ice cream. Her udders were so low, so worn out, she actually stepped on one of them and crushed it. They kept milking her anyway, until her mastitis was so bad they determined that the only thing left was to let her go.

Mastitis is a painful infection of the udders, common in dairy cows. It is an inflammation of the mammary gland, most often caused by bacterial infection. Experts estimate that approximately one-third of cows have mastitis at any one time in the US. It's the most common disease for dairy cows.[18] Dairy cows are milked as frequently as two to three times per day, the strategy being that more milking causes more milk production.[19] But as a result of this continual handling of the cows' udders in the dirty settings of a factory farm, mastitis is all too common.

A neighbor of the dairy farm where Autumn was kept talked the owners into letting her and another cow named Rose go at the same time. "I wish people could have seen [Autumn]," recalled pattrice, "because so often people focus on what her horrible udders looked like and all the pain and the suffering, but she was so full of spirit regardless. She just looked you right in the eye and was like, 'Okay, who are you and what are your plans?'"

In order to treat her, VINE staff had to milk Autumn out, so that she could then receive the antibiotics in her teats. It was painful, and Autumn kicked and wailed. In pattrice's view, they already felt they were violating Autumn, but this experience only made her all the more aware of what it must be like to have your teats pulled like this twice a day, every day, year after year—the humiliation, the pain, the violation. It took two months before Autumn was completely healed of her mastitis. "It was such an intimate act, and I knew that I was doing it to help, but even then, I felt like I was violating her," pattrice says. "And so, to be doing that, and thinking of how that violation happens every day, twice a day, it just viscerally affected me."

"Autumn, you are the best!" she shouted now from across the field to the aging cow on the pasture. Pattrice told me that Autumn is the most charismatic leader you could imagine, although now she was declining a bit mentally and had "gone down" twice. "Going down" means a cow has collapsed and has difficulty getting back up. Sometimes they can't get back up at all. This happens as cows age—or as their conditions and health de-cline prematurely in industrial settings. It's an all-too-common ailment for industrial dairy cows who are milked relentlessly.[20] Industry veterinarians will cite many causes for what is known as "downer cow syndrome," but in reality, these cows have simply been pushed beyond their physical and metabolic limits. Most dairy cows operate in a negative energy balance in the early stage of lactation, after they give birth. They suffer injuries, muscle damage, nutrient deficiency, mastitis, and liver disease. These are all the consequences of the brutal pace of industrial farming and the voracious demand for the cows' milk.[21]

Cows must stand upright in order to digest, or they bloat and die. When they can no longer get back up, they are at their end. Autumn got back up both times she went down, but pattrice feared the time was coming when she wouldn't be able to rise again, despite her incredible resilience. She was twenty-one, after all, an advanced age for this beautiful being.

We wandered further up the mountainside, calling out for Norma. Alpacas, goats, sheep, quail, geese, and a solitary pig all filled the landscape. A sheep named Shadow nudged me, like a cat insisting on being massaged. We rolled under an electric fence, careful not to touch the wires, and headed into the back field where we hoped to find Norma. But she was not among the half a dozen cows there standing on the hillside, staring down at us. We didn't approach them. We were respectful when we read their body language. If they approached us, that was fine. But otherwise, we understood they wanted us to keep our distance.

We trudged further through the woods, mushrooms and ferns and wild berries emerging from the ground below. The damp cool air contrasted with the warmth of the sun. We arrived at another hillside and found another small herd lying in the sunshine. They were too far to see very clearly at first, so we walked over more rocks and mud to see if we could make out exactly who was there.

Just as we were about to give up, far up the hill, a horned, cinnamon-colored cow raised her head to look at us. She was sitting on her own, in the sunshine. She craned her head to check us out, but then relaxed, under-standing we were no threat. It was Norma. Twenty feet in front of her was a darker brown cow, with small horns beginning to sprout, sitting equally unconcerned. This was Nina, her daughter. At last we had found them.

It was hard to believe this gentle, quiet being was the very same that sent a worker to the hospital, and pattrice agreed: "When she came, we thought this is going to be a really fierce person. And we had this whole protocol set up. We moved her into the barn so that she couldn't get at anybody and had them cut off a part of the barn just for her and Nina. We just didn't know. She sent people to the hospital." But Norma was not fierce, she was not violent or aggressive in nature. She had just been pushed to her limit.

"When she got here," pattrice said, "she just had no interest in hurting anybody. To me there's something extra poignant about a peaceful person provoked, pushed to that extent, pushed by taking their child." But today, Norma is grazing in fields, napping in the sun, and living out her life with her final daughter, Nina.

PART THREE

THE COMMUNITIES

CHAPTER EIGHT

EASTERN NORTH CAROLINA COMMUNITIES OF COLOR

Rosemary and René

OFF A DIRT ROAD, tucked behind a line of trees, Rosemary Batts opened the door of a white trailer home. The mid-August heat was stifling, so she wouldn't stay outside long. She was wearing an eggplant-purple headband, snug at the edge of her forehead. Tidy in appearance, her coffee-colored skin gleamed with youth and health even though she was sixty-nine. Her almond-shaped eyes were discerning, carrying the weight of experience.

She let me in and then sat straight-backed on the couch next to the kitchen. With the window blinds pulled shut, there was no natural light in her home, but there was a sense of warmth regardless.

Rosemary's great-grandmother was enslaved and had a son by a white man, Mr. Parker. The Parker family were big landowners right where she sits now, in Duplin County. Rosemary's great-grandmother was enslaved by the Parkers and worked in their house. Rosemary can't say exactly what happened, but she speculates, "I have heard stories, how the Black lady got pregnant by the white owner because she needed food or she just worked for this white guy. It's just like you see in movies. And that's how it was here," she says. "She worked for 'em on the farm and she may have needed money or food or something."

Her grandfather was lighter skinned as a result, and this afforded him some advantages, though not many. Her grandmother on her mother's side came from Georgia, also the descendant of enslaved people. During the Great Migration, when so many Black folks were escaping the oppression of the South, she moved to New York as a single mom. There she raised Rosemary's mother. Rosemary's father's family had also moved north with the rest of the wave. Rosemary's parents got married and had two children in New York, one of which was Rosemary, born May 4, 1953. Eventually two more siblings joined the family.

Then, they decided to make a change. Life wasn't so easy in the city, especially with two babies. They would need space to roam, to be free. So they moved back to where Rosemary's father had grown up—back to Duplin County, North Carolina. Thus began Rosemary's childhood in a tobacco sharecropper family. Life was hard, fraught with obstacles out of their control. Once their house burnt down to the ground. Back then they had wood heaters, and the kerosene her father was using to light a fire caught fire and spread too quickly to stop.

As a child, Rosemary spent her days in the fields. "I remember when I was younger, we picked strawberries, we picked cucumbers and blueberries," she tells me. "And of course, we worked in the tobacco field."

Sometimes her job was to ride on the back of the planter and then jump off to put the plants into the ground. Other times she went through the field picking off the white flowers so the plants would keep growing. Row by row, they'd work the fields as a family. "It was hard and tiresome, but it didn't seem so bad, you know? Because we were children and that was all we had to do. So we were content with it, you know. I didn't ever hate growing up in the fields," Rosemary says now.

As sharecroppers, her parents worked the tobacco in exchange for staying on the land. They tried to save money, but never got ahead. However, Rosemary recalls that they always had food on the table, and they went to school. "I was kind of good at school," she says. The US Supreme Court's landmark 1954 ruling in *Brown v. the Board of Education of Topeka* had officially ended racial segregation in public schools. But Southern states remained resistant to integration. On November 14, 1960, at the age of six, Ruby Bridges became the very first African American child to attend an all-white public school, William Frantz Elementary in

New Orleans, escorted by federal marshals. North Carolina was slower. It wasn't until 1969 that Rosemary would enter a desegregated school. After having gone to an all-Black school her whole life, as a teenager, the mandate changed, and she had to go to the closest high school to her home. Despite concerns for her safety, Rosemary's parents knew this would bring her an education they had never had access to. Rosemary found it harrowing to be in a desegregated school for the first time. "People would pick fights and beat you as you walk down the halls, and they wanna push you out of the way. And everybody was prejudiced. Because east Duplin is a Klan area," she says, referring to the Ku Klux Klan. She recalls that even the principal would call her and the other Black kids names over the loudspeaker.

But all four kids made it through high school, which was a point of pride for her parents. As soon as Rosemary could, she left. "I just wanted to get away from this farmland. My mother had lived in New York, and my goal was always to go to New York and get away from here," she says. She lasted two weeks. She laughs: "I tried to stay, but I just could not stay with the noise and the sirens all night. I had to come back to the country."

She began working as an EMT in her community. One day, one of the other workers, who worked at the sheriff's office, said they needed somebody to work in the jail. Would she consider it? "I told him yes, because I was really ready to get away from the community service job."

After working in the jail for two years, she went to law enforcement academy to become a police officer. Her first job was working in the courtroom. But the sheriff at the time wanted community police officers, so she shifted to that. "You would just patrol that community and stay in touch with the people in that community," she explains. "I loved that because I was really interacting with people. I would go to their homes, and we would sit on the porch and talk. I loved that, you know."

It was through these long talks with people that she began to understand the impact of the hog industry on her community. People talked about the sprays, the smell, the flies. Having a barbeque was impossible for any families next to a spray field. You could not predict when the sprayers would come on and shower the field in hog waste—and nobody wanted their burger doused in fecal matter. Life was lived indoors, and people felt captive on their own properties. Where once children had roamed the edges of the woods, looked up at the sky in wonder, and sat in the long grass, they now peeked through blinds and cracked doors before setting foot outside.

In Rosemary's own lifetime, the hog industry exploded in Duplin County, growing until the county held the highest number of pigs anywhere in the country, with a total of nearly two million pigs.[1]

HOG FARMING'S UNSAVORY BY-PRODUCT

"The American hog kingdom was built by the genius, ruthlessness, and blistering ambition of two men: Wendell H. Murphy and Joseph Luter III," writes Corban Addison in his book *Wastelands*. It was at this time that Earl Butz, under Richard Nixon, was put in charge of the USDA and made the infamous statement, "Get big, or get out." Copying the way the poultry industry had grown by outsourcing production to contract growers, Murphy began to reshape American hog farming.

"The day the first Duplin County farmer became a Wendell Murphy grower," writes Addison, "was the day the modern hog industry was born. The growing agreement radically reshaped the allocation of risk in commodity markets that had always been supplied by independent producers." Most farmers at the time didn't have the means to get big, so they joined the ranks of Wendell Murphy farmers, under contract. Word spread of his contracts, and soon he had to grow his feed order to meet the demand from his many suppliers.

It was then that he realized his biggest bottleneck to expansion: the pig waste. Pigs produce up to ten times as much feces and urine as a human being. As the farms under contract expanded, so did the waste. Although the waste of humans is treated with expensive inputs, for pig waste Murphy was looking for a cheap way out. Enter the cesspool.

Cesspools are cavities dug into the earth and filled with waste. People once kept human waste this way, until we identified the health risks. But when Murphy started building cesspools for hog waste, it would change the trajectory of the pig industry and the communities of North Carolina.[2]

Overcrowded pigs in farms stand over slatted concrete floors, and their waste sloshes through the slots, and into pipes that then lead into cesspools. Today, anaerobic bacteria in these pools "digest" the waste, giving them a bold pink color. But in the early days, in the 1970s, cesspools were straight-up lakes of feces and urine. Rainwater would mix in and the pools would fill to the brim, threatening to overflow onto the farmers' surrounding land and homes. So, to relieve the overflow, Murphy's team came up with the idea to pump and spray the waste onto fields in the area. They actually presented the waste as "fertilizer."[3] Murphy came across as a hero, and state regulators were eager to support the effort, signing off on the initiative with little debate. It's worth noting that Murphy himself later became a state representative and then senator. He successfully helped pass laws worth millions of dollars to his company and his industry, paving the way for unabated expansion.[4]

The location of the farms and the dumping of the waste were not a mere oversight or accident. Spray fields were not built in wealthy white communities. It's almost certain that environmental racism was at play, as shown in Dr. Steve Wing's research, which established the geographic pattern of CAFOs being sited disproportionately in Black and Brown communities. The industry likely chose these areas because of the lack of political and economic power of their communities. The operations were on land adjacent to the homes of those who were mostly poor and Black, the children of sharecroppers. People like Rosemary and her neighbors.[5]

The Murphy model proved so successful that it became an empire: Smithfield Foods. In the 1980s, he started contracting farmers to grow pigs and expanded into the Midwest, with a standard herd size requirement of two hundred. As time went on, Smithfield started figuring out economies of scale, increasing the herd size to five hundred, and then eventually, in the case of a farm in Oklahoma, to eleven thousand pigs.[6] By the 2010s, the company had more than forty thousand employees and fifty slaughter-house facilities, making it the largest pig producer in the world. In 2013, it was bought by WH Group (formerly known as Shuanghui International Holdings) for a total value of $7.1 billion, considered at the time the largest acquisition of a US company by a Chinese business.[7]

And, over the decades that that empire was built, the people of Rosemary's community suffered the consequences of the spraying of literal feces into the air they breathe, onto the mailboxes where they collect their mail, the porches they wish they could sit on, and the windshields of the cars they drive. You see, the sprayers shoot the waste into a field, but the breeze takes it where it will. And it doesn't just travel through the air.

Because they so severely over-apply it to the land, and because lagoons can leak and breach, it travels through the ground and surface waters as well, contaminating the water people depend on for drinking.[8]

One study actually found hog feces in the communities' homes. Samples "contained tens of thousands to hundreds of thousands of hog feces DNA particles." The study said: "It is far more likely than not that hog feces also gets inside the clients' homes where they live and where they eat."[9] Imagine an invisible film of feces on your countertops, your stove top, the table where you eat. The spray had a way of wandering. It lifted in the air and snuck through keyholes and door cracks. It clung to laundry innocently hung outside to dry. Children were made fun of for smelling like pig poop.[10] But how could they not, when the air their laundry dried in smelled of it?

For years, scientists have been trying to measure the extent of the harm from hog farms on local communities. In 2009, a comprehensive review of the existing literature regarding the impact of hog farms on communities shed light on that issue. Importantly, the review found that "citizens from exposed rural communities experienced a greater sense of inequality in the distribution of harms and risks, including those connected with health, the environment, and quality of life."[11] This couldn't be more true for residents of rural North Carolina.

Dr. Wing, an epidemiologist at the University of North Carolina, conducted sampling with a team of local residents whom he engaged in the work, a unique approach known as community-based participatory research. Between September 2003 and September 2005, they sampled 101 non-smoking volunteers living within 1.5 miles of industrial swine operations in sixteen neighborhoods in eastern North Carolina. Twice a day, over two weeks, these volunteers recorded their "odor diaries." The results were clear: "This study indicates that malodor from swine operations is commonly present in these communities and that the odors reported by neighbors are related to objective environmental measurements and interruption of activities of daily life."[12]

Another study showed that life expectancy, even after adjusting for socioeconomic factors, for those in North Carolina near industrial hog farms remained low. The study was an astounding verdict on the prospects of a healthy life for the residents: "North Carolina communities located near hog CAFOs had higher all-cause and infant mortality, mortality due to anemia, kidney disease, tuberculosis, septicemia, and higher hospital admissions/ED visits of LBW [low birth weight] infants."[13] Pig waste was an ever-present malice for those who lived near the farms or the spray fields.

SURROUNDED, BUT FIGHTING BACK

One such resident was René Miller. She had lived for decades surrounded by this malice. She had inhaled it when she woke up each morning and exhaled it when she went to sleep. Pig and chicken farms encircled her home in every direction. At first, she accepted that this was her reality. What choice did she have? But over time, as the farms kept cropping up around her, René knew she had to fight back. She met Rosemary thirty years ago, and she found solace and strength in their shared purpose—to protect their community from the harms of this industry.

René was a school bus driver and grandmother. She was not in good health. She had chronic sinus infections and endless respiratory ailments, which she attributed to decades of exposure to air polluted by the hog feces sprayers. How could it not affect her health? She had a machine in her home that helped her with her breathing, whenever things got bad and the tightness in her chest became overwhelming. Her home was separated from a spray field only by a narrow road—Daisy Miller Lane, an ironically cheery name for her address. Just down the road was her family cemetery. Within a stone's throw from that cemetery were lines of pig warehouses, crowding her ancestors' spirits. A bit further down the road were turkey and chicken farms. The dead, and the living, were surrounded.

This land belonged to her mother, her grandmother before that. The house was built in 1960. Owning land, having that stability, that independence, was significant for a Black family, and for René's it was a point of great pride.

René was living in New Jersey when she got the call in 1978: her mother had had a heart attack. Would she come home? René didn't hesitate. She packed up and began a new life, caring for her ailing mother. After her mother had passed, she began to notice the hog houses. At first it was just a house or two, tucked back in the woods. But then they kept coming. The smell, the sounds, they were awful, and persisted day and night.

In front of her house sits a 750-foot hog waste sprayer. It is the first thing she sees when she walks outside, and the last when she returns. "That's my life, that's where I live," she says. "I don't even eat meat no more. I'm against eating meat. I've seen so much hog decomposing in those boxes"—referring to the dead boxes where farmers put pigs who die on the farm—"chickens burning, that stuff stinks. If my mother were to come back now, she'd say, 'God, I want to die all over again rather than to live through all of this.' 'Cause it's awful, but every day I put up with it."[14]

When she started to look around, it was all she could see—people getting sick from the hogs, the sprayers, and the buzzards on the dead boxes. Eventually, trucks came to take the dead hogs away to a rendering plant. "Rendering" is yet another industry euphemism, hiding the true nature of what the plant does. It takes in dead and diseased farmed animals, and even roadkill and euthanized pets, for the production of animal by-product materials such as tallow, grease, and high-protein meat and bone meal.[15] René saw these trucks rattling by at all times of the day and night, carrying dead and decomposing pigs.

And then there were the sprayers. There was the one in front of her house, shooting pig feces into the air. It aims for the fields but inevitably the spray ends up on her front porch, her mailbox, her car. But she discovered she was not the only one. Hundreds of her neighbors suffered, having been robbed of their quality of life, with no agency to change the situation. Or so they thought. René told me: "It makes you a little ashamed because you are in your area, but then there's nothing I can do about it. But I've always had a saying that if you can't solve the problem, don't let it get you high blood pressure. Just leave it alone. Let God take it."

By the late 1990s, René started joining community meetings held by the Rural Empowerment Association for Community Help (REACH) to see what could be done. Rosemary worried for René. But Rosemary didn't feel able to speak out in the same way René did because of her position working for the sheriff of Kenansville.

René's neighbor, the hog farmer, was this very sheriff. René said that having a neighbor who was both the sheriff and a pig farmer had made life difficult for her for years. A sheriff is supposed to serve and protect, and as a hog farmer, he was contributing to the decreased quality of life that so greatly affected her and her community. He also tried to expand his farm operation over René's family cemetery.

René shared that she consistently felt unsafe within her own community. "Someone keyed my car. Someone keyed my husband's truck. You might find the gas tank on the car open," she says. She hears gunshots outside sometimes. "That's why we keep that cardboard." She pointed to the cardboard in her windows, which she placed there so that in case of a drive-by shooting, people can't tell where she's sitting.

Filmmakers Jamie Berger and Shawn Bannon felt intimidated when they came to interview René and her family for their film *The Smell of Money*, about the impact of the hog industry on their community. At one moment, while Jamie and Shawn were parked and filming a herd of cows near René's home, several police cars surrounded them and blocked them from all sides, with little warning or explanation. The crew filmed the incident, and they said that one of the officers, bent over and leering into the driver's window, simply said, "A lot of different things are going on in this area. So we are trying to make sure everyone is legitimate."[16] There was no just cause, no charge. There was only what Jamie and Shawn felt to be an assertion—that they were being watched.

But René was not alone in her efforts. There was someone else who had come before her and inspired her: Elsie Herring.

STEPPING OUT ON FAITH

Like so many in the area, Elsie had inherited her home, her land passed down through the years from her granddaddy, Immanuel Stalling, who was born into slavery. He, like René's great-grandfather, had a white father, Marshall Stalling of Duplin County. Immanuel does not remember his mother. Enslavement tore families apart, and Immanuel believed she was sold away. Immanuel would be light skinned enough that he was afforded some advantages, but, with a Black mother, it was never enough. And although he lived through Emancipation, he remained in the South and suffered the repercussions of enslavement.

He was, however, afforded one grace: his father's sister, Emily Stalling Teachey, took him in and loved him like the family he was. She sold Immanuel his first fifteen-acre tract of land in 1891, the land that Elsie's home stood on now, and gave him another three acres before she died. This was all he needed to get a start in the world, a start that would radiate down the generations, creating a foundation for all who came after Immanuel, including Elsie.[17]

The youngest of fifteen children, with a good head on her shoulders, Elsie left Duplin County in 1966, riding the wave that took so many ambitious Black folks up north, escaping the oppressive Jim Crow rule of life in her hometown. There was no place for her in rural North Carolina. So she forged a successful career in finance in New York, only returning in 1992, with enough money to retire early. Her mother was then in her eighties.[18]

Elsie could hardly believe what had happened in the time she had been away. As a child, she had roamed the fields and forests and sensed the beauty and freedom her ancestral land had bestowed upon her family. It gave her strength. But then one day she walked outside with her sister onto her mother's land—the same land that had given her such peace and fortitude in her childhood—to feel a mist on her face. The moisture didn't make sense—it was a sunny, cloudless day. To her shock, her sister just shrugged and said it was pig waste. "What gives one human being the right to blow animal waste on another human being?" Elsie later reflected.[19]

Throughout the South, the demonic residues from the enslavement of a people remain. An indefensible belief in white supremacy persists, to the detriment of our entire society. But none perhaps is as apparent as the practice where a farmer legally sprays Black neighbors with hog feces.

René and Elsie worked toward the same goal, speaking out publicly, raising awareness, rounding up petition signatures, meeting with community members, and realizing their collective power to make a difference. "A lot of people were afraid, they were afraid for me," said Elsie of her activism. "But you have to step out on faith. You just have to sometimes. If it's worth fighting for, you have to equip yourself for the fight."

She had plenty of run-ins with the hog folks, especially when things got serious and the community took Smithfield to court.

René has just as much fight in her as Elsie. Speaking admiringly of René, Rosemary said: "I know when she puts her mind to doing some things, she's gonna do it. I would go visit her and see the sprayer out in front of her yard. I was just amazed at, you know, how strong she was and what she was doing. I would just say, 'René, how are you doing this? It's dangerous.' I told her, 'You are riding by yourself, up, down the streets, and anything could happen to you.'"

But the work—and the risk—paid off.

René and Elsie were part of an epic, nine-year legal battle consisting of over twenty-five cases against Smithfield. Jurors unanimously sided with the residents. The five trials and five verdicts landed in favor of the plaintiffs, as juries charged Smithfield nearly $550 million total in punitive damages to North Carolina residents, mostly Black, living near hog farms for the smell, bugs, and other nuisances that plagued their lives. In the end, Smithfield would get away with a much smaller financial penalty. The plaintiffs won what seems a whopping amount. But North Carolina's state cap on punitive damages limited the amount to $97.9 million—a cap that was put in place by industry-friendly lawmakers.[20]

After the five losses in court and losing its appeals, Smithfield moved to settle the remaining cases. René and Elsie's cases never went to trial. Theirs were among the twenty-one additional cases settled out of court after the five trials. After the money was split between the lawyers and the different plaintiffs, what remained barely paid for René's medical bills. She had to continue as a school bus driver. And the sprayers still loomed outside her front yard.

But the lawsuit gave them hope. The verdict confirmed that the hog industry was causing suffering, something Smithfield could not take back. But it was not the end for René and Rosemary. "My plan is to still talk about what's going on to other people and just hope. It might be slow, but I just hope that things change," René says. She tells people to keep taking pictures and collecting facts on the hog industry and their spraying, because, despite the lawsuit's settlements, it has not stopped.

When asked what she would say to the pig industry if she got the chance, her response was blunt: "I would ask them to sell out and pack up." She carefully adds that they should not just pack up and go to another state, but pack up completely.

In August 2022, René and Rosemary head together to a community meeting. They're going to a screening of *The Smell of Money*, about the impact of the hog industry on their community. Many of the people in the crowd are in the film, and this is the first time they'll be seeing it.

It's midday at Truth Tabernacle church in Rocky Mount, in the eastern part of North Carolina. A bus has already arrived, carrying fifty people or so from Duplin County, the county with the highest concentration of hog farms in the entire country; all the bus riders are Black. The majority of the two hundred people attending the screening are also Black. It has been a dream of Jamie and Shawn's to be able to share the film that they poured their hearts and souls into with the very community that the hog industry was impacting.

There is a vegan spread of mac and cheese and barbecue "chicken," salads, and cookies. People dig in, hardly knowing the food is plant-based. A jazz band plays. The sun beams down and people stay in the shade, fanning themselves and talking about where they've come from and how the hog industry affects them.

I sit next to someone named Anthony. He is in his sixties and has come from Duplin County, from a city about two and a half hours away. He tells me his granddaughter couldn't come. She is thirty or so, and has asthma because of the pig industry. Growing up with this pollution all around her, her whole childhood, has affected her quality of life. He hopes things will change, and he's excited to see the film.

The auditorium is filled with people who are anticipating that finally they will be heard. I sit next to Jamie. As we watch the film, I hear her sniffling, reliving the pain that she endured in telling this story. When she's on stage later and someone asks her if she was afraid when they were surrounded by cop cars, she pivots quickly. She says that because of her privilege, because she is white, she feels it's important to note that any fear she has ever felt is nothing in comparison to the fear that others in the community have endured. And that she's lending what power she has, that others don't have, to try to change things. "We have to use the means that we have to help tell this story and help shine some light on this issue and elevate the voices of the people in this community," she says.

During the film, I see Will Butler put his arm around his father, Tom Butler, the hog farmer who has spoken out against his own industry after twenty-two years of polluting his community. He, too, has come here out of respect for the film and the community, a community he knows he has harmed. Will and Tom have had their differences, but Tom has done a brave thing in speaking up, and Will is proud of him for standing up and doing the right thing.

The room is filled with people who once thought that nothing could be done to change the hog industry. But still, even knowing the odds, they felt an irresistible pull to stand up for what was right. The fight has been mostly led by Black women in this community who, for whatever reason, from a young age were described as "difficult" or "rebellious" or "independent-minded." Those qualities served them well when they saw that the pig industry had surrounded their families, the land that they and their ancestors had lived on since they were freed from enslavement. They knew what was happening wasn't right. And even if they weren't sure if they could do anything about it, they would try.

But despite their commitment to the fight, and despite their victory in the Smithfield lawsuit, these activists feel keenly that they must do more. "It's good to have the money, but what good is it to have the money if you are living in an environment that is killing you? This is nothing but a slow death for us. You can't keep living here without it messing up your lungs," Elsie says.[21]

René's respiratory health continues to decline, as her medical bills surge. And in the spring of 2021, Elsie was diagnosed with pancreatic cancer, a disease linked to air pollution. The stoic woman that she is, she had pushed away a feeling that something was not right until her niece noticed a yellow color in her skin and eyes and insisted on taking her to the hospital. The first time Elsie went to the hospital, it was her last. She did not come back.[22]

Although Elsie Herring has passed now, her spirit lives on through the women who've fought with her and through the next generation of women. A younger woman with a two-year-old sitting on her lap, who is from Sampson County, spoke during the Q&A session after the film. She said that she grew up surrounded by the pig industry, but it wasn't until she left the county and went to do her PhD at the University of Maryland, where she was assigned to read a paper talking about the impacts of the pig industry's air pollution on her own county, that she realized what was going on. She had a pig farm next door growing up, right behind her grandmother's house.

"It wasn't until I went to school and I had a professor who gave us an article to read about hog farms—and it was about Sampson County and Duplin County! And I'm like, my whole life, and I had no idea," she said. "I think sometimes when you say, What can we do?, some of the practical things we can do is actually talk to our neighbors. Talk, number one, for anything that's ever been successful for Black America, it happened through the church. And if you think about the civil rights movement, the NAACP, they were trying to take cases to the Supreme Court that took years and years, just like you saw with these settlements. So what happened? Some young preachers—Reverend Dr. Martin Luther King being one of them—took it to the streets. And I know, some of our older generations, you know, you've been there."

She called upon young people now to step up—young pastors, college students from North and South—to help support the efforts here. She called upon school nurses. She called upon the power of the community. "If you live in rural spaces, you're not talking amongst each other. So you have to take the small steps of educating your neighbor, talking to your neighbor, talking to your pastor, the people who have any kind of influence—the barber shop! You gotta connect with folks because everything that we saw happening, it's happening in Sampson County as well, and probably a whole lot of other places, but we're operating in silos because we're waiting for the big people, the big politicians to do what we need to do on the local level."

They discuss electing officials who aren't corrupt, who aren't bowing to the hog industry, aren't in lockstep with it, but rather officials who look like them and will really represent their needs.

There is an energy in the room that I am certain will lead to change. The people here accept that change will take a long time and they may not see it while they are alive—as Elsie did not—but they know they have to continue fighting. They have to keep continuing to prepare their communities. And they have faith that a higher power is guiding them and, over time, will lead them to victory, to protection, and to peace.

CHAPTER NINE

IMMIGRANTS

Sandra, Leticia, Marisol, and Carmen

S ANDRA BARRIENTOS NEVER wanted to move to the US. Unlike her husband, who had grown up in poverty, she had always enjoyed being part of a family running a successful business. But in the first decade of the 2000s, El Salvador was a place of violent uncertainty. "We were being robbed almost every day, every week, every year," Sandra said. "They stole everything from us. We had three cars stolen."

"We were running away from that very difficult situation," her husband, Walter Ramon Abrego, said in agreement.

There was no future in El Salvador. Sandra recalled her father warning her of the dangers, the prospects of murder. "*Mija*, your mom and I are old. Go. Think of your children. Think of your husband," he told her. She did think of her children—Ernesto and Maggy. She dreamed of them not suffering, of fulfilling their potential and making their way in the world, without the suffocating constraints of violence and political destabilization. But these were not just dreams she had for them. These were dreams she also held for herself.

So they decided to take their chances in the United States—a decision that Sandra would, in those first years, deeply regret. Sandra would cry inconsolably, screaming with rage, sorrow, and loneliness, wanting with all her heart to return to her home country, knowing that she could not. She had gone from being a land and business owner to not even being able to communicate with the people outside her family. She didn't speak English, and locals did not treat her with the respect she knew she deserved.

Sandra and Walter arrived in the United States in the heart of the recession that had begun in 2008. They learned that the construction jobs they'd been promised were not available. They started first in Los Angeles, then Arizona with an uncle, but couldn't find work in either place. Finally, they heard from a cousin that there were jobs in Denison, Iowa, in the pig and cattle slaughterhouses and packing plants. Back at home they had run a small farm, killing a couple animals a day and then selling the animals' meat at the town market. So this felt familiar and like something they might even be good at. Little did they know, the farms and slaughterhouses they were headed to would bear no resemblance to the ones they had known.

For the first year, Sandra and Walter and their two kids all lived in an aunt's home. They slept in a tiny room, taking turns on who would sleep on the bed and who would sleep on the inflatable mattress. It was a huge change from their six-bedroom home back in El Salvador. Walter and Sandra would barely see the children, who had started at Denison High School. Their shift at the bacon packing plant started at 3 p.m. and ended at 1 a.m. They had to travel an hour and a half each way for that first job. "I would leave them food—sometimes I would make pupusas, and I would leave their little pupusas there in the room," Sandra remembered.

Tired of the long commute, in 2010, Sandra began working at a large slaughterhouse for pigs, and Walter at a large slaughterhouse for cows. These plants were far closer, just a couple miles away from their apartment. They hoped the change would be a step forward, but it turned out to be anything but.

Walter lasted only a year and a half before a debilitating injury made it impossible to continue. His job was to trim sections of fat in the cow stomach. This had to be done very quickly and with great force, but also very carefully, so as not to break the stomach bag, which was full of excrement. He'd wear protective gloves, but the repetition of the movement caused him excruciating pain. He recalls: "I raised my hand above my head constantly, to reduce the pain and swelling. I didn't even sleep in bed anymore. I couldn't sleep."

Sandra begged to return to El Salvador. "I told him, 'Let's go to El Salvador, you're going to die here. Let's go, let's go back, let's go back.' I felt horrible anger," she recalled. After a year and a half of enduring the pain, the tendons in Walter's hands were permanently damaged, and he could no longer continue. He looked for other work.

Sandra, too, endured unbearable physical pain, along with emotional turmoil. Her job in the slaughterhouse was to separate the intestines, working alongside nine other women. They would stand over a metal table as the lines shot pig guts at them at an unimaginable pace. She explained that her job was to separate the large intestine. "It was filled, excuse the word, with shit. When that burst, which it often did, it went everywhere." They didn't wear protective gear on their faces. It was very hot, and the gear would have suffocated them, she said. She continued: "We'd only have gloves. I would get filthy and return home. If Walter went out to kiss me when I came home from work, he would hold his breath because of the smell."

After work, she would soak her nails in vinegar, trying to protect them from the bacteria and fungus that she had been told would grow there from the work, despite the protective gloves she wore. "The glove breaks when it hits the metal table, and the nails tend to get infected with fungus," she said. "My hands hurt so much. With that job my hands, my fingers, my shoulders began to ache. I cried from the pain." But she carried on.

She continued to work in the hot section of the plant, being transferred wherever she was needed, until she had a major accident. "It was very hot and the fan was over there and I was working here," she said, indicating a distance between herself and a ventilator. She moved the fan to increase the air circulation. "When I moved it, it sucked my glove, and my finger went with the glove. I only heard a noise. I didn't feel anything." It was only when she took off the glove that she saw all the blood and realized part of her finger was gone.

She filed a workers' compensation claim but came back to work the very next day because she felt she might lose her job. She was put on "light duty," in the cold part of the plant. As bad as the warm part of the plant was, she hated the cold part even more. Since she was from a warm climate, working in the cold felt unbearable. She felt that this was a kind of revenge from the company. She fought her way back into the hot part of the plant.

After two years, the company, through workers' compensation, sent Sandra a check for losing her finger: $2,000. The Abrego Barrientos family sat around the table speculating about whether there is a list itemizing what each body part is worth. They wondered how much you would be sent for losing a hand, an arm, or a leg. State workers' compensation systems and state law—whether by code or case law—indeed set out the value of body parts. Insurance claims administrators then usually make a decision on the compensation amount.

Sandra was clear about the root of the problem: "It's a dangerous job. Why? Because the line goes too fast. They force you to go fast. The line goes here, I'm standing here, I'm working with a knife, I have the sharpener here, then cut here." She took an athletic stance at the kitchen table to demonstrate the process, moving her hands back and forth quickly. "There are 10,500 or 10,700 pigs that pass through my hands each day."

She talked about having to hold her bladder for hours and hours, witnessing people urinate on the floor in desperation. In a ten-hour shift, workers are only allowed two 15-minute breaks and one 30-minute unpaid lunch break, which must include the time it takes to take off and put back on the protective gear they wear.

But Sandra, despite her personal suffering, still thinks it was worth it. "I was able to help my children, I was able to help my parents, we were able to pay for the house, I was able to afford the trips to see my parents. It was worth it," she said. "Because thank God, I didn't get hurt in other parts of my body, because there are many people who lost more, and then got fired."

In this statement, Sandra reveals how strategic she has been, how she's worked hard to manage her pain and avoid debilitating injury. She's lasted over a decade in an inconceivably cruel and dangerous job, through chronic pain and fatigue.

AN INDUSTRY BUILT ON PERCEIVED DISPOSABILITY

Today slaughterhouses rely heavily on immigrant workers.[1] According to the US Census Bureau, slaughterhouse workers are "overwhelmingly made up of people of color, with a large percentage of immigrants and refugees." Most do not have citizenship, and there is an unknown percentage of whom are employed without authorization to work in the country.[2]

Why and how did this come to be? A schoolteacher in Denison, Iowa, where Sandra and Walter live, told me that up until the late 1980s slaughterhouse workers were not immigrants. Once, in fact, there were no slaughterhouses in Denison at all, and it was rare to find large commercial slaughterhouses in rural areas.

In the first half of the 1900s, slaughterhouses were largely located in cities, and slaughterhouse workers made decent wages and had powerful unions protecting them. But in the 1960s, the industry started to move outside the city to rural areas, in order to leave behind "the urban unions and their collective bargaining agreements and to operate, as nearly as possible, in a union-free environment," according to William Whittaker, a specialist in labor economics.[3]

By the early 1990s, the majority of slaughterhouse workers across the country were Black. But when Black workers in slaughterhouses started to unionize and a labor movement started to emerge there as well, the industry started to search again for an alternative cheaper workforce.[4] At the same time, American demand for chicken started to skyrocket and the industry needed cheap solutions fast. The industry's solution was to acquire a more malleable, vulnerable workforce: immigrants escaping poverty, war, and violence.

According to Angela Stuesse, an anthropologist at the University of North Carolina at Chapel Hill, speaking of Mississippi's slaughterhouse workforce: "The prominence of Latinos in Mississippi's chicken plants and communities today was not accidental. It was calculated, strategic and intimately related to deeply rooted structures of labor exploitation in the region."[5] One of the earliest efforts to shift the workforce came from a slaughterhouse in Morton, Mississippi, which advertised in Miami's Cuban stores and newspapers in the early 1990s in an effort to recruit a cheaper labor force than the Black workers who were now asserting their rights as laborers.

One worker, Pablo Armenta, from Veracruz, Mexico, recalls: "I was in Florida picking oranges. One afternoon I went to a Cuban store . . . and when I was walking home, a van pulled over, [and this guy says to me,] 'Hey, do you want to work in Mississippi?' And I told him, 'Well, that depends.' So he explained what it was about, a chicken plant, a factory where they process chicken, the work is like this, they pay this much. They were offering housing and everything . . . so yeah, it sounded good to me."[6]

Workers in Florida willing to accept lower wages than the current workforce were sent on a Greyhound to the slaughterhouse in Mississippi. It only took a week to find enough workers to fill up the first bus. They were housed in dilapidated and overcrowded trailers. Fees were deducted from workers' paychecks, often reducing earnings to below minimum wage. It would be called the Hispanic Project and would change the makeup of communities of the South in the decades that followed.[7]

Observing the success that this worker recruitment strategy achieved, one plant began offering a $600 finder's fee to anyone who brought on a new worker who stayed at least three months. Stuesse reports: "In its roughly four years of operation, the Hispanic Project recruited nearly 5,000 workers to two Mississippi towns with a combined population of less than 10,000. Not everyone stayed, but this scheme caught on, and other plants began recruiting Latinx immigrant workers from Florida, Texas, and even farther afield."[8] The project proved so successful, it was replicated across the South.[9] At first, the workforce had authorization to work but soon were outpaced by those without authorization.[10] The rise of the poultry industry became inextricably linked to the rise of cheap, vulnerable immigrant labor from Mexico and Central and South America. Soon the rest of the animal agriculture industry caught on, and today people of color and immigrants make up the majority of slaughterhouses' and farms' workforces.[11]

Today's headlines detail Immigration and Customs Enforcement raids on poultry slaughterhouses that end in the removal and deportations of immigrant workers. These are often seen as politically motivated actions, with no real intention of solving the immigrant policy challenges faced by the United States. In these ICE raids, what is forgotten is that the immigrant workforces may be here through incentives, invitation, and recruitment by the industry. The industry usually gets away with a small financial penalty, all the while continuing its recruitment of this vulnerable and unprotected workforce that sustains our country's supply of cheap chicken, pork, and beef.[12]

In his review of the history of slaughterhouse workers, Whittaker states that over time, "the workforce was transformed from high-wage, stable, and union, to lower-wage and often non-union, and came to be characterized by a high turnover rate."[13] According to the US Bureau of Labor Statistics, there are 86,450 slaughterers and meat packers, and 132,100 meat, poultry, and fish trimmers employed today (these numbers don't include the many workers who do not have authorization to work).

Today many slaughterhouse workers are still unionized—60 percent of all pork and 70 percent of all beef in 2020 came from United Food and Commercial Workers unionized plants, for example. But unions today are weaker than those of the past.[14] In an article in *New Labor Forum*, Daniel Calamuci writes: "The once strong and militant union disappeared, replaced by a union that bargained concessionary contracts, failed to organize new plants, and had no response for these extraordinary changes. The industry, emboldened by its success, has fought the union using legal challenges, violence, race baiting, and immigrant bashing."[15] In addition, as so many of the workers are noncitizens, they can't influence political power to change the situation. They can't vote or run for office, and therefore they can't have a voice in changing policies that are harmful to them.

Pay also has gotten worse over time. In 1979, for example, the average wage for a slaughter worker, at roughly $28 per hour (adjusted for inflation), was 14 percent *above* the national manufacturing average.[16] Today, they make roughly $18 per hour—about 17 percent *below* the national manufacturing average.[17] This, despite profits skyrocketing for mega-meat companies. In addition, the conditions have gotten worse. The line speeds for poultry, for example, have doubled in the last half century.[18]

I'd come here to meet with Sandra, Walter, and some of their friends at the invitation of Ernesto, their son. At the end of winter in Iowa, the landscape looked like a patchwork quilt made in shades of brown. The trees were bare. On both sides of the highway, monoculture fields stretched to the horizon. The corn had been cut in November, and now only gold stalks poked out from the earth. Flat land turned to rolling hills as I headed north out of Des Moines to Denison.

Train lines cut through the fields with purpose. They stopped at feed mills, collecting and transporting crops across the countryside to the Mississippi River, where soy and corn were loaded onto ships and sent to factory farms around the world. This land, once prairies where buffaloes roamed, was now a massive factory, devoted to producing either animals or animal feed.[19]

On the empty highway coming out of Des Moines, it was hard to imagine there was a town somewhere in these barren beige fields. But as the highway turned through a crossroads, Denison emerged on the other side of the hill. Purple flags for Denison High School—the Monarchs—hung on the side streets. Some 63 percent of students in the local schools are from historically marginalized groups, and 68 percent of students are economically disadvantaged.[20]

Despite its racial and ethnic diversity, this is the high school that produced former congressman Steve King. He has a long history of insults and offensive comments about immigrants, and has publicly defended the concept of white supremacy, for which he was ousted by his party from a key committee and eventually voted out of office.[21] The town has just over eight thousand people, half of whom are from Mexico or Central America, according to the US census.[22] The people who live here will tell you the real number is higher, because the census does not count the many people who are here without authorization. Approximately two thousand people are employed at the slaughterhouses, and most of the immigrant community here has ties to these establishments.

This is an industry that relies on perceived disposability—of workers, animals, and the land—to drive the rapid, efficient output that puts profit into shareholder pockets and cheap meat on our plates. Our government policies allow for it, even encourage it, creating these politically, socially, and economically vulnerable groups. Government policies leave these communities exposed and ripe for exploitation by corporate and political interests.

For decades, the United States has allowed for a broken immigration system. This broken system is working to provide cheap, disposable workers who lack the agency to demand more pay or rights or fair treatment. Immigrant workforces are used first in fields and slaughterhouses to produce cheap food, as well as in restaurants, construction sites, and manufacturing sites. Then they are used again as scapegoats in political campaigns to drive up poll numbers and media views. Nothing sells like fear and hate. If immigrant workers don't have a pathway to become citizens, then they will never be able to vote and thus have full political agency to participate in society or be able to elect representatives who will advocate for better conditions for them.

Corporations pave the way for these immigrants, lining the pockets of politicians through political campaign contributions to ensure nothing is actually done to change the immigration system. The result is a steady supply of workers who are vulnerable enough to take on the worst, most dangerous jobs in America, including delivering cheap meat, dairy, and eggs at enormous profit for corporations.

Sandra and Walter lived in a typical American home, painted cool mint green, with a small front lawn of tidy grass and potted plants. They had just paid it off, with Ernesto's help. When I visited, the warm, tidy home was filled with the smell of fried foods. Yuca and pastel sat neatly in bowls on the table along with pickled vegetables, chilis, and vinegary coleslaw.

When I interviewed her in the early spring of 2023, Sandra's intelligence was visible. When she spoke, she performed her stories, articulating them with clarity and conviction. She got up from her chair to illustrate how cuts in the slaughterhouse were made on the large intestine, how cutting other pieces might happen, and how she would sharpen her knife. When she stood, her strength was obvious. Had she been born in a different place, with different resources, no doubt she could have been a philosophy professor, or perhaps a trial lawyer or politician. Her animated gestures were captivating. She wagged her fingers, banged the table to make a point, and leaned forward, squinting her eyes and pursing her lips for dramatic impact.

Sandra's friends often call her "La Vieja." The nickname literally means "the Old One," but the connotation is one of wisdom. Many people also call her "La Abuela," though she is only in her early fifties and is no one's grandmother, unless you count Remi, Ernesto's pit bull mix (whom she does lovingly refer to as *nieto*, or grandson). Over the years, her home has become a place of refuge for other women who have endured misfortune, suffering, and pain. The week of my visit, she had gathered three friends—Leticia, Marisol, and Carmen—from the slaughterhouse to share their stories. These women in Denison were fighting for their lives, their rights, and the future of their children.

Sandra has played a critical role in each of these women's lives—providing sanctuary, strength, and even strategy on how to make this difficult life work. She is a connector, a thread weaving the community into one. Together these women help each other, whether it be through strategies to lessen the pain they endure, claim justice for themselves, or be a safe haven during dangerous times. Together they think about how to protect their bodies, lessen each other's suffering. Together they work to recreate for their children a life that has a strong sense of community, when most have had to leave their family of origin somewhere far away, places they cannot return to. Despite all the suffering, they are not defeated. They see purpose. It is not just about their children, but their own agency to fight and succeed in what most would find an impossibly difficult situation.

LETICIA

Leticia,[23] from Campeche, Mexico, had a dimple when she smiled. Her voice was gentle and sweet. She lived within walking distance of the slaughterhouse where she worked. Not that anyone should walk there. The route crossed over a highway and had no sidewalks.

Three to four cars were parked in front of each trailer home, an indication that many people live in these small homes—and that you need a car here. Leticia referred to Sandra and Walter as "Abuela" and "Abuelo." Though they are not family in the strict sense, they are what family should be, and they are the only family she had. She had built a family and community for her children, connecting with Sandra and Walter, filling the hole that her family back home had occupied.

Here she lived with her young children—her older children were at college. She had succeeded in getting them out, in pushing them forward—one of the main reasons she came here, for a better life for her children. They'd spent years with her in the trailer park, caring for the younger kids while Leticia worked at the slaughterhouse in the early hours. Her husband had left her, gone back to Mexico, and she now did her best to manage alone.

The first time she came to the United States she was eighteen years old, with her husband, escaping dire poverty. They worked in a slaughterhouse in Nebraska for five years, using papers with someone else's identity. After five years, they returned to Mexico, having saved a bit of money. When that money ran out again three years later, Leticia and her husband came again, leaving their children with family. They would send for them later.

She recalled, "This last time we suffered a lot, we spent a month at the border. The *migra* (slang for border patrol) caught us all the time. A coyote helped us get through the border." (*Coyote* is the term for smugglers who take migrants across the borders without authorization.)[24] "We jumped the fence, slipped down the other side. Our hands got all cut up, as did our clothes. We ran across the desert." They spent a month in the desert, trying to survive, until a coyote picked them up and placed them in an abandoned house, where Leticia said she nearly died.

"We were in Phoenix," she told me. "We stayed in an abandoned house with no water or electricity for three days. We were already weak from trying, trying and not eating anything. There the coyote abandoned us." Finally, neighbors came by. Two girls arrived, a brunette and a blonde, Leticia recalled. Leticia's husband saw his skeletal wife languishing on the bed and felt he didn't have a choice but to answer the door, despite the risks. Leticia told him, "Let the migra catch us and send us to Mexico, because I can't take it anymore." She couldn't even walk.

The girls asked if they had eaten, and Leticia's husband said, "My wife is dying because we haven't eaten anything." The girls returned with food. Then they told their mom, who helped Leticia and her husband to recover. "Thanks to that lady we survived. We spent more than a month there," Leticia recalled.

From there, they headed to Iowa, where, like Sandra, Leticia had heard there were jobs. And she's been working now for years at a slaughterhouse. Last year she received a plaque commemorating her length of service. "That plaque is a slap in the face, with the pain I feel in my hands." She massaged her hands as she shook her head. They had a blue tinge to them. "As if giving a plaque to someone will take away the pain, right?" Sandra said in agreement.

Leticia had recently switched to a new placement in the slaughterhouse. She used to work side by side with Sandra on the intestines. But the pain in her knees became unbearable. She had to stand all day with one leg out in front of the other, in a catch position. But the new job was no better: using an air pistol to shoot air up the rectum of the pig. She held out her pinky, ring, and middle fingers and showed how she'd have to pull the trigger over and over again, more than ten thousand pigs a day. In just three weeks, the pain had become excruciating.

If you have a desk job, it's hard to understand this kind of pain. But imagine taking a hole puncher and punching it for ten hours a day, six days a week, with only two 15-minute breaks and one 30-minute unpaid lunch. Just try squeezing your hand, squeezing nothing but air—in just a few minutes, your hand will begin to ache. And yet, Leticia reported that the line keeps getting faster, in an effort to pass more and more animals through. "They are speeding up the line little by little. They are now at 10,500, 10,600 pigs a day," she said.

Leticia's body swelled up, and her joints hurt. She felt heat in her knees, in her feet. She visited a specialist, who told her she had a thyroid problem and needed to do cardio exercise, rather than stand in one position. "I decided to try the gym. Now I get up at 3:30 a.m. I leave here at 4:00 a.m., at 5:00 a.m. I come back from the gym to shower, get my things ready and everything." She prepares her children's breakfast, combs their hair, and sets an alarm for when they need to brush their teeth and head out to catch the school bus. "I go to work at 5:40 a.m., I leave the house here. You see, we start work at 6:30 a.m. I work ten hours, then I come home to take care of my children, feed them, make lunch, and get ready for the next day."

Leticia worked through pregnancies while at the plant. Breastfeeding at work was an impossibility. "No mother of a newborn can breastfeed if they work at the plant," she said. There are hardly any breaks to go to the bathroom, let alone express milk. And she had to string together money for a babysitter for her long hours. "Children also pay a heavy price," Leticia lamented.

"I would not recommend the 'American dream' to anyone." Leticia sighed. Like Sandra, she never learned English, despite now being in the country over twenty years. When could she have had the time, or how could she have had the money to do so? She's contributed to the economy here for two decades, but still has no path to citizenship. Like Sandra, Leticia will endure it all to ensure her children's future. She, too, plans to keep going, until all her children are on the road to success.

MARISOL

Marisol[25] also worked side by side with Sandra. She often stopped by Sandra's home on her day off with her young children, to visit with the abuelos, though they, like Leticia, were not family in the strictest sense. Today, Marisol wore a line of self-adhesive gems under her perfectly sculpted eyebrows, accompanied by a red wave of makeup lining the gems. She still had youthful energy, despite all that she had seen and endured. The gems, along with her high-bubble ponytail, gave her the look of royalty from Star Wars. But her tailored beauty hid her deep trauma. She held her toddler on her lap, wiped her mouth. Having young daughters was a heavy burden for someone who knew all too well the dangers for women in this world. She kept them close.

When Marisol sat down to talk, the tears swelled almost immediately. "Maybe I should not tell you the things I have endured," she said. "They are so ugly."

A relative had paid for her trip from El Salvador when she was five months pregnant. Between the violence and the dire poverty, she had to get out of El Salvador, for the sake of her future child. She crossed the border without authorization, brought by a coyote. She thought being pregnant would protect her, but still the coyote tried to rape her repeatedly during the crossing. The others in the group tried to protect her. She lived in constant fear.

Her first job was in the *lavada*—the cleaning shift at the slaughterhouse. She cleaned guts, muscle, fragments, fat, and bone from the equipment. It is the very worst job in the slaughterhouse, reserved for those who live truly in the shadows—including children. In February 2023, the Department of Labor uncovered major violations of child labor laws in the industry. One hundred and two children between the ages of thirteen and seventeen were employed by Packers Sanitation Services Inc., which offered cleaning services under contract to major meat and poultry processing companies.[26] The Department of Labor found these children working hazardous cleaning shifts at thirteen meat-processing plants in eight different states, including plants run by Cargill, Tyson, Maple Leaf, and JBS. Marisol found it unsurprising that there was widespread use of child labor. She felt that given the lack of rigor in checking paperwork, the companies wouldn't see a difference between employing those without employment authorization and employing children.

The company that oversees the lavada was willing to hire Marisol without her having employment authorization. Her job was to use a high-pressure hose full of hot water to spray down the equipment. Her hand and wrist burned with pain from holding the heavy hose. She mixed and sprayed toxic chemicals to sanitize the machines. She'd arrive at 9 p.m. and finish by 6 a.m.—in time for the day shift that Leticia and Sandra worked starting at 6:30—returning to her newborn baby each morning.

But the paychecks were never hers. Her family member insisted she owed him for bringing her to the US and demanded she hand it all over, even long after she had paid him back for the journey. He constantly threatened to report her to the authorities. Marisol said she had reason to believe that he abused his own wife, and when Marisol helped his wife escape her marriage, he turned his abuse to Marisol. Marisol told me that he began sexually and physically abusing her. "We had never lived together as family, so he didn't see me that way," Marisol said. Tears welled up again in her enormous brown eyes.

A kind woman in the lavada took pity and invited Marisol to stay with her, giving her and her newborn shelter. Others started harassing Marisol for staying with the woman, who happened to be a lesbian, for being too close with this woman who had given her an escape from abuse. Marisol sank into depression. She pointed to her wrists and said, "I did a *locura* (something crazy)." She sliced the inside of each wrist with her finger to indicate she tried to die by suicide. She entered a psychiatric hospitalization program. She sent her baby, the one she had crossed the border five months pregnant with, to stay with Sandra for a time, afraid of her own instability, and then back to Mexico to stay with her mother, while she tried to make sense of the world she had found herself in.

Unable to take the harassment on the lavada shift any longer, she took a job in a pig factory farm, the signing bonus allowing her to move into her own place. Finally, she had a place of her own. But to her horror, the work was worse than she could have imagined. Here pregnant mother pigs were kept in crates. After babies were born, Marisol was told her job was to kill any of the piglets that didn't meet the standards—the runts, the sickly. "I didn't want to, but I had no one to turn to, nowhere to go," she said. She was told to smash the piglets' heads on the concrete—a method known as *blunt force trauma* and the standard way to kill piglets in the industry. She said it made her vomit, that she had nightmares every night and still had nightmares about it. Tears welled again. "What choice did I have?"

In psychology, what Marisol was made to do is termed *moral injury*: the act of forcing someone to do something against their moral code or values. It's a concept usually studied in veterans, who can experience moral injury during war. The result is trauma and PTSD, requiring treatment and ongoing management, something that is not considered for slaughterhouse workers or farmworkers, but no doubt they are in deep need of. It has been referred to as "a deep soul wound that pierces a person's identity, sense of morality, and relationship to society."[27]

As I sat interviewing her at Sandra's kitchen table, Marisol told me she was only looking forward now. Just months earlier, in February 2023, after years of filling in paperwork and paying lawyers to help her, she was granted her authorization to work and live in the United States through her marriage to a man with a green card. With her new status, she had started to work at a tax office, and said the work was interesting. She was clever, quick with numbers, and hardworking. She had endured unimaginable trauma. But she still had big dreams. She wanted to start a vegan makeup line, a shop that sold clothes, and do makeup for people. She'd recently got her beautician's certificate. She was weary but determined.

CARMEN

Carmen was also trying to look forward after many years working in the slaughterhouse plant. She too had worked side by side with Sandra. Now she and Sandra had both found new work at Pella, a manufacturer of windows and doors. It paid a little less, with fewer hours, but the work didn't put them in danger or pain. Anyone in Denison who could was looking to work at Pella.

Carmen was infected with COVID three times in the slaughterhouse. She was not alone. According to the Center for Economic and Policy Research, "People of color, immigrants, and people in relatively low-income families are disproportionately employed in meatpacking plants," and during the pandemic, the Centers for Disease Control and Prevention reported a sharp rise in COVID-19 outbreaks among meat and poultry processing facility workers; 87 percent of those reported cases were among historically underrepresented racial or ethnic groups.[28]

The death and despair COVID-19 caused in these facilities in the United States came to dominate national headlines, only adding to already terrible conditions that marginalized, vulnerable communities work in. Instead of coming to the aid of workers, the government took the side of protecting and bolstering Big Ag. President Trump indemnified the industry against responsibility for any illness or death during COVID-19. On April 28, 2020, he released an executive order that compelled slaughter plants to stay open.[29] Trump invoked the Defense Production Act, usually used during wartime to secure the production of essential goods and protect companies from getting sued for manufacturing faulty products.

By invoking the Defense Production Act, the president deemed slaughterhouses "critical infrastructure." Instead of holding them accountable for their workers' illnesses and deaths, the president further endangered workers by ordering these companies to continue operations. The slaughterhouses may have been shielded from liability for workplace exposure to COVID-19 during this time, preventing slaughterhouse workers or their loved ones from the financial recourse owed to them. Indeed, Smithfield immediately used the executive order to its advantage: *one day* after Trump's order, the company asked a federal judge to toss out a lawsuit in which a worker claimed the company's failure to comply with CDC guidelines resulted in his illness.[30] In the end, the case against Smithfield was dismissed.[31]

When illness rates began to skyrocket at the Smithfield Foods pig slaughterhouse in Sioux Falls, South Dakota, the governor and mayor urged the company to temporarily suspend operations. Smithfield refused. Shortly after, officials traced 40 percent of the state's cases to this single plant.[32] Rather than take responsibility for ignoring the advice of public health experts and elected officials, Smithfield later blamed the spread of the virus on its employees, citing the "living circumstances of certain cultures" as the primary cause.[33]

Nearly all other large meat companies followed in Smithfield's footsteps, refusing to protect their employees from COVID-19. Workers reported that they were denied or not provided masks and other protective gear and were forced to stand shoulder to shoulder.[34] As a result, the

CDC reported in July 2020 that among twenty-three states reporting COVID-19 outbreaks in slaughterhouses, there were 16,233 cases in 239 facilities, including 86 COVID-19–related deaths.

Carmen considered herself lucky to have survived. Not everyone in the plant she worked with had. But she still paid a heavy price. Because of her illness, she was unable to visit with her father in his final days and she never got to say goodbye in person.

Carmen was originally from San Pedro Sula, Honduras. Like Sandra, when asked about her childhood, her eyes lit up and she shared nothing but happy memories. As an adult, she worked for Chiquita, separating bad fruit and packing the rest into boxes for export around the world. She was a party girl at heart and spent her first thirty years enjoying life to the fullest. But at thirty, she fell in love and married a man who had US citizenship, whom she met in Honduras. It took over six years for her to gain residency in the United States, but when she did, she moved with her husband to Miami. She wanted her future children to be born in the United States, where she knew they'd have better opportunities.

She worked an array of jobs. "In this country, I have done things that in life I never thought I would do," Carmen told me. "I worked in a factory where televisions were assembled in Miami. Then I took care of children, then I took care of adults, I did house cleaning, I worked in a factory where beds were made. I've even been a carpenter," she said.

But in 2010, the ripple effects of the 2008 recession caught up with her. Jobs became difficult to find. She had been cleaning houses, but that work dried up when disposable income grew short. "Miami is a beautiful, beautiful city, but for someone who doesn't have a degree, they don't have the education, you are just surviving. I got desperate," she said. She told her husband, "We can't go on like this. If we leave our country, it is to improve ourselves and try to have something better." As the bills piled up and the opportunities dried up, she found herself turning toward Perry, Iowa, where she had family.

Carmen started in Perry at an egg processing factory, on the night shift cleaning the equipment and arriving back home in the early hours of the day. After sleeping a few hours, she'd get up at 7 a.m. to get her daughter ready for school. But the lack of sleep was too hard, and she looked for other work. She applied at McDonald's, at Burger King, but she had no luck. Finally, after a week of dead ends and desperate to start working, she let a cousin convince her to apply to a slaughterhouse. She was hired immediately.

Her job, like Sandra's, was to separate the intestines. She recalled sometimes seeing rashes or pimples inside the intestines of the pigs. "If the abscesses accidentally burst, we had to wash and clean the whole area," she said. Like Sandra, she can describe in intricate detail the anatomy of the pig gut. Like Sandra, she endured pain from repetitive motions.

The pain became unmanageable seven years into her job. She was diagnosed with fibromyalgia, a disorder that causes full-body musculoskeletal pain along with fatigue and mental health issues. While scientists do not understand the cause, symptoms often begin after physical trauma or significant psychological stress. Sufferers have a heightened sense of pain, among other afflictions.[35] "I couldn't even walk. I would look like I was a hundred years old when I got out of bed," Carmen told me. "It has many symptoms—it gives you anxiety, depression, migraine, inflammation, pain, decay." She had little choice but to continue working with the pain and fatigue.

She also saw and was subject to sexual harassment on the job. As Carmen worked on the line, a manager would brush against her and grab her body parts. One day she couldn't take it anymore and burst out yelling at him not to touch her anymore. Other workers told her later that he'd done the same thing to them. Some women are starting to fight back. In 2018, for example, nine women sued Smithfield Foods, stating that supervisors engaged in "the most extreme acts of sexual harassment." They stated that supervisors "brushed their genitals against them and grabbed their breasts and buttocks; promised a promotion and even a 'cheap car' in exchange for sexual liaisons; and prodded the women for sexual favors such as fellatio and a lap dance."[36] When harassment was reported, women were fired, ensuring other women thought twice before making a complaint. Like so many of these cases, the suit never reached a jury and was settled out of court, with no disclosure of the settlement.

Smithfield is hardly alone in sexual harassment claims and lawsuits. Most firms in the industry have been sued. Koch Foods, a poultry company in Mississippi, for example, settled a $3.75 million sexual and racial harassment lawsuit in 2018. Supervisors, according to the suit, "touched and/or made sexually suggestive comments to female Hispanic employees, hit Hispanic employees," and then fired workers who complained.[37] Experts agree that sexual harassment in the general workforce is still underreported. And that's doubtless even more true in the animal agriculture slaughter industry, where workers are vulnerable, afraid to speak up and lose authorization to work, or be deported.

About a year ago, Carmen couldn't take the conditions at the slaughterhouse anymore. Like Leticia, she had thyroid problems. She had to have surgery and just couldn't bear the thought of going back after the procedure. She managed to get a job where Marisol and Sandra worked. It paid less and gave her fewer hours, but it's what she could handle now. Looking back, she knows she gave her children a better life. The schools in Denison are decent. One daughter is in the navy and the other still in high school. Like Sandra, Leticia, and Marisol, when she looks at the path she's provided for her children, she can endure the pain and suffering.

THE NEXT GENERATION

Since entering the country at age forty, Sandra has never learned English. As a result, she can't, according to US policy, take the citizenship test until she's fifty-five or has been in the country for fifteen years (in her case, at that point she will satisfy both criteria). That's only one year away now. She's endured this much and will stick it out a little longer. But as soon as she gets her citizenship, she plans to go back to El Salvador to live. Was it worth it?

Sandra is clear that she would have sacrificed much more than a finger to secure her children's future. Her son, Ernesto, made good on his parents' sacrifice. That was the trade—their misery in exchange for his sister's and his freedom and fulfillment. Ernesto told me: "There was an explicit expectation that you were going to come and do something. Especially when you start adding all the suffering that I was seeing."

Ernesto wasted no time in learning English and excelled at school in the first year after he arrived. "I was taking honors classes by my second or third year. I took an English class at this community college my last year, so that counted as college credit," he recalled. He received a full scholarship to the University of Northern Iowa, his ticket out of Denison. It was in university that Ernesto really took off. He felt totally uninhibited and got involved in everything he could. He recalled thinking, "No one knows me here now. No one knows that I didn't know English before." He got involved with the Hispanic-Latino Student Union and then with student government, which led him to politics. He then decided to do a master's degree in public administration at Texas Tech and found somebody to pay for it. He was employed as a resident assistant, which gave him room, a meal plan, and paid for tuition. While doing his master's, he worked in the congressional office of Sheila Jackson Lee, the representative from Houston. It was a safe district where her incumbency was secure, and he found it uninspiring. So he decided to support a campaign in a West Texas district where a Democrat was running for Congress—the first time a Democratic candidate had contested the district in twelve years. Ernesto had always been attracted to fighting for the underdog. He was hired as the campaign's communications director. "It was a scrappy little campaign," he smiled.

He returned to the Midwest after finishing his master's, after trying out politics. He decided to try the nonprofit space, where he finally found his home, first at the Center for Victims of Torture, and eventually settling into working for a foundation, giving strategic advice on where to distribute funds. "I wanted to work in the social impact sector, but I didn't want to work in government," he said.

He's now thinking deeply about system change and how to speed up the transition away from industrial animal agriculture. Although he's a vegan, he's clear that his stance is not just about the animals. It's also about people like his parents and the community he grew up in. Seeing how important the jobs have been to his parents and his own journey, he's also clear that a transition plan is critical: "We are not going to go from CAFOs [concentrated animal feeding operations] to no CAFOs. There's no way. That's not how the systems change. That's not how systems operate. In my mind, I think you have to create a different pipeline of work around it. I think that's why we need to invest in an alternative supply chain."

In Ernesto's mind, vegan advocacy is part of the solution, but it is more complex than that. He believes that policy plays a critical role—specifically, policy that builds something even as it takes something away. "We need policy to help us do better," he said, "and at the same time, we need to take down the bad things that are currently happening. We need to build broad allyship with everyone from those advocating for clean water, to clean air, to those who don't like monoculture, all of whom might or might not care about animals."

The root of the problem is a system that treats all of those involved as widgets in a machine rather than individuals with intrinsic value. Ernesto thinks back to his mother, and her finger, valued at $2,000. One of the policies he believes will immediately help people in his community is to slow down the slaughter lines.

Magaly Licolli, founder of Venceremos, a group fighting for poultry workers' rights in the South Central and Midwest United States, including Iowa, agrees with Ernesto. "Line speed is one of the top priorities—to regulate the line speed, the bathroom breaks and the chemicals," she told me. She helps poultry slaughterhouse workers organize to raise standards. Along with a slower line speed and more bathroom breaks, workers want regulation of the chemicals used in the plants. Many suffer from acute respiratory and neurological problems as a result of constant exposure to toxic chemicals. Magaly has less faith in the strategy of pushing for government policies. Instead, she believes it is more effective to directly hold corporations accountable. Through pressure campaigns, she wants companies that purchase from Smithfield and Tyson, like McDonald's, Kroger, or Walmart, to make commitments to higher standards. She believes that will achieve faster results, and that way, the workers inside the slaughterhouses can directly monitor whether the companies are following the commitments or not.

Ernesto believes that in the near future, a crisis point is needed to force change for these mega-meat companies. He thinks that crisis is coming, noting, "What they're doing is not sustainable. If it's not sustainable for our world, it's not sustainable for them, and that's why they're invested in the alternative protein sector." While shareholders are still demanding growth from the companies now, that growth will eventually run out, because arable land and our planet's resources will run out if we continue business as usual. The question is, can we create a viable transition in time?

Ernesto is determined to build a pipeline to that better world. He returns from time to time to Denison, if only to remind himself of not just where he comes from, but who he's fighting for. Whether it be Marisol's tears and her children, whom he cuddled and offered unconditional love, or his mother's missing finger and her fierce battle to build opportunities for her children, or his dog Remi, who reminds him of how much he loves animals, Ernesto knows his path. He feels that this path has, in fact, chosen him to help end a system of oppression, a system that treats everyone in its wake as disposable and destroys the planet. For him, there is no clearer wrong to right. And with patience and determination, and a unique insight that only a son of slaughterhouse workers could embody, Ernesto no doubt will be crucial to the dissolution of this cruel system and the creation of something better.

CHAPTER TEN

REFUGEES

Tom, Mykia, and Maykeu

CLARKSTON, GEORGIA, located a few miles from my home, calls itself the "Ellis Island of the South." The town claims to be one of the most diverse in America. The high school welcomes students from over fifty countries.[1] Clarkston has received tens of thousands of refugees in the past few decades.

The United States has a long history of taking in the weary and the oppressed. Right from its founding as a nation, the flow of new people has included those escaping famine, religious persecution, poverty, or political turmoil, as well as those seeking economic opportunities. A major part of the growth of the US owes to immigrants and their descendants.[2] Immigrants, including refugees and asylum seekers, come hoping to change the trajectory of their children's future.

The United States also has a dark history of *creating* the weary and the oppressed—one only has to look at our history of enslavement and racism to be clear on that, not to mention the recent history of immigrants in slaughterhouses. Just as with our immigrant workforce, in our treatment of our refugee communities, we have often done both—taken people in only to oppress them again.

It should have been no surprise to me when I saw the Pilgrim's Pride transporter vans pull into the parking lot of the apartment complex where a new refugee family was settling in. Pilgrim's is one of the largest poultry companies in the US. The Clarkston complex was made up entirely of resettled refugees. People trickled wearily out of the van and shuffled across the parking lot and into their respective apartments. I then realized what was happening. They were slaughterhouse workers, returning from a day's work. Tomorrow and the next day and every day after, they would do it again.

At the Global Village Project, a nonprofit middle school serving the refugee girls of Clarkston, the majority of the students' parents are poultry slaughterhouse workers. When the girls talked about what they wanted to be when they grew up, they'd say anything but what their parents do, their parents who have lost fingers and limbs at the plants.

In US poultry slaughterhouses, 76 percent of the workforce are noncitizens, according to the Economic Policy Institute. EPI experts put it well: "One of the most dangerous and exploitative industries in the country, the slaughter and processing of the meat we eat relies heavily upon rural workers—disproportionately immigrants, refugees, and people of color—who have few better options."[3]

According to Oxfam, "In recent years, the poultry industry has been turning to an especially vulnerable population: refugees who come to the US seeking asylum. In a plant in Texas, Pilgrim's employs refugees from Burma, while other companies employ refugees from Sudan, Iraq, Eritrea, and Somalia. Refugees are apt to be paid even less than other workers because the poultry industry often uses labor contractors to find these refugees; contractors pay wages directly to the workers—usually less than the plant would pay."[4]

It's not just the slaughterhouses. As awareness spreads in rural farming communities about the false promises of contract poultry and pig farming, fewer and fewer residents want to take up the job. As they become clearer about what the job entails—crippling debt, toxic waste, suffering animals, and a lack of freedom—the next generation wants nothing to do with this exploitative industry. So the industry is finding a new cohort to take on its exploitative contracts: refugees. The industry's lack of transparency makes it hard to find good data on the trend, but there is some evidence that refugees are being engaged through the exploitative contract farming system.[5]

I got my first clue about this connection in Duplin County, North Carolina, home of one of the largest chicken farms in the United States, maybe the world. To see it, though, I had to go two thousand feet up.

As I stepped onto the tarmac, I got a whiff of what was to come—the smell of pig feces blew in from the west, the direction we were about to fly. Between that and the blazing heat, I was already feeling dizzy and overwhelmed. We were at Duplin County Airport. The airport itself had been created to service the hog industry. It was first established by Wendell Murphy, the man credited with building the modern pig business. The preparations were quick and the instructions few: *Do you get airsick? Here's your headset. Here's your seat belt.* When I inspected the flimsy red strap that was my seat belt, I realized that in a plane like this, a seat belt wasn't the thing that would save you. I sized up the pilot, Aaron, who looked confident, and put my life in his hands.

I was handed a small handheld camera and told how it worked. We were heading up and out in a small three-seater plane to get a real sense of the size and impact of the hog and poultry industry. With us was Rick Dove, an activist and senior adviser at the Waterkeeper Alliance. We'd met before, and he'd been up many times. But today, we were searching for something new and menacing that was just emerging in North Carolina. We were determined to get photos and video to try to get to the bottom of it. We headed fifty miles west to the edge of Fayetteville to find the biggest, newest poultry farms in the world.

As we ascended, we could immediately see hog farms. At first, we saw small ones with small lagoons full of sludge—islands of poop forming in the middle and on the sides where the land couldn't process it. We weren't quite low enough to smell it. I spotted a trailer home next door to the lagoon. I imagined what it would be like to live next door to a pool of feces. We kept flying west. Rick pointed out a sprinkler throwing some of that hog waste into the air and onto the land. It was an insane way to try to get rid of it, yet totally legal and normal. It didn't fertilize anything; it was just a method to get rid of all that poop.

Some of the lagoons were pink, some brown, some black. Some had sludge. Some had algae growing on them. Rick told me a lagoon should be pink. Anything other than that, and especially any indications of algae and islands forming, meant the waste was not being managed correctly. And it only takes one big rain to turn a poorly managed lagoon into a toxic disaster.

Rick pointed out snaking lines of trees below us. This meant there were creeks and rivers. Hog farms sprouted on either side of those snakes of trees, meaning waste could easily get into those rivers and into the water supply. We flew over huge wetlands, full of ancient cypress and shimmering waterways. I could see white egrets flying far below us. These swamps are home to some of the oldest trees on the planet—2,700-year-old cypress trees. Any minute, all of that natural beauty could be overwhelmed by waste.

As we charged across the sky, the hog farms began to acquire menacing neighbors—broiler chicken farms. Right next to a hog farm, we could see lines of chicken warehouses, with tens of thousands of birds locked inside. Some of the warehouses were clearly older, derelict and with rusted roofs. But I could also see lots of shiny new silver warehouses, lined up like sardines in a can. Some of them had bright, easy-to-spot red doors—the tell-tale sign of Sanderson Farms, the third-largest poultry company in the US.[6] Others had green fronts, more likely from Mountaire, the fourth-largest poultry company in the US.[7] These bright lines of brand-new warehouses were the visible proof of a rising trend in chicken production and consumption. New animals would suffer, new habitats would be polluted, and new communities would inhale those fumes and ingest that water. From two thousand feet up, it was clear the industry was not giving up. It was doubling down.

There were so many new facilities as we moved across the land. Broiler farms lined up next to hog farms, both surrounded by fields. Some of the fields grew soy, others had rotating sprinkler systems—land used for nothing but absorbing hog waste. I asked Rick if things were getting better or worse. He said he thought there were fewer hogs but that there was more poultry. He said poultry was unregulated and they were expanding in an unbelievable way in North Carolina. It was frightening. North Carolina literally does not allow a county to restrict where a chicken farm can be set up, nor does it require an environmental permit for a new farm.[8] It's a gross free-for-all. As a *Charlotte Observer* article stated: "Environmental regulators almost never inspect the state's 4,600-plus poultry farms. They can't monitor where all the waste goes. They don't even know where most of the farms are."⁹ So there is no record, no paper trail. Finding out who is running these farms and how they are being run is nearly impossible. You can't file a Freedom of Information Act request because there simply isn't any paperwork to examine. There's the paperwork from the loans farmers take out to establish their farms, but that is private.

Because of this lack of regulation, the industry has exploded here. Georgia is still the country's top producer when it comes to the number of individual chickens, at 1.3 billion per year, equaling 7.9 billion pounds of meat. But North Carolina is quickly catching up. It produces just under a billion birds annually, but these birds are heavier, for a total of over 8 billion pounds of meat.¹⁰

As we approached the place Rick had brought me to see, I thought at first it must be a car manufacturer, or an Amazon storage site. I opened the window next to me so I could get a better view. The window flew up with the hundred-mile-per-hour winds. I was too distracted by the horrors below to be scared. Below were forty-eight houses in total, in three rows of sixteen. Each one of these houses could fit forty-five thousand birds. That makes for 2.16 million birds at any one time on this one property. I've seen tiered systems in Russia and China that house hundreds of thousands of birds. I've seen properties in the US with up to twelve houses, but I had never seen a farm with forty-eight houses in one spot.

Who would look after all those birds? Walking one house takes about half an hour, and a farmer has to do that twice a day. That's one hour per house—with forty-eight houses, that means forty-eight hours of work per day. And that's just to pick up the dead birds—normal stuff. What happens when something goes wrong? When the generator goes out, or something like a big hurricane hits the South? It's not out of the realm of possibility—in fact, you have to be prepared for these things to happen.

How did the financing work? When Craig Watts opened up two houses, he had to take a loan out for $250,000—and that was back in 1993. What I was looking at would cost tens of millions of dollars to build. Who is facilitating that loan? Was it backed by the taxpayers? No single individual could handle this. Was it split among many families?

As we circled over the warehouses, I tried to imagine what 2.16 million animals would look like. I tried to imagine what it would be like to move them onto the farm and off the farm into the slaughterhouse. Usually, a big slaughterhouse can only handle 1.25 million, maybe 1.6 million birds a week. The scale was unimaginable.

I asked about new slaughterhouses in the area. All these birds would have to be sent off to slaughter, and usually the farms weren't far from the processing plants. That might give us a clue to try to understand who was behind these mega-farms. It turned out two poultry companies had in recent years either upgraded or set up new slaughterhouses: Sanderson and Mountaire.[11]

With these unanswered questions swirling around in my mind, the plane veered away. We were now near St. Pauls, North Carolina, over the Little Marsh Swamp, a tributary of the Lumber River. We passed over yet another mega-farm—forty-eight houses. There was nothing to do but take in this horrific sight.

As the plane headed back to the airport, we passed over one area that looked like a patchwork of different colored piles below—aqua, green, blue, brown, black, and yellow. When I asked Rick what they were, he said that it was chicken litter, stored for way too long and likely toxic by this point. He said the Waterkeeper Alliance had filed a complaint and report and turned it into the state. But nothing had happened. As we landed, Aaron made jokes with Rick about rating his landing. I was just glad to be on the ground and give him a 9.8. Apparently, Rick gave him a 2. I said to him, "I'm just glad I lived to tell the tale, because I have a tale to tell."

I later asked Craig Watts and Rick Dove about the ownership of the mega-farm we had flown over. They confirmed that the company or persons contracted for that farm were from Vietnam, thought to be refugees, growing for Mountaire. Rick sent me photos of the Mountaire signs, which listed four names as contractors: Han Farms, Sweet Farms, Yang Farms, and Ming Farms. Remembering the trailer homes right next to the warehouses, I imagined that a large family lived on the farm on trailers and split the work. But I have yet to find any way to confirm this.

The property features clearly posted "No Trespassing" signs—hence the need to visit the operation from two thousand feet above. After calling journalist after journalist, begging for someone to take up an investigation, I decided to take a different route to understand the connection between refugees and contract farming. I decided to meet with a few refugees contracting with the industry and hear their story. Tyler Whitley, the head of our Transfarmation Project, had been working with and supporting the North Carolina refugee farming community for years, and brought me to meet some of his contacts.

A KHMER REFUGEE SETTLES IN NORTH CAROLINA

It was 9 a.m. on a late summer morning in 2022, and already 85 degrees. The sun beat down as we rounded a bend and six gleaming warehouses met our eyes—chicken farms. A truck approached us from the opposite direction, full of chickens stacked in crates, heading to their end. I watched them in the rearview mirror as feathers whipped off the truck.

We drove up to the house: clean white clapboard siding nestled in a riot of red roses. There was a wide fern hanging on the porch and a magnolia tree at least a hundred years old shading the front yard. Lining the driveway were Asian persimmon and jujube trees. These were signs of a life that reached beyond North Carolina, a story that began somewhere else. We walked to the back of the house and a lush garden erupted into view—in every direction, buckets and hanging pots and the ground were filled with plants with smells I didn't recognize. Tom Lim appeared, gentle in spirit and stature. He extended a hand and began to introduce his plants.

We rubbed leaves and inhaled their residues on our fingertips. Lemongrass extended to my chest and energized me as we walked by. A lotus pond held hidden frogs singing and pink buds blooming. Tom told us he'd planted crab apples twenty years ago, and they now have branches heavy with thousands of fruit. I touched an herb that smelled like basil, lemon, and licorice all at once. A Korean herb called shiso, Tom told me. We passed a Thai basil plant and an Asian lemon tree. Tom told me it was called *smiling lemon*, and they used the leaves in traditional dishes. Loofah fruit hung overhead. This was a magic garden transporting us to another country—to Cambodia, where Tom and his family are from.

In the distance, four chicken warehouses stood erect and unnatural, juxtaposed against this wonderland. Tom Lim had raised chickens for twenty years before the company he contracted with terminated him without warning in 2018. Since then, he and his wife, Sokchea, have been working multiple jobs to try to pay off the debt they still carry.

We walked away from the coolness of the garden and into the grass toward the warehouses. We entered a now disused warehouse, and Tom told me his story as we stood in the vast empty space. Even though the house had not held any animals for two years, the smell of ammonia rose up from the ground. I knew it would cling to my hair and skin and clothes.

Tom is a Khmer immigrant from Cambodia who grew up in a farming family. When he was a young boy, he fled the Khmer Rouge's genocidal regime. He lived in a refugee camp in Thailand for ten years before coming to the United States. Upon his arrival, he lived in a California resettlement camp, where he worked during the day and attended Christian religious meetings in the evening. Eventually, an extended-family member sponsored his move to North Carolina, where he bought his farm with his siblings in 1999.

Tom and Sokchea initially became farmers to care for the land and provide food for others. Chicken farming seemed like an attractive option, so he took the loan that all farmers do.

When he was active in chicken farming, Tom, at the instruction of the company he contracted with, had 108,000 chickens per flock at his farm. In a typical year, he raised 540,000 chickens, according to his poultry company's specifications. "The money side of things was good, but not the rest. I lived in constant fear that they would let us go and we couldn't pay the bills. That's what ended up happening," he said.

All at once the smell of ammonia was too much, so we left for the sanctuary of the garden. We settled in the shade of the loofah vines. A gray and white hummingbird sat on a line just above Tom. Songs of cicadas and frogs rose and fell. A swallowtail butterfly hung above us on the breeze for a moment before moving on. We spoke to Tom about joining our Transfarmation Project, and he was excited about bringing his now disused warehouse back to life. We hatched a plan and began the first steps toward transition. We promised to return in winter.

We left Tom brewing his plans for a revitalized future. The heat rose to 98 degrees that afternoon before the skies erupted with rain. A tree fell on the road, and we had to weave back around through back roads to make it to our next destination. Next, we were meeting with Hmong poultry farmers, a community of refugees from Laos. For months I had been working with Tyler to gain their trust.

Two sisters, Mykia and Maykeu, who were contacts of Tyler's, invited us to meet a few members of the Hmong community. Tyler had once helped the sisters with a dispute with the poultry company, so they trusted him. They were all chicken contract growers. "I didn't really invite a lot of people, because I know some of them may not want to share or were a little bit afraid," Mykia explained. "So I selected a few from each area—though I know we have about thirty-five or thirty-seven families."

"What are they afraid of?" I asked.

"They have debt," was her only response.

Around the room, people nodded. This was the only explanation.

They introduced themselves. They had escaped the Vietnam War and genocide. They had lived in refugee camps in Thailand for a couple of years. And then they had entered the United States as refugees. They had moved all over the country, from Madison, Wisconsin, to Fresno, California, until the people who sat before us settled in North Carolina. Perhaps something about the humid foothills of North Carolina reminded the Hmong people of their homeland. North Carolina boasts the fourth-largest Hmong population in the United States. It is estimated that around three hundred thousand Hmong have made the US their home, spanning three generations, with some fifteen thousand living in North Carolina alone.[12]

The Hmong people were recruited by the CIA in the early 1960s to fight against the North Vietnamese and the Communist Pathet Lao in the United States' "secret war." The Hmong served the CIA faithfully, providing intelligence and even rescuing downed American pilots. But they paid a heavy price for their role fighting against the Communist regime.[13] When the war was over, the Hmong were targeted by the Communist governments of Laos and Vietnam. Their villages were sprayed and bombed with chemicals and napalm. Many of them were forced into concentration camps. More than 10 percent of the entire Hmong population was murdered in Laos during this time. Those who remained, including the ones who sat in front of me now, survived, but not without physical, mental, and emotional scars.[14] They fled to refugee camps in Thailand, where many lived for years before being resettled to countries around the world, including the US, France, Australia, and the UK.[15]

The Latehomecomer, a memoir by Kao Kalia Yang, tells the story of her family's harrowing experience escaping genocide, foraging in the jungle, crossing a dangerous river, finding their way to Ban Vinai Refugee Camp in Thailand, and eventually being resettled in St. Pauls in the United States. Yang depicts what her family endured, both in surviving genocide and in settling in a new country with a new language and way of life. Once in the United States, Yang experienced poverty and bullying. But her connection to her community and culture remained an anchor for her always. This is true for so many refugee communities. Though life is no doubt safe in comparison to what they have fled, it is hardly easy. Despite their hard work and incredible fortune in surviving the most unimaginable persecution, they continue to face struggles and obstacles in their new country. So, when offered our most unwanted jobs, they take them. They have little choice. They hope that their children will never have to make such choices. They look only forward, never back.

Tyler picked up fried tofu and beans from a local restaurant, keen to ensure we showed up with an offering. When we stepped through the front door our nostrils were filled with smells of spices, garlic, and onions. On a table was an array of familiar foods such as watermelon, but also vegetables I didn't recognize. No Hmong gathering happened without food, I was told. The home was clean and bright, a far cry from the darkened warehouses these people worked in day-to-day. Chairs were set up in the living room in a circle in which members were already settled. We took plates of food and found places in the circle.

Tyler explained that we were working on a program called the Transfarmation Project, with the goal of providing a means for farmers to transition out of chicken farming. We were meeting with farmers all over the country who were unsatisfied with the exploitative contract systems. We wanted to hear their perspectives, to understand if this was their view, too, and if they were also looking for a way out.

The Hmong farmers were reluctant to speak ill of the job that enabled their kids, first-generation Americans, to go to college, especially with my recording device on. They talked about wanting to "give their kids strong wings to fly." The afternoon turned into evening, and we kept skimming along the surface of their lives. One farmer told me of arriving in Madison. "I remember driving down the highway and I was asking my father, 'Is this the way all these trees are? What happened to all the leaves? Are they dead?' My father said, 'No, no, no. In the summertime, the leaves come

back, everything turns green.' That was my first experience of winter."
They switched between English and Hmong often, calling it Hmongish,
deciding among themselves how much to say.

It was a job, after all, that gave them homes, and a safe life, after fleeing
war and genocide. They didn't want to bite the hand that had fed them.
This is the dualistic nature of this industry. It provides to those who have
nothing but an unbreakable will to survive, but it also takes so much. The
two truths exist simultaneously: it builds and it destroys. This is precisely
why we need to help farmers transition, not simply to pull the plug on this
brutal industry. These families did not enter chicken farming because they
dreamt of being chicken farmers. They dreamt of stable and safe homes,
education, a better trajectory for their children.

They talked of wanting to retire. One family lost their home to a fire,
and that set them back. COVID was challenging, with an unsteady supply of
chickens and difficulty finding workers to help on the farm. That set them
back too. There was always something that kept them on the treadmill.

When I asked, "Do you want to do more farming or do you want to do
something else?" a farmer offered, "I just want to go on vacation." This is
a near impossibility for these farmers. The job is year-round, 24/7.

They told me that in order to succeed in this business, you had to be
ruthlessly careful with money, precise in budgeting. You must be willing
to work hard and sacrifice. One farmer told me that people fail because
they lack the ability to stick to a budget. "If you don't, you are gonna dig
your hole bigger," he said. The group agreed they had done well, sent kids
to college and bought homes, because they had worked hard, they had
managed difficult budgets, and they had sacrificed.

But as the conversation continued, this narrative unraveled. They
started to talk about things they saw as unfair, ways the system was stacked
against them. These were factors outside their control that affected their
income despite their very careful planning and budgeting. They spoke of
difficult relationships with service techs, the poor quality of the birds they
received, an unexpectedly long downtime between flocks, robbing them
of expected payments. It was only later, when the recorder was off, that
they began to elaborate on these frustrations.

After nearly six hours of talking, we had made a breakthrough. I was
asked to turn off the recording device. I was told the reality of their lives

in certain detail, details I have promised not to print here, names I have promised not to share. These families have been through enough. They have worked hard to nearly pay off debt, made every sacrifice, and emerged strong. They can't take risks. But that doesn't mean they don't have strong views on the ways the system has cheated them. Their story is no different from the other farmers I've met with. They just have even more to lose.

Many rural farmers whose families have been farming American soil for generations have come to see the truth behind the oppressive contract systems offered by the poultry and pig industry; however, if we are not careful, the industry will simply continue to find another vulnerable workforce. Refugees and immigrants seeking a better life in the United States will be among them. We need ironclad regulation that does not allow such exploitative moves. We need regulation that puts the responsibility for animals—from birth to end of life—back on the industry, rather than allowing huge corporations to externalize risk and debt on the backs of the most vulnerable among us. Until that stops, the industry will always find a vulnerable population to prey upon.

TOM'S NEW BEGINNING

Tyler Whitley, Transfarmation's director, Katherine Jernigan, its farmer outreach manager, and I returned to the farm six months later in February to check on Tom's progress. It was a vastly different day to the one in June—just above freezing temperatures and raining. But as we pulled up, Tom was out to greet us, arm extended, full of energy, ready to shepherd us to a new container that would soon hold mushrooms. He was now a grandfather to two-month-old Luke. Every weekend he would drive to see his daughter and help her out. He showed me photos of Luke in a sweet Santa outfit and glowed with pride.

We walked up wooden plank steps into a fridge container, 53 feet long and about 7 feet wide. This type of container is usually hitched to a truck to transport goods that need to be kept cold—no doubt, meat included. Now it was hitched up and ready to grow mushrooms. Tom had already installed the water lines and pump, and as soon as the rain stopped he would put up the shelves. He planned to install seven shelves on each wall. He pointed overhead to where he'd put in the LED lighting, and then to the boxes of more lights on the ground waiting to be installed. He pointed to the planks outside the container that would make the shelves. When I asked him what the hardest part was, he just said waiting for materials to arrive, getting started, moving fast enough. His excitement was palpable. His face lit up when we asked him about the mushrooms.

He'd be working with local mushroom log supplier Haw River Mushrooms and had been in conversation with Ches and Laura, the owners. Ches had even said he'd buy back the mushrooms from Tom once he got going. Three weeks from now, Tom would have the container ready and Ches would come out and do a final check before the logs would go in and the mushrooms would start.

The poultry industry's recent shift toward refugee, immigrant, or asylum-seeking contract farmers is a story not uncommon in America—a vulnerable community seeks safety and new opportunities, an industry offers visas with strings attached. No doubt it is better than whatever they've left behind. But certainly, America can do better than exploit people who have already lost everything. Tom's journey illustrates one way to stop the problem before it starts—to avoid the same injustice all over again, of refugees and immigrants who have been in this country for decades saddled with the same debt that American-born farmers are burdened with today. Now is the time to offer alternatives, before the trend becomes entrenched.

HARVESTING CHANGE

A Vision Toward a Humane, Sustainable, and Just Food and Farming System

NINE YEARS AFTER I FIRST MET CRAIG WATTS, I twirled a shiitake mushroom in between my thumb and fingers and marveled. Here in my hands was tangible proof that change was possible.

It was winter in North Carolina and a fog sat heavy on the fields. Craig and I walked down the clay dirt road between the two warehouses. For twenty years, up until 2016, those houses had been packed full of chickens. About halfway down the road, we entered what once served as the control room to one of Craig's chicken warehouses. We stepped into a tidy space. Tools hung on the wall in rows. Cobwebs, once thick here, had been cleared away. Cracks filled. Craig opened the door that once led to where the chickens were contained. I recalled that when that door opened years ago, I was hit with a wall of ammonia and dust from the chicken feces. Now it smelled of freshly dug earth. He'd covered the floor with clay. Piece by piece, signs of his old life were being buried, covered in new growth.

In the middle of the warehouse sat a white shipping container. An HVAC unit hummed on its outside wall. A white pipe snaked across the ceiling of the warehouse and into the container through a hole, bringing water to the organisms within.

Craig wrestled with the hinges of the shipping container door, shifting them left and right until the heavy metal door began to break loose. He opened the door and we stepped into the warm humid air within, reveling in the earthy smell and soft lights. I could not help but be delighted. It felt like we'd been on a long journey and, after feeling lost, we'd finally seen a sign that we were going the right way. Two long shelves lined with blocks of mushrooms sat erect and knowing in their space, as if they were waiting for us to arrive. A tube of LED lights hung above them, illuminating the growing fungi on blocks of spongy white substrate, made of soy hulls and saw dust. From each block, a forest of shiitake mushrooms emerged, popping out on all sides of the block, in all sizes. Craig's first batch of mushrooms comprised sixty blocks, each of which would give way to one to two pounds of shiitakes.

Craig had bought each inoculated log for $8.50 from Laura and Ches at Haw River Mushrooms, about a two-hour drive from him. Their mushroom operation stood on fields where hogs were once raised. They were working not just to sell mushroom starter logs, but also to remediate the land and water that pig farming had harmed. In their longer-term vision, they talked about maybe buying back grown mushrooms from farmers to supply the tinctures and jerky they were now experimenting with. On the wall of their facility hung a sign that said "There's so mushroom [much room] for everyone."

Craig planned to sell his shiitakes at $15 per pound and hoped to make a profit. But if this first time he just broke even, he'd be happy. By the end of the week, he'd clip the mushrooms off. Mushrooms had to be kept cool to ship, so he planned to dehydrate them and sell them dried to avoid the cost and loss that could come with shipping them fresh.

When Craig first quit chicken farming, he couldn't make himself come down to the warehouses for a good year or two. The grass became overgrown, and wasps and fire ants took over. Then he started growing just a few rows of crops in his front yard—corn, okra, watermelon. He got the bug to grow again. Farming is just in his veins. Chicken farming had made him forget that, because that's not farming. Farming is about deep breaths of fresh air, innovation, creation, and freedom. Industrial chicken farming is the exact opposite.

This is Craig's first full crop of mushrooms after his experiment in the tent. He says: "I've transitioned now. This is it. I've done it." He leaned in close, examining his yield and his labors. He had awakened early—4:30

a.m.—worried about his mushroom babies, and had come down to check on them, just like he used to worry about his chickens. But they could not suffer. Within this container, the apocalypse could be happening outside, and the mushrooms wouldn't be bothered. They were future-proof. The shelves that now held mushrooms had once served as dividers in his chicken houses, separating the chicks when they were small. Now they held shiitakes.

We stepped out of the warehouses into the mild January day. Craig had one more task in mind for today. In 1992, he had taken out a ten-year loan of $250,000 to start raising chickens. The money would allow him to build two warehouses and buy all the necessary equipment. As time passed, he kept getting into more debt, which then brought more pressure to get bigger and upgrade. It wasn't until December 2022, thirty years later, that finally he paid off the last cent of what he owed for the chicken houses, four years after he'd stopped chicken farming. We stood in the center of his farm, with all four warehouses that once kept chickens in our sight. Craig pulled out an envelope and handed it to me. I pulled out its contents. It was the loan papers with an official stamp reading that he had paid off the loan in full. He was finally free, after thirty years. He pulled out a box of matches, struck one. The flame flickered for a moment, reflected in his eyes. He took a breath and brought the flame to the first paper. Sheet by sheet we burned those papers, laughing and hooting as we did. Everything they represented—the debt, despair, and lack of freedom—went up in smoke, never again to plague this farmer.

REAL CHANGE TAKES A LONG TIME

I met Craig in 2014, when we first came together as so-called enemies to expose the cruel realities of industrial animal agriculture. Our story went viral and was picked up by the *New York Times*. In 2016, Craig stopped chicken farming forever. In 2018, we stood together in his empty chicken warehouses and looked out from the doors. We spent hours that day talking about what else we could do with these houses. Squinting our eyes, looking at the walls and ceiling, trying to see something else. We ran into a lot of dead ends in those first years. But dead ends are just data, each step closer to the right answer.

In 2018, I brought the idea of transitioning farmers to Mercy For Animals, and in 2019 we launched the Transfarmation Project. We built a team led by Tyler Whitley and, working with farmers like Craig across the country, in 2023 we broke ground on the first two Transfarmation Hubs, one in Iowa at Tanner Faaborg's farm, and one in North Carolina at Tom Lim's farm. These hubs will serve as resource sites and models where any farmer, anywhere in the country, can come to learn about how to transition their factory farm to a plant farm. They will also be research and education centers for community members, policymakers, and advocates to learn and advance the Transfarmation model together.

More than anything, real change simply takes people consistently showing up day after day, over years, pushing for change, trying a million different ways, but never once thinking it isn't possible. Change makers are optimists, but not complacent. They are active in their optimism. Making change requires a steady, relentless march across time. The opposing force in social justice work almost always has more power and money. But they never have more passion and conviction.

Factory farming as a model of food production and farming has failed us. It's failed animals, farmers, our planet, and our communities. It promised to feed the world. Sure, anyone can get a chicken nugget in the United States now. But at what cost? The trade-offs are too high. It's now time to look at what our current and future selves need to not just feed ourselves but sustain ourselves and thrive.

Public policy has failed us. Yet policy still has the greatest capacity to create the biggest changes. As we saw during COVID, the government chose to protect the industrial animal agriculture industry over the workers in slaughterhouses. In North Carolina, following the big Smithfield loss against over four hundred plaintiffs, among whom included René and Elsie, the government chose to create protections for the hog industry by making it even more difficult to bring future nuisance lawsuits, rather than creating further protections for communities harmed by factory farming.[1]

Can voters simply vote out politicians who protect industry over their constituents? Unfortunately, campaign contributions and their influences can be hard to follow. Without elected officials who are willing to turn away the money the industrial animal agriculture industry lines their pockets with, our farmers, communities, animals, and planet will continue to be devastated by factory farming. The suffering that factory farming causes should be squarely on the conscience of these politicians, who need to be held accountable to their voters and the communities they represent.

Corporations must be held accountable so they do not continue to benefit from cruelty, labor exploitation, and environmental degradation. They profit from this exploitation, drive down their costs, and make small-scale options uncompetitive, which increases their profits even more. According to White House economic advisers, speaking in 2021, "Four of the biggest meat-processing companies, using their market power in the highly consolidated US market to drive up meat prices and underpay farmers, have tripled their own net profit margins since the pandemic started."[2] This at the same time we were all experiencing record high prices at the grocery store and many were struggling with food insecurity. We must no longer stand for this absurdity. The time has come to construct a kinder, more just, and more sustainable food system, not just for today, but for generations to come.

The true cost of factory farming is mostly externalized by the industry and often paid by the most vulnerable among us. This damage, this harm, is borne by farmers, workers, communities, consumers, the environment, and animals, but not the industry that stands to make profits by externalizing these risks and liabilities. Yes, meat, eggs, and dairy appear cheap at the point of purchase. But they are anything but cheap. They are coming at a very dangerous price to us all. From Craig Watts the farmer to René Miller the neighbor to Felix the pig to Marisol the worker, the cost could not be higher. And because this price is hidden from us, we are not actively consenting to the harm caused by the purchasing and eating of animals and their products. We need regulations and legislation to ban the worst practices and force the industry to internalize the costs, harms, risks, and liabilities that they have externalized to us all.

In early February 2023, negotiations for the Farm Bill, which is reauthorized every five years, gathered steam, and a coalition came to Capitol Hill to begin this work in earnest at the Food Not Feed Summit, highlighting the urgent need to transition away from industrial animal agriculture and toward a kinder, more just, and more sustainable system. This was a growing coalition of advocates, representing academia, agriculture, animal rights, the environment, faith, food, health and nutrition, social justice, and workers, who all were united to demand a transition away from industrial animal agriculture.

We walked the corridors of Congress and met, one by one, with elected officials, explaining the deep need for change. Together, Tanner Faaborg and our Transfarmation and Government Affairs staffers, along with members from the entire coalition, marched in and out of offices, repeating over and over again, through some ninety meetings in total, that transition plans were needed and wanted, but would be difficult without the financial, political, and technical support of Congress.

What follows are some suggestions, some of which we did get to speak to members of Congress about, and some we have not yet presented. They are not utopian by any means; rather, they show how we can begin the process of forcing the industry to take on the real cost of the production of meat, dairy, and eggs. These steps would put more pressure on the need to transition and make new models of food and farming more viable as alternatives.

IMPROVING ANIMAL WELFARE STANDARDS

I am often asked if I am open to a compromise between the extreme of not exploiting animals at all in our food system and the current reality of eating them en masse. Can any common ground be found with those who believe that animal agriculture can be done morally, humanely? I find myself unable to answer this directly, but instead unpack the current reality.

Last year saw the largest number of farmed animals in human history killed. As this trend continues, and until it doesn't, we have a moral obligation to do everything we can to reduce the suffering of animals trapped in our food system. This comes by way of standards to improve their welfare—banning the worst practices, which means getting rid of close confinement, extreme growth rates, and standard mutilations. Animal welfare measures are not so much a compromise but rather a stepping stone to reduce the suffering of animals trapped in the system until a day when they are not there at all.

No doubt the world is moving in the right direction when it comes to animal welfare. This book has largely focused on public policy solutions and opportunities. But it is important to recognize that in the United

States and around the world, corporate policies and commitments to animal welfare have been paving the way for public policy. A critical mass of corporate policies often precedes government action, thereby reducing resistance to a public policy's implementation.

A decade ago, hardly a company in the world had any kind of animal welfare policy. Today, almost every company in the world has one, and thanks to pressure campaigns from animal activist groups, over three thousand farmed animal welfare corporate policies have been established in the last two decades or so. Today more than a third of egg production in the US is cage free—meaning egg-laying hens are guaranteed enough space to spread their wings and perform natural behaviors such as dust bathing. The USDA predicts that by 2025, cage-free eggs will represent more than half the total market in the United States.[3]

This trend extends beyond the US and EU to other parts of the world, with major pledges being made from Brazil to Thailand. Activists have secured global cage-free pledges from 150 multinational corporations, including the world's largest hotel chains and food manufacturers. This has been heralded as major progress by Lewis Bollard of Open Philanthropy, who writes: "165M more hens are already cage-free in Europe and the US today than were a decade ago, and advocates are on track to help over 300M more just by getting companies to follow through on their existing policies."[4]

All of this is a testing ground for a much bigger target—broilers, or chickens raised for meat. Roughly 70 billion are slaughtered globally each year and 90 percent of all factory-farmed animals on land are broilers, so this is a critical issue in terms of reducing suffering. Progress has been slower and harder for chickens raised for meat. And this makes sense—they constitute nearly all factory-farmed animals. If we undo broiler farming in its current form, we undo almost all of factory farming.

An important corporate animal welfare policy eliminating cruel practices includes the Better Chicken Commitment, which requires chickens raised for meat to be given more space, be grown from healthier breeds, and be given enrichments, among other things. These measures not only reduce the suffering of animals trapped in these systems, but they also raise costs and decrease efficiency. Adding space means that instead of squashing thirty thousand birds into a warehouse, now there might only be twenty thousand. It inevitably means that the cost of the meat will go up. And when cost goes up, we know consumption tends to go down. Producers estimate cage-free brings an 8 to 19 percent increase in annual costs.[5] This is a direct result of "internalizing" the costs the industry previously externalized through animal suffering. While it is a far cry from ensuring that the animals live a life worth living, it is a step in the right direction.

Legislation, which, again, often comes after corporate initiatives in the US, is following suit. Since 2002, fourteen states have passed laws banning close confinement systems such as cages and crates for hens, calves, and pigs.[6] California's Prop 12 was upheld by the Supreme Court. The status quo, factory farming, is being questioned and disrupted. This trend must continue.

Simply banning cages by no means ensures a decent life for these animals, but it represents a positive trend that I hope will continue. The more standards we can raise, the more costs that can be internalized, the less efficient the system becomes, and the more apparent become the true costs of the products coming out of the system.

IMPROVING LABOR STANDARDS FOR WORKERS AND FARMERS

One of the most resounding cries for change for workers is to slow down the line speeds at the slaughterhouses. Not only would it result in fewer animals being slaughtered, but workers would have more time to repeat the same motions over and over, and it would also allow them to physically spread apart more from one another, to reduce the risk of diseases spreading.

The industry still has a long way to go and arguably is going in the wrong direction, never seeming to be able to stand up to pressure caused by competition. In 2019, the Trump administration finalized a rule allowing pig slaughter plants to run without any line speed limits. It also let pig slaughter plants use some company inspectors instead of government ones, the equivalent of being able to grade your own papers. After the enactment of the pig slaughter plant rule, an equivalent poultry plant rule was proposed, though never was put into effect. The new Biden administration immediately withdrew the poultry plant line speed proposal. The pig slaughter plant rule was harder to change, given it was already in effect.

But then the United Food and Commercial Workers Union, arguing that faster line speeds compromised worker safety, brought a lawsuit against the USDA, and the rule was finally overturned.[7]

Unfortunately, the Biden administration created a loophole, no doubt caving to industry pressure.[8] It allowed for faster line speeds in some cases if a plant obtained a USDA-issued waiver. On June 30, 2021, under the New Swine Inspection System, the Food Safety and Inspection Service reinstated the maximum line speed of 1,106 pigs per hour.[9] That is approximately a pig every three seconds. However, in November that same year, the USDA invited processors to apply for a "time-limited trial" that would allow for processors to run slaughter at an even faster speed. At the time of writing this book, this so-called trial has been extended for a second time to November 2023, and there were six processors participating in the program allowing for even faster speeds.[10] For chickens, the maximum line speed for the waiver program is 175 birds per minute, which is 3 birds per second (without the waiver, it is 140 birds per minute). At this writing, forty-nine poultry slaughter plants have obtained such a waiver.[11]

The pace is unimaginable to the layperson, yet this maximum speed is being permitted more and more. For animals, fast line speeds lead to improper shackling and stunning, leaving countless animals conscious throughout the slaughter process. For example, many birds miss the kill blades and are still alive when they reach the scalding feather-removal tanks. It is all too common for birds to enter scald tanks fully conscious and die by drowning and being boiled alive. Thereafter termed *cadaver birds*, the actual number who die this way is difficult to pin down.[12] Inspectors are not always present when violations happen, and reports are only made when more than six animals are deemed to be harmed via ineffective slaughter at one time.[13] According to the USDA, in 2018 more than six hundred thousand young chickens drowned in these tanks.[14]

In the same way that we have seen reform sweep through the country in securing cage-free egg commitments, tackling change at the corporate level regarding slaughterhouses could quickly improve conditions for workers and animals alike. The government should immediately revoke waivers allowing slaughterhouses to operate without line speed restrictions and reduce the current maximum line speed. There are so many reasons to do this: it would prevent harm to vulnerable communities, promote worker and consumer safety, minimize environmental impacts, and prevent increased animal cruelty, to name just a few. And there is one reason not to: it would maximize corporate profits, at the expense of everyone else. Pressure campaigns to gain commitments from retailers and restaurants to slow down the lines could help build momentum toward legislative change.

We need to update the Packers and Stockyards Act. It was once one of the greatest pieces of legislation created to protect our nation against abuse from corporate consolidation in our food system. It desperately needs an overhaul to break the stranglehold that massive, vertically integrated meat, dairy, and egg companies have on our food systems.[15]

There are many other measures that would reduce the suffering of workers—more required bathroom breaks, paid lunches, proper compensation for injuries, banning toxic chemical use in plants, and preventing the use of incarcerated people as slaughterhouse workers, to name a few.

Ensuring that slaughterhouse workers are given the same severance packages as supervisors when slaughterhouses shut down would also change the equation considerably. Currently, when a slaughterhouse shuts down, it is all too common that the workers are simply let go without severance, or given a much smaller severance package than supervisors, even if they have built a life around the plant and have been employed for a decade or two. Management, however, often receives generous severance pay. For example, when a Tyson plant in Arkansas closed, company supervisors reportedly received a full severance package but workers on the floor did not. Tyson also reportedly refused to pay out unused vacation time and would not allow workers to take any vacation days before the closure.[16]

Treating farmers as employees instead of contractors is one option that might force a rapid change in the system. Employees are protected by state and federal law in ways that contractors are not. Companies would care far more about why animals are dying and getting sick if they, rather than the farmers, were the ones who had to incur the cost for this loss. If farmers were paid by the hour, or better yet, were paid a salary for their work as other employees of the mega-meat companies are, this, too, would make companies far more accountable to the liability and risk inherent in raising animals on a farm, thereby increasing motivation to improve standards. In addition, paying for all the infrastructure required to raise animals would cost the industry billions of dollars. That cost is borne by the farmers—$5.2 billion in the poultry field alone, according to one USDA study.[17] What if the industry were to have to pay for the property, buildings, and land?

Another option, and perhaps one far preferred by farmers, is that they are true independent contractors, with true choices about who to sell to and how to run their business. At the moment, contract farmers are extremely limited—they usually only have one integrator they can sell to, and that integrator determines nearly all of the inputs—the breeds, the living conditions of the birds, the feed inputs, and the time to slaughter. Farmers should not be pitted against each other via the tournament system, and the contracts should be less restrictive.

A very similar problem occurred in the past with brewers. It was known as a "tied house," which referred to a pub that was tied to a single brewer and couldn't sell any other beer. This resulted in lower competition and consumer choice. After Congress repealed Prohibition in 1933 through the Twenty-First Amendment, the government stepped in and solved the problem by enacting some version of laws designed to prohibit and minimize tied houses.[18] It's time for the government to do something similar with contract farming in the industrial animal agriculture industry.

MEAT TAXES

Many products are taxed based on the damage they cause and as a way to discourage their use. As mentioned in chapter 3, tobacco and soda taxes in the United States work to deter consumption of these products. When the city of Berkeley, California, raised taxes on soda by a penny an ounce, rates of consumption, at least according to one study published in the *American Journal of Public Health*, dropped 21 percent.[19] In 2022, New Zealand introduced a plan to tax livestock production based on carbon emissions, to be implemented in 2025.[20] The idea is to tax livestock production in an effort to meet emissions targets. Former prime minister Jacinda Ardern called it "an important step forward in New Zealand's transition to a low emissions future."[21]

An Oxford University research team published a paper in the *Review of Environmental Economics and Policy* arguing that taxes on meat could help mitigate some of the negative environmental and public health impacts of meat consumption.[22] They argued that an environmental tax covering greenhouse gas emissions and nutrient pollution alone would increase the current retail price of meat in high-income countries by roughly 20–60 percent. In fact, they suggested this was likely an underestimate.

It's an intervention well worth considering. Taxes for products that adversely affect our health, like those on soda and tobacco, along with taxes on high-emission items, would cause both consumers and producers to reconsider their choices.

BROAD REFORM

Ultimately, we need major corporate and legislative reform that reflects the simple truth that factory farming at its core is the wrong food and farming system for our future.

The alternative protein market is rapidly developing viable alternatives to meat on the product side. But we also need alternatives for the people in the system—farmers and workers—that show what life beyond factory farming could look like.

One of the lead reformers in the nation who is working on those alternatives at the government level is Senator Cory Booker. He first introduced the Farm System Reform Act in 2019, which would put a moratorium on factory farms of a certain size. Critically, the act would also provide debt relief for farmers and set aside federal funds to help transition farmers out of factory farming. This first attempt started a discussion in the halls of Congress about what is possible.

In 2023, Senator Booker led another effort. Once every five years, the Farm Bill is reauthorized—this means that the same legislation from five years ago is reintroduced, and members of Congress have the opportunity to propose amendments to it. If the amendments don't pass, the existing Farm Bill goes into law. This federal legislation has an impact on national policies for agriculture, nutrition, conservation, and forestry. Booker in the Senate and Jim McGovern in the House introduced a multi-title amendment to the Farm Bill in 2023, calling it the Industrial Agriculture Accountability (IAA) Act. Their proposal called for the industry to be held accountable for the external harm that it does to our environment and communities. Some of its components included the following:

Restricting the use of ventilation shutdown, water-based foam, and other cruel methods of mass on-farm killing. These systems, used during COVID when slaughterhouses were backed up because of worker shortages, should not be permitted, and tax dollars should not be used to pay for them.

Making industrial operators responsible for all costs associated with animal depopulation, including buying the equipment for depopulation, providing compensation to contract growers, and providing worker compensation. Our current livestock indemnity program allows big meat companies to recover 75 percent of the fair market value of the lost cost when many animals must be killed yet fails to require them to make disaster prevention plans. After COVID, in 2023 the country saw record egg shortages as a result of avian flu and the mass killing of hens on farms. But companies continued to make record profits, recovering the majority of their lost costs, and were not required to make any changes to their practices, even though avian flu is known to be a regular, almost annual, disaster event in the egg industry. This is an absurd handout to the corporate meat and egg industries, and it must end.

Prohibiting the use of incarcerated workers in the livestock and poultry systems during disasters. A captive workforce in the literal sense, prisoners, who are disproportionately Black and Brown, frequently receive wages as low as 25 cents an hour for backbreaking, traumatizing work.[23]

Setting minimum labor standards for contract farmers and slaughterhouse workers.

Covering poultry under the Humane Methods of Slaughter Act. Chickens are currently excluded, despite making up 90 percent of all slaughtered individuals in our land-based food system.

I'm sure this bill will continue to be debated well after the completion of me writing this book. But holding this debate, in the corridor conversations and meetings with members of Congress, was an important step toward adding some accountability and discussing the need to internalize the true costs of meat production.

SHIFTING THE FEDERAL DOLLAR

A disproportionate amount of our taxpayer dollars in the form of crop subsidies goes to support crops grown to feed beef and dairy cattle, chickens, and pigs—not humans. This, in a very real way, artificially gives these industries a leg up that no other product line enjoys in the market. By keeping the costs of factory farming inputs such as corn and soy down, meat, egg, and dairy companies gain a market advantage over fruits, vegetables, grains, nuts, and seeds, and these artificially low prices influence our purchasing habits.

According to Farm Action, about 30 percent of American farm subsidies go just to produce feed crops for dairy, eggs, and meat. That is about double the amount that goes to feeding people. Only 13 percent of farm subsidies go to food grains like rice, corn, and wheat, while a mere 4 percent go to fruits and vegetables and 2 percent to nuts and seeds.[24] This is reflected back to us in the way we eat. When fast food chicken nuggets are cheaper than an apple, it's hard to choose the latter. According to the CDC, only about 10 percent of the US population consumes the recommended dietary allowance of fruits and vegetables.[25] This is in no small way a result of where federal support goes in the form of subsidies.

As the saying goes, you are what you eat. And a healthy diet supports everything from a healthy immune function to preventing major chronic diseases that plague the United States right now—type 2 diabetes, cardiovascular diseases, and some cancers.[26] According to the American Hospital Association, nearly half of all Americans today suffer from at least one chronic illness such as hypertension or heart disease. That number is 15 million higher than it was just a decade ago and set to continue rising in the decade ahead.[27]

In addition to what is covered in the IAA Act, there are many policy opportunities in the fight ahead. We need a federal food policy that prioritizes producing food, not feed for factory-farmed animals—one that will ensure our neighbors and communities are well fed and will put profits back in the pockets of our family farmers. We need to shift government support away from feed grains for industrial livestock production and toward vegetables, fruits, nuts, legumes, mushrooms, and cereal grains.

We must also increase the financial and technical resources available for farmers who want to transition away from industrial agriculture and toward models that empower producers to grow food for their communities and treat animals, workers, and our environment with respect.

Our elected officials should also include requirements in the Farm Bill for farmers to meet certain conservation standards in order to participate in our nation's farm programs, such as the federal crop insurance, commodity/price support, and disaster payment programs.

We need legislation that addresses the terrible history of the USDA and its discrimination against farmers of color and communities of color.[28] A whole book could be written on this subject alone. The USDA has a history of discriminatory lending practices, making it difficult for Black farmers to get a start and, when times are hard, remain in the business. These practices include, according to NPR's coverage of the issue, "barriers to access to programs ranging from incorrect denials, to cumbersome paperwork, to a failure to know what applicants could qualify for to begin with." There have been multiple class action lawsuits, and Congress has had multiple hearings on the discriminatory practices. In 2023, Congress, led by Senators Cory Booker and Raphael Warnock, approved a large debt relief program, and the USDA created an Equity Commission.[29] The government needs to continue its focus on this area.

THE END OF FACTORY FARMING—A CALL FOR TRANSITION

Ultimately, we need a moratorium on industrial animal agriculture, and we need pathways for farmers and workers who wish to leave this system. This system serves no one, save the corporate executives and shareholders who stand to make record profits while the rest of the nation struggles to find healthy food.

There are so many opportunities to do better by our farmers, our communities, the animals, and our planet. As we survey the country and note the state of our food and farming system, it's clear that we need new policy. We need new champions unafraid to stand up to corporate power, champions like Paula Boles, Elsie Herring, Ernesto Abrego, and the others portrayed throughout this book.

The clearest precedent for the kind of farm transitions we're calling for is tobacco. As discussed in chapter 3, the Tobacco Transition Payment Program, colloquially known as the "Tobacco Buyout," paid out $4.11 billion directly to tobacco growers and $5.85 billion directly to former quota owners over the ten-year transition period between 2004 and 2014.[30] The result was that the number of tobacco farmers declined by 51.5 percent in the year after the legislation took effect in 2005, according to research firm IBISWorld. The numbers of farmers growing tobacco in total dropped from 56,879 in 2002 to only about 4,268 in 2015, when the payments ended.[31] The swift change made it clear that tobacco farming had been largely sustained by government payments. Removal of government support via federal payouts to industrial animal agriculture would likely result in the same shift. During the tobacco transition, as federal support for tobacco farming shifted, so, too, did public use of tobacco. The program worked.

Farmers aren't factory farming because they love the idea of being under the thumb of corporate entities and picking up dead and dying chickens. They do it because they are trapped in debt and have few other economic options. This form of farming is largely sustained by government payments and lack of choice.

Let's choose better. Let's choose farming that benefits the most people, supports the most communities, reduces the most suffering of animals, and builds a planet we want to hand over to the next generations. Let's choose a just transition away from this unfair, cruel, and unsustainable food and farming system we have found ourselves in.

Imagine a food system where farmers have freedom. Imagine farmers waking each morning with a sense of hope, as Craig Watts now does as he checks on his mushrooms. Imagine warehouses scattered across our country that once kept chickens and pigs in despair, instead holding shelves of shiitakes and microgreens in greenhouses. Imagine a day when communities near farms aren't plagued by flies, terrible smells, carcasses, and aerial feces, like Rosemary Batts and her neighbors are. Imagine, instead, that she can sit on her porch and enjoy a glass of lemonade as the sun sets. Imagine a food system where workers are paid fairly, are part of the political system, and have safe labor standards. Imagine workers like Leticia never suffering any pain from the rapid and relentless pace of the slaughterhouses. Where workers are treated as a respected workforce, rather than disposable. Imagine a day where farmed animals never live a day in fear or pain. Where cows like Norma never have to fight for their babies. Where, rather than seeing their flesh as a commodity, we make them a part of our hearts and homes, as Henrietta was.

This is the hope we must hold up in front of us like a guiding light. We are not going to go from factory farming to no factory farming. As with all systemic change, it won't happen overnight. We must build pipelines for markets, jobs, farms, and even mindsets. And we must have conviction in this task.

This is the fight we are in now, and our futures depend on it. Billions of dollars are poured in to preserve a status quo, this system of oppression, this industrial animal agriculture model of food production. But as we have seen clearly from our nation's history, organized people always beat organized money.

This is a system that keeps so many oppressed—from the farmer to the rural impoverished community, the immigrant worker, the sentient farmed animal, and the parent trying to feed their family a healthy meal. The task before us is to undo this system of oppression. It may take many attempts. It may take decades. This fight will demand perseverance. But it is a worthy fight. Because what can matter more than the food we put in our body and souls to nourish and sustain us? What can matter more than the way our communities thrive, and the way we treat the beings we share the planet with? This is a sacred task. This is the moment we decide who we are as a nation, who we are as a species, and the kind of future we want to carve out for all those who come after us.

ACKNOWLEDGMENTS

WRITING A BOOK IS NOT AN INDIVIDUAL EFFORT. It is the coming together of many—a collective will to bring forth an idea whose time has come, stories that are ready to be told. This book is no different and is the result of a network of people who all believe in the words within these pages.

The most important beings to thank within this book are those who have shared their stories, hardships, and dreams with me. They trusted me to tell their story and I can only hope to have done them justice. To the farmers, the workers, community members, advocates, animal rescuers, and to the animals themselves, who told me their story in their own way, I am deeply and eternally grateful. I hope this helps move us toward our collective liberation where we are all free from the pain and suffering factory farming causes.

I am deeply grateful to my agent Stacey Glick, who believes in projects addressing animal rights and food justice. Thanks to her, stories like this have a platform. Thank you to my editor Joanna Green, and Beacon Press, who truly believes in the ideas within this book and gave the most insightful feedback. Joanna's passion and skill made me work hard to communicate better and deliver the best narrative possible.

I'm deeply grateful to the people at Mercy For Animals who gave me space and support to write this book and who shared in the vision that we must change the dominant narrative about factory farming: the Transformation team—Katherine Jernigan and Tyler Whitley—you have tolerated my slowing us down in the field to interview and dig deeper; the video team—Jenn Murphy, Stephanie Lundstrom, and Shawn Bannon—who captured so many of these conversations I used as dialogue in the book;

Jamie Berger, who provided valuable feedback, contacts, and insights; the editing team—Brooke Mays and Eric Ford—who sorted out my horrific formatting for my citations with patience and professionalism; the legal team—Jodi Medoff and Abbey Jay—who kept me out of hot water while ensuring there was still bite to my book; to the MFA board of directors for supporting me in doing this project, in particular T. L. Gray, who read the book and gave valuable feedback; the internal feedback team—Chelsie Schadt, A. J. Albrecht, Alex Cragun, Michael Gagné, Jesse Marks, Katherine Jernigan, Tyler Whitley, Matthew Scheer, and Steph Woman, and to Steph Woman again for being a deep thinker and magical scheduler, keeping me on track.

Thank you to my dear friend Nan Schivone, a legal champion and veteran of defending immigrant rights, who read the chapter on slaughterhouse workers and helped ensure the accuracy and clarity of the narrative. I am deeply grateful to Walter Ernesto Abrego Barrientos, who trusted me and brought me into his family and community in Iowa, and to Daniela Medrano, who stood with me to hear the stories there. Thank you to the people and places that gave me space to be alone and write. I am deeply grateful to the Mesa Refuge in Point Reyes Station, California, where I was a writing fellow, for giving me the most fruitful weeks to focus on my ideas and writing. That place is magical, and some of the writing I am most proud of came from that time as a result of the environment they cultivate for "writers on the edge." I am also grateful to Sarah Pickering and Lauren Gould, who gave me time in Maine, and Andy and Stephanie Williams, who gave me time in New Smyrna Beach, Florida. These were times where I was really able to go inward and find the truth and story I wanted to tell.

Finally, I thank my family—Ben, Ruben, Asher, and Andrea—who understood that I had to do this, and never once questioned my need for more time and space to learn, travel, think, and write in order to create this book. I am so lucky to have you.

NOTES

INTRODUCTION

1. Hannah Ritchie, Pablo Rosado, and Max Roser, "Animal Welfare," Our World in Data, 2023, https://ourworldindata.org/animal-welfare.

2. Leah Garcés, "Are We on the Cusp of a Pandemic Flu?," *Mercy For Animals* (blog), January 17, 2020, https://mercyforanimals.org/are-we-on-the-cusp-of-a -pandemic-flu.

3. Food and Agriculture Organization of the United Nations, "Surge in Dis-eases of Animal Origin Necessitates New Approach to Health—Report," Decem-ber 16, 2013, http://www.fao.org/news/story/en/item/210621/icode.

4. Food and Agriculture Organization, "Surge in Diseases of Animal Origin."

5. Rob Wallace, *Big Farms Make Big Flu: Dispatches on Influenza, Agribusiness, and the Nature of Science* (New York: Monthly Review Press, 2016).

6. Bill Gates, "Responding to Covid-19—a Once-in-a-Century Pandemic?," editorial, *New England Journal of Medicine* 382, no. 18 (April 2020): 1677–79.

7. Harvard School of Public Health, "Red Meat Consumption Linked to In-creased Risk of Total, Cardiovascular, and Cancer Mortality," news release, March 12, 2012, https://www.hsph.harvard.edu/news/press-releases/red-meat-consumption -linked-to-increased-risk-of-total-cardiovascular-and-cancer-mortality.

8. World Health Organization, "Stop Using Antibiotics in Healthy Animals to Prevent the Spread of Antibiotic Resistance," news release, November 7, 2017, https://www.who.int/news-room/detail/07-11-2017-stop-using-antibiotics-in -healthy-animals-to-prevent-the-spread-of-antibiotic-resistance.

9. World Health Organization, "Stop Using Antibiotics in Healthy Animals."

10. Henning Steinfeld et al., *Livestock's Long Shadow: Environmental Issues and Options* (Rome: Food and Agriculture Organization of the United Nations, 2006).

11. "Tackling the World's Most Urgent Problem: Meat," UN Environment Programme, September 26, 2018, https://web.archive.org/web/20220425033918 /https://www.unep.org/news-and-stories/story/tackling-worlds-most-urgent -problem-meat.

12. Sky Chadde, "Tracking Covid-19's Impact on Meatpacking Workers and Industry," Investigate Midwest, April 16, 2020, https://investigatemidwest.org /2020/04/16/tracking-covid-19s-impact-on-meatpacking-workers-and-industry.

13. Christina Cooke, "Injured and Invisible," Civil Eats, accessed May 16, 2023, https://civileats.com/injured-and-invisible.

14. "CAFOs and Environmental Justice: The Case of North Carolina," *Environmental Health Perspectives* 121, no. 6 (June 2013): 182–89.

15. Dan Cunningham, "Contract Broiler Production: Questions and Answers," The Poultry Site, April 30, 2004, https://www.thepoultrysite.com/articles/contract-broiler-production-questions-and-answers.

16. Christopher G. Davis et al., *U.S. Hog Production: Rising Output and Changing Trends in Productivity Growth* (Washington, DC: US Department of Agriculture, Economic Research Service, 2022), iv.

17. Ezra Klein, "Farmers and Animal Rights Activists Are Coming Together to Fight Big Factory Farms," *Vox*, July 8, 2020, https://www.vox.com/future-perfect/2020/7/8/21311327/farmers-factory-farms-cafos-animal-rights-booker-warren-khanna.

18. Klein, "Farmers and Animal Rights Activists."

19. This is a reference to Edward S. Herman and Noam Chomsky, *Manufacturing Consent: The Political Economy of the Mass Media* (New York: Pantheon, 1988).

20. Jacy Reese Anthis, "US Factory Farm Estimates," Sentience Institute, last modified April 11, 2019, https://www.sentienceinstitute.org/us-factory-farming-estimates. The Sentience Institute estimates that 99 percent of farmed animals in the United States live in factory farms. By species, it estimates that 70.4 percent of cows, 98.3 percent of pigs, 99.8 percent of turkeys, 98.2 percent of chickens raised for eggs, and over 99.9 percent of chickens raised for meat live in factory farms.

21. See Raj Patel and Jason W. Moore, *A History of the World in Seven Cheap Things: A Guide to Capitalism, Nature, and the Future of the Planet* (Berkeley: University of California Press, 2017).

22. "10 Things You Should Know About Industrial Farming," UN Environment Programme, July 20, 2020, https://www.unep.org/news-and-stories/story/10-things-you-should-know-about-industrial-farming.

23. "Unchecked Corporate Power and Exploitation: The Truth About Contract Growing," Food Integrity Campaign, December 14, 2021, https://foodwhistleblower.org/unchecked-corporate-power-and-exploitation-the-truth-about-contract-growing.

CHAPTER ONE: FROM CHICKENS TO HEMP AND DOG RESCUE

1. "Per Capita Consumption of Poultry and Livestock, 1965 to Forecast 2022, in Pounds," National Chicken Council, last modified December 2021, https://www.nationalchickencouncil.org/about-the-industry/statistics/per-capita-consumption-of-poultry-and-livestock-1965-to-estimated-2012-in-pounds.

2. Lisa Held, "Just a Few Companies Control the Meat Industry. Can a New Approach to Monopolies Level the Playing Field?," Civil Eats, July 14, 2021, https://civileats.com/2021/07/14/just-a-few-companies-control-the-meat-industry-can-a-new-approach-to-monopolies-level-the-playing-field.

3. Pew Environment Group, *Big Chicken: Pollution and Industrial Poultry Production in America* (Washington, DC: Pew Environment Group, 2011), 3–5.

4. Mike Callicrate, "Obama's Game of Chicken," No-Bull Food News, November 20, 2012, https://competitivemarkets.com/obamas-game-of-chicken.

5. "Feeding the World with America's Poultry Farmers," Tyson Foods, accessed April 11, 2023, https://www.tysonfoods.com/who-we-are/our-partners/farmers/contract-poultry-farming.

6. "Feeding the World," Tyson Foods.

7. Callicrate, "Obama's Game of Chicken."

8. Callicrate, "Obama's Game of Chicken."

9. White House, "Fact Sheet: The Biden-Harris Action Plan for a Fairer, More Competitive, and More Resilient Meat and Poultry Supply Chain," news release, January 3, 2022, https://www.whitehouse.gov/briefing-room/statements-releases/2022/01/03/fact-sheet-the-biden-harris-action-plan-for-a-fairer-more-competitive-and-more-resilient-meat-and-poultry-supply-chain.

10. White House, "Biden-Harris Action Plan."

11. Bruce Derksen, "Thinking of Starting a Poultry Business? Here's What You Need to Know," The Poultry Site, April 9, 2019, https://www.thepoultrysite.com/articles/thinking-of-starting-a-poultry-business-heres-what-you-need-to-know.

12. Pew Charitable Trusts, *The Business of Broilers* (Philadelphia: Pew Charitable Trusts, 2013), 26.

13. FarmEcon LLC, *Live Chicken Production Trends* (Washington, DC: National Chicken Council, 2022), 3.

14. Taylor Meek, "How Many Chickens Does Tyson Kill per Day?," Sentient Media, August 8, 2019, https://sentientmedia.org/tyson-foods.

15. "Texas Industrial Hemp Program," Texas Department of Agriculture, accessed March 23, 2020, https://www.texasagriculture.gov/regulatoryprograms/hemp.aspx.

16. "Laboratory Testing Guidelines U.S. Domestic Hemp Production Program," US Department of Agriculture, Agricultural Marketing Service, accessed May 1, 2022, https://www.ams.usda.gov/rules-regulations/hemp/information-laboratories/lab-testing-guidelines.

17. Cora Peterson et al., "Suicide Rates by Industry and Occupation—National Violent Death Reporting System, 32 States, 2016," *Morbidity and Mortality Weekly Report* 69, no. 3 (January 24, 2020): 57–62, https://www.cdc.gov/mmwr/volumes/69/wr/mm6903a1.htm.

CHAPTER TWO: FROM CHICKENS TO MUSHROOMS

1. Organization for Competitive Markets, "Packers and Stockyards Act Reform," 2022, https://competitivemarkets.com/gipsa.

2. James M. MacDonald, *Technology, Organization, and Financial Performance in U.S. Broiler Production* (Washington, DC: US Department of Agriculture, 2014), 15.

3. Farm System Reform Act of 2021, S. 2332, 117th Cong. (2021).

4. David Robinson Simon, *Meatonomics: How the Rigged Economics of Meat and Dairy Make You Consume Too Much—and How to Eat Better, Live Longer, and Spend Smarter* (San Francisco: Conari Press, 2013), xv.

5. "19th Amendment: Topics in Chronicling America," Library of Congress, https://guides.loc.gov/chronicling-america-19th-amendment.

6. Highland Economics, *Specialty Mushroom Production*, report for Transformation (Los Angeles, Mercy For Animals, 2023), 3, https://file-cdn.mercyforanimals.org/mercy4animals.wpengine.com/sites/450/2023/06/Final-Specialty-Mushroom-Crop-Analysis.pdf.

7. "Monopolies Are Giving Chicken Farmers a Raw Deal. We're Urging States to Act," op-ed, Civil Eats, May 2, 2022, https://civileats.com/2022/05/02 /op-ed-chicken-farmers-raw-deal-monopoly-consolidation-meat-industry-beef -pork-prices-inflation.

8. FarmEcon LLC, *Live Chicken Production*, report for National Chicken Council (Washington, DC: National Chicken Council, 2022), 7, table.

9. Manuel Bojorquez, "Inflation or 'Corporate Greed'? Meat Prices Increased by Double Digits During Pandemic," CBS News, March 9, 2022, https://www .cbsnews.com/news/meat-prices-pandemic-inflation-corporate-greed.

10. Tyson Foods, "Tyson Foods Reports First Quarter 2022 Results: Delivers Strong Operating Results Driven by Strong Consumer Demand," news release, February 7, 2022, https://www.tysonfoods.com/news/news-releases/2022/2/tyson -foods-reports-first-quarter-2022-results; *Investor's Business Daily* and James Detar, "Pilgrim's Pride Stock Sizzles as Profit Shoots 124% Higher," *Investors Business Daily*, April 18, 2022, https://www.inkl.com/news/stocks-to-watch-ahead-of -earnings-dow.

11. Chloe Sorvino, "Higher Chicken Prices Expected After $4.5 Billion Poul-try Merger Wins U.S. Approval," *Forbes*, August 5, 2022, https://www.forbes.com /sites/chloesorvino/2022/08/05/higher-chicken-prices-expected-after-45-billion -poultry-merger-wins-us-approval/?sh=37ad20bf67b9.

12. Sorvino, "Higher Chicken Prices Expected After $4.5 Billion Poultry Merger Wins U.S. Approval."

13. Alison Moodie, "Fowl Play: The Chicken Farmers Being Bullied by Big Poultry," *Guardian*, April 22, 2017, https://www.theguardian.com/sustainable -business/2017/apr/22/chicken-farmers-big-poultry-rules.

14. United States' Explanation of Consent Decree Procedures, America v. Cargill Meat Solutions Corp. et al. (2022).

15. Food Integrity Campaign, "U.S. Department of Justice Takes Landmark Action Against Poultry Companies for Deceptive Grower Payment Practices," news release, July 25, 2022, https://foodwhistleblower.org/press-release-u-s -department-of-justice-takes-landmark-action-against-poultry-companies-for -deceptive-grower-payment-practices.

16. Food Integrity Campaign, "U.S. Department of Justice Takes Landmark Action Against Poultry Companies for Deceptive Grower Payment Practices."

17. US Department of Justice, "Justice Department Files Lawsuit and Pro-posed Consent Decrees to End Long-Running Conspiracy to Suppress Worker Pay at Poultry Processing Plants and Address Deceptive Abuses Against Poultry Growers," news release, July 25, 2022, https://www.justice.gov/opa/pr/justice -department-files-lawsuit-and-proposed-consent-decrees-end-long-running -conspiracy.

CHAPTER THREE: FROM CHICKENS TO GREENHOUSES

1. Wilma V. Davis and Gary Lucier, *Vegetables and Pulses Outlook: November 2021* (Washington, DC: US Department of Agriculture, Economic Research Ser-vice, 2021), 12. Figures are averages of imports and exports from January through September, 2018–21.

2. Sarah Baskins, Jennifer Bond, and Travis Minor, *Unpacking the Growth in Per Capita Availability of Fresh Market Tomatoes* (Washington, DC: US Department of Agriculture, Economic Research Service, 2019), 1.

3. Highland Economics, *Indoor Tomato Production*, report for Transfarmation (Los Angeles: Mercy For Animals, 2023), 6–7, table 2, https://file-cdn.mercyfor animals.org/mercy4animals.wpengine.com/sites/450/2023/06/Final-Indoor -Tomato-Budget-Analysis.pdf.

4. Datassential, "Flavor of the Week: Microgreens Add a Healthy Touch," *Nation's Restaurant News*, January 27, 2020, https://www.nrn.com/consumer-trends /flavor-week-microgreens-add-healthy-touch.

5. Highland Economics, *Microgreen Production*, report for Transfarmation (Los Angeles: Mercy For Animals, 2023), 6, https://file-cdn.mercyforanimals.org/mercy 4animals.wpengine.com/sites/450/2023/06/Final-Microgreen-Production.pdf.

6. Highland Economics, *Indoor Cucumber Production*, report for Transfarmation (Los Angeles: Mercy For Animals, 2023), 8, https://file-cdn.mercyforanimals.org /mercy4animals.wpengine.com/sites/450/2023/06/Final-Indoor-Cucumber -Budget.pdf.

7. Highland Economics, *Indoor Strawberry Production*, report for Transfarma- tion (Los Angeles: Mercy For Animals, 2023), 7, https://file-cdn.mercyforanimals .org/mercy4animals.wpengine.com/sites/450/2023/06/Final-Indoor-Strawberry -Production.pdf.

8. Highland Economics, *Indoor Tomato Production*, 7.

9. This analysis does not yet take into account the cost of conversion and the corresponding debt-service coverage ratio analysis that is included in the other crop analyses. It is still expected to be the most profitable of the crops.

10. Highland Economics, *Specialty Mushroom Production*, report for Transfarm- ation (Los Angeles, Mercy For Animals, 2023), 3, https://file-cdn.mercyforanimals .org/mercy4animals.wpengine.com/sites/450/2023/06/Final-Specialty-Mushroom -Crop-Analysis.pdf.

11. Donald D. Stull, "Tobacco Barns and Chicken Houses: Agricultural Trans- formation in Western Kentucky," *Human Organization* 59, no. 2 (Summer 2000): 151–61.

12. Katie Algeo, review of *When Tobacco Was King: Families, Farm Labor, and Federal Policy in the Piedmont*, by Evan P. Bennett, *AAG Review of Books* 5, no. 4 (October 2017): 268–70.

13. Nathan Bomey, "Thousands of Farmers Stopped Growing Tobacco After Deregulation Payouts," *USA Today*, September 2, 2015, https://www.usatoday.com /story/money/2015/09/02/thousands-farmers-stopped-growing-tobacco-after -deregulation-payouts/32115163.

14. Bomey, "Thousands of Farmers Stopped Growing Tobacco After Deregu- lation Payouts."

15. "What Does the End of the Tobacco Buyout Mean?," Farm Progress, No- vember 27, 2013, https://www.farmprogress.com/tobacco/what-does-end-tobacco -buyout-mean.

16. Bomey, "Thousands of Farmers Stopped Growing Tobacco After Deregu- lation Payouts."

17. David Robinson Simon, *Meatonomics: How the Rigged Economics of Meat and Dairy Make You Consume Too Much—and How to Eat Better, Live Longer, and Spend Smarter* (San Francisco: Conari Press, 2013), xx.

18. H. Charles J. Godfray et al., "Meat Consumption, Health, and the Environment," *Science* 361, no. 6399 (July 2018): eaam5324.

19. James McWilliams, "Why Our Food Choices Are Determined by Price—and Not Ethics or Morals," *Pacific Standard*, August 30, 2016, https://psmag.com/news/why-our-food-choices-are-determined-by-price-and-not-ethics-or-morals.

20. France Caillavet, Adélaide Fadhuile, and Véronique Nichéle, "Could a Tax on Animal-Based Foods Improve Diet Sustainability?," *Academic Insights for the Thinking World* (Oxford University Press blog), April 10, 2016, https://blog.oup.com/2016/04/tax-animal-based-foods-diet.

21. Eliza Barclay, "Americans Should Eat Less Meat, but They're Eating More and More," *Vox*, last modified October 1, 2016, https://www.vox.com/2016/8/18/12248226/eat-less-meat-campaign-fail.

22. Barclay, "Americans Should Eat Less Meat."

23. Parija Kavilanz, "U.S. Places $40 Million Chicken Order," CNN Money, August 16, 2011, https://money.cnn.com/2011/08/16/news/economy/chicken_prices/index.htm.

24. US Department of Agriculture, Farm Service Agency, "USDA Issuing Approximately $270 Million in Pandemic Assistance to Poultry, Livestock Contract Producers," news release, November 18, 2021, https://www.fsa.usda.gov/news-room/news-releases/2021/usda-issuing-approximately-270-million-in-pandemic-assistance-to-poultry-livestock-contract-producers.

25. Jared Hayes, "USDA Livestock Subsidies Near $50 Billion, EWG Analysis Finds," Environmental Working Group, February 28, 2022, https://www.ewg.org/news-insights/news/2022/02/usda-livestock-subsidies-near-50-billion-ewg-analysis-finds.

26. Simon, *Meatonomics*, 248.

27. Paula Boles, grant application, July 2022.

CHAPTER FOUR: THE LAST PIGS

1. Hannah Ritchie, "How Much of the World's Land Would We Need in Order to Feed the Global Population with the Average Diet of a Given Country?," Our World in Data, October 3, 2017, https://ourworldindata.org/agricultural-land-by-global-diets.

2. Ritchie, "How Much of the World's Land Would We Need in Order to Feed the Global Population with the Average Diet of a Given Country?"

3. Carly Cassella, "US Soil Could Be Eroding Up to 1,000 Times Faster Than It Should," *Science Alert*, December 13, 2022, https://www.sciencealert.com/%E2%80%8B%E2%80%8Bus-soil-could-be-eroding-up-to-1000-times-faster-than-it-should.

4. "Food and Agriculture Data," FAOSTAT, 2020, https://docs.google.com/spreadsheets/d/1ufCLYkj2D1Z-52euGg0HcDzSBrrdWV7EfGIJV9HfRJY.

5. Ritchie, "How Much of the World's Land Would We Need in Order to Feed the Global Population with the Average Diet of a Given Country?"

6. Food & Water Watch, *Factory Farm Nation: 2020 Edition* (Washington, DC: Food & Water Watch, 2020), 2.

7. "Iowa Pork Facts," Iowa Pork Producers Association, accessed May 3, 2023, https://www.iowapork.org/news-from-the-iowa-pork-producers-association/iowa -pork-facts.

8. Sierra Club, Iowa Chapter, *Iowa's Nutrient Problem—Iowa Is the Major Contributor to the Dead Zone in the Gulf of Mexico* (Des Moines: Sierra Club, n.d.), 7.

9. Sierra Club, *Iowa's Nutrient Problem*, 1.

10. Sierra Club, *Iowa's Nutrient Problem*, 1.

11. Christopher Ingraham, "Americans Say There's Not Much Appeal to Big-City Living. Why Do So Many of Us Live There?," *Washington Post*, December 18, 2018, https://www.washingtonpost.com/business/2018/12/18/americans -say-theres-not-much-appeal-big-city-living-why-do-so-many-us-live-there.

12. "Something Special Is Happening in Rural America," *New York Times*, September 17, 2019, https://www.nytimes.com/2019/09/17/opinion/rural -america.html.

13. North Carolina in the Global Economy, "Hog Farming: Establishments, Workers & Wages," https://ncglobaleconomy.com/hog/overview.shtml, accessed February 8, 2024.

CHAPTER FIVE: THE YEAR OF HENRIETTA THE HEN

1. Name changed to protect their identity.

2. Memorandum from the majority staff of the Select Subcommittee on the Coronavirus, House of Representatives, Congress of the United States, to the members of the subcommittee (October 7, 2021) (on file with the US House of Representatives Committee Repository).

3. Centers for Disease Control and Prevention (CDC), "Questions and Answers," last reviewed February 16, 2023, https://www.cdc.gov/campylobacter/faq.html.

4. World Health Organization, "Campylobacter," May 1, 2020, https://www .who.int/news-room/fact-sheets/detail/campylobacter.

5. European Food Safety Authority, "Campylobacter," accessed August 13, 2020, https://www.efsa.europa.eu/en/topics/topic/campylobacter.

6. European Food Safety Authority, "Campylobacter."

7. CDC, "Questions and Answers."

8. CDC, "Questions and Answers."

9. Centers for Disease Control and Prevention, "Antibiotic Resistance," last reviewed June 27, 2022, https://www.cdc.gov/campylobacter/campy-antibiotic -resistance.html.

10. CDC, "Questions and Answers."

11. CDC, "Questions and Answers."

CHAPTER SIX: FELIX THE PIG

1. Hrisanthi Kroi, "Florence Rainfall Totals for North Carolina: 8 Trillion Gallons," *Fayetteville Observer*, September 20, 2018, https://www.fayobserver.com /story/special/special-sections/2018/09/20/florence-rainfall-totals-for-north -carolina-8-trillion-gallons/10249499007.

2. Stacy R. Stewart and Robbie Berg, *National Hurricane Center Tropical Cyclone Report: Hurricane Florence* (Miami: National Hurricane Center, 2019), 9.

3. Stewart and Berg, *National Hurricane Center Tropical Cyclone Report*, 12.

4. Charles Bethea, "Could Smithfield Foods Have Prevented the 'Rivers of Hog Waste' in North Carolina After Florence?," *New Yorker*, September 30, 2018, https://www.newyorker.com/news/news-desk/could-smithfield-foods-have-prevented-the-rivers-of-hog-waste-in-north-carolina-after-florence.

5. Kendra Pierre-Louis, "Lagoons of Pig Waste Are Overflowing After Florence. Yes, That's as Nasty as It Sounds," *New York Times*, September 19, 2018, https://www.nytimes.com/2018/09/19/climate/florence-hog-farms.html.

6. "Hurricane Florence: Carolina Pig Waste Lagoons Overflow," BBC.com, September 19, 2018, https://www.bbc.com/news/world-us-canada-45578485.

7. Michael Graff, "Millions of Dead Chickens and Pigs Found in Hurricane Floods," *Guardian*, September 21, 2018, https://www.theguardian.com/environment/2018/sep/21/hurricane-florence-flooding-north-carolina.

8. Humane Society of the United States, "Pigs," accessed October 15, 2022, https://www.humanesociety.org/animals/pigs.

9. Mercy For Animals, "Animals Under Attack," accessed October 15, 2022, https://animalsunderattack.com/?_ga=2.82765270.198010753.1665856060 -1066860770.1625158130.

10. Humane Society of the United States, *State Farm Animal Protection Laws* (Washington, DC: Humane Society of the United States, n.d.), 1, https://www .humanesociety.org/sites/default/files/docs/HSUS_state-farm-animal-protection -laws.pdf.

11. "The Supreme Court Upholds California's Prop 12 Declaring It Serves 'Moral Interests,'" media release, Brooks McCormick Jr. Animal Law & Policy Program, Harvard Law School, May 11, 2023, https://animal.law.harvard.edu /news-article/prop12-serves-moral-interests.

12. US Courts, "About the Supreme Court," accessed October 15, 2022, https://www.uscourts.gov/about-federal-courts/educational-resources/about -educational-outreach/activity-resources/about.

13. Oral Argument, National Pork Producers Council & American Farm Bureau Federation v. Ross, et al., No. 21-468 (US, argued October 11, 2022).

14. Socially Responsible Agriculture Project, "Socially Responsible Agriculture Project Submits Amicus Brief to U.S. Supreme Court Supporting California's Prop 12," news release, August 24, 2022, https://www.globenewswire.com/news -release/2022/08/24/2504124/0/en/Socially-Responsible-Agriculture-Project -Submits-Amicus-Brief-to-U-S-Supreme-Court-Supporting-California-s-Prop -12.html.

15. Brief of Agricultural and Resource Economics Professors as Amici Curiae in Support of Neither Party, National Pork Producers Council & American Farm Bureau Federation v. Ross, et al. (US, filed June 17, 2022).

16. Holly Cook and Lee Shulz, *The United States Pork Industry 2021: Current Structure and Economic Importance* (Washington, DC: National Pork Producers Council, 2022), 2.

17. Graff, "Millions of Dead Chickens and Pigs Found in Hurricane Floods"; "Hurricane Florence," BBC.com.

18. Zoë Schlanger, "What Will Happen When Hurricane Florence Hits North Carolina's Massive Pig Manure Lagoons?," *Quartz*, September 11, 2018, https://qz.com/1386629/hurricane-florence-threatens-north-carolinas-pig -manure-lagoons.

19. "Nesting During Pregnancy," American Pregnancy Association, accessed November 3, 2023, https://americanpregnancy.org/healthy-pregnancy/pregnancy -health-wellness/nesting-during-pregnancy; Jinhyeon Yun and Anna Valros, "Benefits of Prepartum Nest-Building Behaviour on Parturition and Lactation in Sows—a Review," *Asian-Australasian Journal of Animal Sciences* 28, no. 11 (November 2015): 1519–24.

20. Yun and Valros, "Benefits of Prepartum Nest-Building Behaviour on Parturition and Lactation in Sows."

21. Per Jensen, "Observations on the Maternal Behaviour of Free-Ranging Domestic Pigs," *Applied Animal Behaviour Science* 16, no. 2 (September 1986): 131–42.

22. "Farmed Animals: Welfare Issues for Pigs," Compassion in World Farming, accessed October 15, 2022, https://www.ciwf.com/farmed-animals/pigs /welfare-issues.

23. G. B. Meese and R. Ewbank, "The Establishment and Nature of the Dominance Hierarchy in the Domesticated Pig," *Animal Behaviour* 21, no. 2 (May 1973): 326–34.

24. Alex Stolba and David Granger Marcus Wood-Gush, "The Behaviour of Pigs in a Semi-Natural Environment," *Animal Production* 48, no. 2 (April 1989): 419–25.

25. Carly I. O'Malley et al., "Animal Personality in the Management and Welfare of Pigs," *Applied Animal Behaviour Science* 218 (September 2019): 104821.

26. National Pork Producers Council et al. v. Ross, Secretary of the California Department of Food and Agriculture et al., No. 21–468, slip op. (Sup. Ct. May 11, 2023).

27. Lewis Bollard, "A Big Supreme Court Win for Farm Animals," *Open Philanthropy Farm Animal Welfare Newsletter*, May 12, 2023, https://farmanimal welfare.substack.com/p/a-big-supreme-court-win-for-farm.

28. Bollard, "A Big Supreme Court Win for Farm Animals."

29. National Pork Producers Council et al. v. Ross, Secretary of the California Department of Food and Agriculture et al., 598 US 356, 393–94 (2023). "California's interest in eliminating allegedly inhumane products from its markets cannot be weighed on a scale opposite dollars and cents—at least not without second-guessing the moral judgments of California voters or making the kind of policy decisions reserved for politicians." (Justice Barrett, concurring in part).

CHAPTER SEVEN: NORMA THE COW

1. Sue Donaldson and Will Kymlicka, "Farmed Animal Sanctuaries: The Heart of the Movement? A Socio-political Perspective," *Politics and Animals* 1, no. 1 (October 2015): 50–74.

2. RealAgriculture News Team, "U.S. Dairy Subsidies Equal 73 Percent of Producer Returns, Says New Report," RealAgriculture, February 9, 2018, https:// www.realagriculture.com/2018/02/u-s-dairy-subsidies-equal-73-percent-of -producer-returns-says-new-report.

3. Victoria Petersen, "Have We Reached Peak Plant Milk? Not Even Close," *New York Times*, February 28, 2022, https://www.nytimes.com/2022/02/28/dining /plant-based-milk.html.

4. Kate Barcellos, "Vermont Expands Farm Grant Eligibility," *Rutland Herald*, June 27, 2019, https://www.rutlandherald.com/news/vermont-expands-farm-grant -eligibility/article_b64387df-734c-5bf0-9a32-a20338f687fb.html.

5. Corinne Gretler, "Danone Reports Weakest Profitability in Six Years amid Inflation," *Bloomberg*, February 23, 2022, https://www.bloomberg.com/news /articles/2022-02-23/danone-reports-weakest-profitability-in-six-years-amid -inflation.

6. Jessica DiNapoli, "Ben & Jerry's Says Unilever Froze Directors' Salaries," Reuters, August 3, 2022, https://www.reuters.com/business/retail-consumer/ben -jerrys-says-unilever-froze-directors-salaries-2022–08–03; Zippia, "Ben & Jerry's Careers," accessed October 14, 2022, https://www.zippia.com/ben-jerry-s-careers -16592/revenue.

7. Jack Kelly, "'The Happiness and Joy Has Been Sucked Out of Me': Wisconsin Dairy Farmers Face Mental Health Crisis," *Daily Yonder*, January 28, 2021, https://dailyyonder.com/the-happiness-and-joy-has-been-sucked-out-of-me -wisconsin-dairy-farmers-face-mental-health-crisis/2021/01/28.

8. Rosalie Eisenreich and Carolyn Pollari, *Addressing Higher Risk of Suicide Among Farmers in Rural America* (Kansas City, MO: National Rural Health Association, n.d.), 1, accessed October 30, 2023.

9. Kimberly Amadeo, "How Farm Subsidies Affect the U.S. Economy," The Balance, last modified April 18, 2022, https://www.thebalancemoney.com/farm -subsidies-4173885.

10. US Department of Agriculture, Animal and Plant Health Inspection Service, Veterinary Services, *Dairy Cattle Management Practices in the United States, 2014* (Washington, DC: USDA, APHIS, VS, 2014), ix.

11. Agnes van den Pol-van Dasselaar, Deirdre Hennessy, and Johannes Isselstein, "Grazing of Dairy Cows in Europe—an In-Depth Analysis Based on the Perception of Grassland Experts," *Sustainability* 12, no. 3 (2020): 1098; Andrew Crump et al., "Optimism and Pasture Access in Dairy Cows," *Scientific Reports* 11 (March 2021): 4882.

12. European Food Safety Authority, "Scientific Opinion on Welfare of Dairy Cows in Relation to Behaviour, Fear, and Pain Based on a Risk Assessment with Special Reference to the Impact of Housing, Feeding, Management and Genetic Selection," *EFSA Journal* (July 2009): 1–75.

13. Annabelle Beaver, Daniel M. Weary, and Marina A. G. von Keyserlingk, "The Welfare of Dairy Cattle Housed in Tie Stalls Compared to Less-Restrictive Housing Types: A Systematic Review," *Journal of Dairy Science* 104, no. 9 (September 2021): 9383–417; USDA, *Dairy Cattle Management Practices in the United States*.

14. Global Animal Partnership, *5-Step® Animal Welfare Pilot Standards for Dairy Cattle v1.0* (Austin, TX: Global Animal Partnership, 2021), 60.

15. Andreas W. Oehm et al., "Factors Associated with Lameness in Tie Stall Housed Dairy Cows in South Germany," *Frontiers in Veterinary Science* 7 (December 2020): 601640.

16. Name changed to protect their identity.

17. Cheryl, "Fair Week," *VINE Sanctuary News* (blog), July 27, 2015, https://blog.bravebirds.org/archives/2784.

18. Cathleen C. Williams, "Mastitis in Dairy Cattle," *Louisiana Agriculture* (Winter 2009): 21.

19. US Department of Agriculture, Animal and Plant Health Inspection Service, Veterinary Services, *Milk Quality, Milking Procedures, and Mastitis on U.S. Dairies, 2014* (Washington, DC: USDA, APHIS, VS, 2014), ii.

20. Maria Puerto-Parada et al., "Survival and Prognostic Indicators in Downer Dairy Cows Presented to a Referring Hospital: A Retrospective Study (1318 Cases)," *Journal of Veterinary Internal Medicine* 35, no. 5 (September–October 2021): 2534–43.

21. Emmanouil Kalaitzakis et al., "Clinicopathological Evaluation of Downer Dairy Cows with Fatty Liver," *Canadian Veterinary Journal* 51, no. 6 (June 2010): 615–22.

CHAPTER EIGHT: EASTERN NORTH CAROLINA COMMUNITIES OF COLOR

1. Jennifer Shike, "America's Top 20 Pig Counties," *Farm Journal's Pork*, July 23, 2019, https://www.porkbusiness.com/news/hog-production/americas-top -20-pig-counties.

2. Corban Addison, *Wastelands: The True Story of Farm Country on Trial* (New York: Penguin Random House, 2022), 40–50.

3. Addison, *Wastelands*, 40-50.

4. "The 1996 Pulitzer Prize Winner in Public Service," Pulitzer Prizes, accessed May 22, 2023, https://www.pulitzer.org/winners/news-observer-raleigh-nc.

5. Steve Wing, Dana Cole, and Gary Grant, "Environmental Injustice in North Carolina's Hog Industry," *Environmental Health Perspectives* 108, no. 3 (March 2000): 225–31.

6. Betsy Freese, "Meet the Man Who Built the Modern Pig Business," *Successful Farming*, February 25, 2019, https://www.agriculture.com/livestock/pork -powerhouses/meet-the-man-who-built-the-modern-pig-business.

7. Jennifer Wang, "This Little-Known Woman Billionaire Built a Fortune Powering Fintech Firms like SoFi and Webull," *Forbes*, October 25, 2021, https://www.forbes.com/sites/jenniferwang/2020/04/16/the-chinese-billionaire-whose -company-owns-troubled-pork-processor-smithfield-foods.

8. I. G. Krapac et al., "Impacts of Swine Manure Pits on Groundwater Quality," *Environmental Pollution* 120, no. 2 (2002): 475–92.

9. Environmental Working Group, "Study: Fecal Bacteria from N.C. Hog Farms Infects Nearby Homes," news release, May 11, 2017, https://www.ewg.org /news-insights/news-release/2017/05/study-fecal-bacteria-nc-hog-farms-infects -nearby-homes.

10. Addison, *Wastelands*, 40–50.

11. Geneviève Brisson et al., *Hog Farms and Their Impact on the Quality of Life of Rural Populations: A Systematic Review of the Literature* (Vancouver: National Collaborating Centre for Environmental Health, May 2009), https://ncceh.ca /resources/evidence-reviews/hog-farms-and-their-impact-quality-life-people -living-rural-areas.

12. Steve Wing et al., "Air Pollution and Odor in Communities near Industrial Swine Operations," *Environmental Health Perspectives* 116, no. 10 (October 2008): 1362–68.

13. Julia Kravchenko et al., "Mortality and Health Outcomes in North Carolina Communities Located in Close Proximity to Hog Concentrated Animal Feeding Operations," *North Carolina Medical Journal* 79, no. 5 (September 2018): 278–88.

14. *The Smell of Money*, directed by Shawn Bannon, written by Jamie Berger, 2022, 23:00, https://www.imdb.com/title/tt18567908.

15. "A Rare Look Inside a Rendering Plant; Shocking First Hand Account," Poisoned Pets, accessed May 22, 2023, https://www.poisonedpets.com/a-rare-look-inside-a-rendering-plant.

16. *The Smell of Money*, 45:00.

17. Addison, *Wastelands*, 9–19.

18. Addison, *Wastelands*, 77–85.

19. Addison, *Wastelands*, 157–67.

20. Jamie Berger, "How Black North Carolinians Pay the Price for the World's Cheap Bacon," *Vox*, April 1, 2022, https://www.vox.com/future-perfect/23003487/north-carolina-hog-pork-bacon-farms-environmental-racism-black-residents-pollution-meat-industry; Addison, *Wastelands*, 333–42; Travis Fain, "Jury Awards $473.5 Million to Neighbors Who Sued Smithfield over Hog Waste," WRAL News, August 2, 2018, https://www.wral.com/third-hog-trial-to-jury-plaintiffs-ask-for-millions/17743873.

21. *The Smell of Money*, 1:12.

22. *The Smell of Money*, 1:13.

CHAPTER NINE: IMMIGRANTS

1. Stephen Groves and Sophia Tareen, "U.S. Meatpacking Industry Relies on Immigrant Workers. But a Labor Shortage Looms," *Los Angeles Times*, May 26, 2020, https://www.latimes.com/food/story/2020–05–26/meatpacking-industry-immigrant-undocumented-workers.

2. Delcianna J. Winders and Elan Abrell, "Slaughterhouse Workers, Animals, and the Environment," *Health and Human Rights Journal* 23, no. 2 (December 2021): 21–33.

3. William G. Whittaker, opening summary, *Labor Practices in the Meat Packing and Poultry Processing Industry: An Overview*, CRS report for the US Congress (Washington, DC: Congressional Research Service, Library of Congress, July 20, 2005–October 27, 2006), https://www.everycrsreport.com/reports/RL33002.html.

4. Groves and Tareen, "U.S. Meatpacking Industry Relies on Immigrant Workers"; Angela Stuesse, "The Poultry Industry Recruited Them. Now ICE Raids Are Devastating Their Communities," *Washington Post*, August 9, 2019, https://www.washingtonpost.com/outlook/2019/08/09/poultry-industry-recruited-them-now-ice-raids-are-devastating-their-communities.

5. Stuesse, "Poultry Industry Recruited Them."

6. Angela Stuesse and Laura E. Helton, "Low-Wage Legacies, Race, and the Golden Chicken in Mississippi: Where Contemporary Immigration Meets African American Labor History," *Southern Spaces*, December 31, 2013, https://

southernspaces.org/2013/low-wage-legacies-race-and-golden-chicken-mississippi
-where-contemporary-immigration-meets-african-american-labor-history.

7. Stuesse, "The Poultry Industry Recruited Them."

8. Stuesse, "The Poultry Industry Recruited Them."

9. Stuesse, "The Poultry Industry Recruited Them."

10. Stuesse, "The Poultry Industry Recruited Them."

11. "Slaughterhouse Labor," *Food & Power*, accessed August 24, 2023, https://
www.foodandpower.net/slaughterhouse-labor.

12. Stuesse, "The Poultry Industry Recruited Them."

13. Whittaker, opening summary, *Labor Practices in the Meat Packing and Poultry Processing Industry*.

14. Daniel Calamuci, "Return to the Jungle: The Rise and Fall of Meatpacking Work," *New Labor Forum* 17, no. 1 (Spring 2008): 66–77.

15. Calamuci, "Return to the Jungle."

16. Claire Kelloway, "Meatpacking More Dangerous Today Than a Generation Ago, Amplifying COVID-19 Crisis," *Food & Power*, May 7, 2020, https://www
.foodandpower.net/latest/2020/05/07/meatpacking-more-dangerous-today-than
-a-generation-ago-amplifying-covid-19-crisis.

17. US Bureau of Labor Statistics, "Occupational Employment and Wages, May 2022," last modified April 25, 2023, https://www.bls.gov/oes/current/oes 510000.htm.

18. Kelloway, "Meat Packing More Dangerous Today."

19. Hannah Ritchie, "Half of the World's Habitable Land Is Used for Agriculture," Our World in Data, November 11, 2019, https://ourworldindata.org/global
-land-for-agriculture.

20. "Denison High School," *U.S. News & World Report*, accessed April 1, 2023, https://www.usnews.com/education/best-high-schools/iowa/districts/denison
-community-school-district/denison-high-school-7589.

21. Trip Gabriel, "A Timeline of Steve King's Racist Remarks and Divisive Actions," *New York Times*, January 15, 2019, https://www.nytimes.com/2019/01/15
/us/politics/steve-king-offensive-quotes.html.

22. "Quick Facts," table on Denison City, Iowa, US Census Bureau, July 1, 2022, https://www.census.gov/quickfacts/fact/table/denisoncityiowa/PST045221.

23. Name changed to protect their identity.

24. Jasper Gilardi, "Ally or Exploiter? The Smuggler-Migrant Relationship Is a Complex One," Migration Policy Institute, February 5, 2020, https://www
.migrationpolicy.org/article/ally-or-exploiter-smuggler-migrant-relationship
-complex-one.

25. Name changed to protect their identity.

26. US Department of Labor, "More Than 100 Children Illegally Employed in Hazardous Jobs, Federal Investigation Finds; Food Sanitation Contractor Pays $1.5M in Penalties," news release, February 17, 2023, https://www.dol.gov
/newsroom/releases/whd/whd20230217-1.

27. "What Is Moral Injury," Syracuse University, Moral Injury Project, https://
moralinjuryproject.syr.edu/about-moral-injury.

28. Shawn Fremstad, Hye Jin Rho, and Hayley Brown, "Meatpacking Workers Are a Diverse Group Who Need Better Protections," Center for Economic and

Policy Research, April 29, 2020, https://cepr.net/meatpacking-workers-are-a
-diverse-group-who-need-better-protections; Centers for Disease Control and
Prevention (CDC), "Update: COVID-19 Among Workers in Meat and Poultry
Processing Facilities—United States, April–May 2020," *Morbidity and Mortality
Weekly Report* 69, no. 27 (July 2020): 887–92.

29. Trevor Bach, "Critics Slam Trump's Executive Order Requiring Meat
Plants to Stay Open," *U.S. News & World Report*, April 30, 2020, https://www
.usnews.com/news/national-news/articles/2020–04–30/labor-advocates-slam
-trumps-executive-order-requiring-meat-plants-to-stay-open.

30. Danielle Nichole Smith, "Smithfield Says Trump Order Should Sink Plant
Safety Suit," *Law360*, April 29, 2020, https://www.law360.com/benefits/articles
/1268795.

31. Mike LaSusa, "Smithfield Nixes Meat Plant Workers' Suit Over Virus
Safety," *Law360*, May 5, 2020, https://www.law360.com/cases/5ea1d06639d5a
402df6db1ee.

32. Dan Charles, "How One City Mayor Forced a Pork Giant to Close Its
Virus-Stricken Plant," National Public Radio, WBEZ Chicago, April 14, 2020,
https://www.npr.org/2020/04/14/834470141/how-one-city-mayor-forced-a-pork
-giant-to-close-its-virus-stricken-plant.

33. Albert Samaha and Katie J. M. Baker, "Smithfield Foods Is Blaming 'Living Circumstances in Certain Cultures' for One of America's Largest COVID-19
Clusters," *BuzzFeed News*, April 20, 2020, https://www.buzzfeednews.com/article
/albertsamaha/smithfield-foods-coronavirus-outbreak.

34. Taylor Telford and Kimberly Kindy, "As They Rushed to Maintain U.S.
Meat Supply, Big Processors Saw Plants Become Covid-19 Hot Spots, Worker
Illnesses Spike," *Washington Post*, April 25, 2020, https://www.washingtonpost.com
/business/2020/04/25/meat-workers-safety-jbs-smithfield-tyson.

35. Mayo Clinic, "Fibromyalgia," October 26, 2021, https://www.mayoclinic
.org/diseases-conditions/fibromyalgia/symptoms-causes/syc-20354780.

36. Lauren Kaori Gurley, "Women in Meatpacking Say #MeToo," *In These
Times*, October 10, 2019, https://inthesetimes.com/features/women_meatpacking
_industry_workplace_sexual_harassment_investigation.html.

37. Gurley, "Women in Meatpacking Say #MeToo."

CHAPTER TEN: REFUGEES

1. Emily Giambalvo, "Refugees, Immigrants Helped a Georgia High School
Build a Diverse Cross Country Dynasty," ESPN, May 19, 2017, https://www.espn
.com/endurance/story/_/id/19389944/refugees-immigrants-help-georgia-high
-school-build-diverse-cross-country-dynasty.

2. Joseph Chamie, "American Migration: 1776 to 2006," *Globalist*, November
29, 2006, https://www.theglobalist.com/american-migration-1776-to-2006.

3. Angela Stuesse and Nathan T. Dollar, "Who Are America's Meat and Poultry Workers?," *Working Economics* (blog), Economic Policy Institute, September
24, 2020, https://www.epi.org/blog/meat-and-poultry-worker-demographics.

4. Oxfam America, "Vulnerable Populations," in *Lives on the Line*, accessed
June 4, 2023, https://www.oxfamamerica.org/livesontheline.

5. Oxfam America, "Vulnerable Populations."

6. "WATT PoultryUSA 2021 Top Broiler Company Profiles," WATT Poultry USA, accessed March 17, 2023, https://www.wattpoultryusa-digital.com/wattpoultry usa/march_2021/MobilePagedArticle.action?articleId=1668376#articleId1668376.

7. "WATT PoultryUSA 2021 Top Broiler Company Profiles."

8. N.C. GEN. STAT. § 160D-903 (2020).

9. Gavin Off, Adam Wagner, and Ames Alexander, "Poultry Farming Has Taken Flight in NC. But at What Cost?," *Charlotte Observer*, November 30, 2022, last modified May 17, 2023, https://www.newsobserver.com/news/state/north -carolina/article267887592.html#storylink=cpy.

10. US Department of Agriculture, National Agricultural Statistics Service, *Poultry—Production and Value 2021 Summary* (Washington, DC: USDA, NASS, 2022), 7.

11. Sanderson Farms, "Sanderson Farms Opens New Facility in St. Pauls, N.C.," news release, January 11, 2017, https://sandersonfarms.com/press-releases /sanderson-farms-opens-new-facility-in-st-pauls-n-c; David Bracken, "Mountaire Farms to Take Over Siler City Poultry Plant," *News & Observer*, last modified May 20, 2016, https://www.newsobserver.com/news/business/article75807177.html.

12. Center for New North Carolinians, "Hmong Students and UNCG," UNC Greensboro, April 4, 2019, https://cnnc.uncg.edu/hmong-students-and-uncg.

13. Hmong American Center, "Hmong History," accessed March 17, 2023, https://www.hmongamericancenter.org/hmong-history.

14. Hmong American Center, "Hmong History."

15. Stanford Medicine, Ethnogeriatrics, "History," accessed May 17, 2023, https://geriatrics.stanford.edu/ethnomed/hmong/introduction/history.html.

CONCLUSION: HARVESTING CHANGE

1. Ryan Rudich, "North Carolina Adds New Protections for CAFOs Against Nuisance Lawsuits," *Environmental Law Next* (blog), June 1, 2017, https://www .environmentallawnext.com/2017/06/north-carolina-adds-new-protections -cafos-nuisance-lawsuits.

2. Andrea Shalal, "Meat Packers' Profit Margins Jumped 300% During Pandemic—White House Economics Team," Reuters, December 10, 2021, https:// www.reuters.com/business/meat-packers-profit-margins-jumped-300-during -pandemic-white-house-economics-2021-12-10.

3. "WATT Poultry Top Companies: Special Report," *Egg Industry* 128, no. 1 (January 2023): 3–31.

4. Lewis Bollard, "Big Wins for Farm Animals This Decade," Open Philanthropy, December 22, 2022, https://www.openphilanthropy.org/research/big -wins-for-farm-animals-this-decade.

5. Vincenzina Caputo, Jayson Lusk, Glynn Tonsor, and Aaron Staples, *The Transition to Cage-Free Eggs* (Lansing: Michigan State University, 2023), ii, https:// static1.squarespace.com/static/502c267524aca01df475f9ec/t/63f62ad67b3be60f 1d3c1fc3/1677077208857/Challenges+Associated+with+the+Transition+to+Cage +Free+Eggs+Study+Feb+2023.pdf.

6. Danielle J. Ufer, *State Policies for Farm Animal Welfare in Production Practices of U.S. Livestock and Poultry Industries: An Overview* (Washington, DC: US Department of Agriculture, Economic Research Service, 2022), 1.

7. Reuters, "US Court Blocks Trump-Era Hog Slaughter Line Speed Rule; Union Cheers," March 31, 2021, https://www.voanews.com/a/usa_us-court-blocks -trump-era-hog-slaughter-line-speed-rule-union-cheers/6204016.html.

8. Tom Polansek, "U.S. to Allow Pork Plants to Operate Faster in Trial Program," Reuters, November 10, 2021, https://www.reuters.com/world/us/us-allow -pork-plants-operate-faster-trial-program-2021-11-10.

9. Ryan McCarthy, "USDA Allows Faster Line Speeds at Two More Pork Plants," *Meat + Poultry*, August 24, 2022, https://www.meatpoultry.com/articles /27122-usda-allows-faster-line-speeds-at-two-more-pork-plants.

10. "Modernization of Swine Slaughter Inspection," US Department of Agriculture, Food Safety and Inspection Service, https://www.fsis.usda.gov/inspection /inspection-programs/inspection-meat-products/modernization-swine-slaughter -inspection; US Department of Agriculture, Food Safety and Inspection Service, "Constituent Update," news release, March 3, 2023, https://www.fsis.usda.gov /news-events/news-press-releases/constituent-update-march-3-2023.

11. "Modernization of Poultry Slaughter Inspection," US Department of Agriculture, Food Safety and Inspection Service, accessed May 23, 2023, https://www .fsis.usda.gov/inspection/inspection-programs/inspection-poultry-products /modernization-poultry-slaughter.

12. US Department of Agriculture, Food Safety and Inspection Service, *Poultry Postmortem Inspection* (Washington, DC: USDA, FSIS, 2019), 8–19.

13. Andrew Wasley and Natalie Jones, "Chickens Freezing to Death and Boiled Alive: Failings in US Slaughterhouses Exposed," *Guardian*, December 17, 2018, https://www.theguardian.com/environment/2018/dec/17/chickens-freezing -to-death-and-boiled-alive-failings-in-us-slaughterhouses-exposed.

14. US Department of Agriculture, National Agricultural Statistics Service, *Poultry Slaughter 2019 Summary* (Washington, DC: USDA, NASS, 2020), 27.

15. Phoebe Galt, "24 Groups to Sec. Vilsack: Strengthen Packers & Stockyards Act," Food & Water Watch, January 30, 2023, https://www.foodandwaterwatch .org/2023/01/30/24-groups-to-sec-vilsack-strengthen-packers-stockyards-act.

16. Jose Carranza, "Why Are Workers at the Van Buren Tyson Plant Protesting?," 5News Online, April 10, 2023, https://www.5newsonline.com/article/news /community/protest-van-buren-tyson-plant-close-strike/527-258f11f3-a213-4415 -bb25-df0b746e9005.

17. James M. MacDonald, *Technology, Organization, and Financial Performance in U.S. Broiler Production* (Washington, DC: US Department of Agriculture, Economic Research Service, 2014), 15.

18. Daniel Croxall, "Let's Make Sure We Are Talking About the Same Things: Tied-House Laws and the Three-Tier System," *Craft Beer Law Prof* (blog), February 6, 2017, https://www.craftbeerprofessor.com/2017/02/lets-make-sure-talking -things-tied-house-laws-three-tier-system.

19. Ronnie Cohen, "First U.S. Soda Tax Cuts Consumption Beyond Expectations," Reuters Health, October 28, 2016, https://www.reuters.com/article/us -health-soda-tax/first-u-s-soda-tax-cuts-consumption-beyond-expectations -idUSKCN12S200.

20. Lucy Craymer, "New Zealand Announces Changes to Agricultural Emissions Scheme to Help Farmers," Reuters, December 20, 2022, https://www

.reuters.com/world/asia-pacific/new-zealand-announces-changes-agricultural
-emissions-scheme-help-farmers-2022-12-20.

21. "New Zealand's Plans for Agricultural Emissions Pricing," Organization
for Economic Co-operation and Development, last modified November 7, 2022,
https://www.oecd.org/climate-action/ipac/practices/new-zealand-s-plans-for
-agricultural-emissions-pricing-d4f4245c.

22. Franziska Funke et al., "Toward Optimal Meat Pricing: Is It Time to
Tax Meat Consumption?," *Review of Environmental Economics and Policy* 16, no. 2
(2022): 219–40.

23. Oxfam America, "Vulnerable Populations," in *Lives on the Line*, accessed
June 4, 2023, https://www.oxfamamerica.org/livesontheline.

24. Farm Action, "References: Federal Farm Subsidies," US farm subsidies pie
chart, accessed February 8, 2023, https://farmaction.us/subsidies-sources.

25. Seung Hee Lee et al., "Adults Meeting Fruit and Vegetable Intake Recommendations—United States, 2019," *Morbidity and Mortality Weekly Report* 71, no. 1
(January 2022): 1–9.

26. Lee et al., "Adults Meeting Fruit and Vegetable Intake Recommendations."

27. American Hospital Association, "Focus on Wellness," in *Health for Life*
(Washington, DC: American Hospital Association, 2007), 1.

28. US Government Accountability Office, USDA Market Facilitation
Program, *Oversight of Future Supplemental Assistance to Farmers Could Be Improved*
(Washington, DC: US Government Accountability Office, 2022), 3–4, 11–14.

29. Ximena Bustillo, "Black Farmers Call for Justice from the USDA," NPR,
February 12, 2023, https://www.npr.org/2023/02/12/1151731232/black-farmers
-call-for-justice-from-usda.

30. Farm Progress, "What Does the End of the Tobacco Buyout Mean?,"
November 27, 2013, https://www.farmprogress.com/management/what-does-the
-end-of-the-tobacco-buyout-mean-.

31. Nathan Bomey, "Thousands of Farmers Stopped Growing Tobacco After
Deregulation Payouts," *USA Today*, September 2, 2015, https://www.usatoday.com
/story/money/2015/09/02/thousands-farmers-stopped-growing-tobacco-after
-deregulation-payouts/32115163.

INDEX

Abrego, Ernesto, 139–42, 171
Abrego, Walter Ramon, 121–24, 127, 129
abuse, 19, 134, 138–39, 165. *See also* suffering; trauma
accountability, xix–xx, 8, 28, 136, 141, 160, 165–69
Addison, Corban, 110
advocacy work, 140–42. *See also* Mercy For Animals; Transfarmation Project (Mercy For Animals)
air pollution, 107–20
Alito, Samuel, 83
Allowed to Grow Old (Leshko), 93
American diet, 38–41, 47
animal law program, 96
animal liberation, 62–71, 95, 98–102. *See also* animal sanctuaries
animal sanctuaries, 84–87, 88–91, 92–96
Animal Welfare Act, 71
Animal Welfare Approved certification program, 98
animal welfare laws, 81–83, 89–91
animal welfare standards, 71–72, 98, 161–63
antibiotic resistance, xvi, 72, 73
antimicrobial resistance, 39
antitrust laws, 9, 27, 29
Ardern, Jacinda, 166
Armenta, Pablo, 125–26
armyworms, 16
asthma, 118
Autumn (cow), 102, 103

bacteria: human disease from, 12, 39, 72–73, 80, 102, 110, 123; in water, 50–51, 58. *See also* foodborne illness
Bannon, Shawn, 5, 115
Barrett, Amy Coney, 83, 90–91
Barrientos, Sandra, 121–24, 127, 129–30, 139
Batts, Rosemary, 107–17, 171
belonging, 52
Ben & Jerry's (company), 98
Berger, Jamie, 115
Better Chicken Commitment, 71, 162
Biden administration, 82, 90, 163–64
Big Animal Agriculture. *See* industrial animal agriculture, overview
Billy Idol (duck), 95
Bishop, Timothy, 82
Black communities, xvii–xviii, 82, 107–20
Black workers in slaughterhouses, 125
blunt force trauma, 135
Boles, Dale, 32, 37, 41–42, 44
Boles, Paula, 32–36, 41–44, 171
Bollard, Lewis, 90, 162
Bomey, Nathan, 38
Booker, Cory, xix, xx, 21, 39, 98, 167, 170
brain drain, 52
Bridges, Ruby, 108
Brown v. the Board of Education of Topeka, 108
Bruno (chicken), 66–71, 75
buffalo, 46
bullying, 152

Burmese refugees, 144. *See also* refugee workforce
Bush administration (G. W. B.), 38, 39
Butler, Tom, 53, 54, 56–57, 118–19
Butler, Will, 56–57, 118–19
Butz, Earl, 110
buyout programs, 38–39. *See also* government subsidies
by-product of animal farming. *See* waste from hog farming

CAFOs (concentrated animal feeding operations), xvii, xix, 111. *See also* industrial animal agriculture, overview
Calamuci, Daniel, 127
California, 81, 82
Campaign for Contract Agriculture Reform (CCAR), 28
campylobacter, 39, 72–73
cancer, 44, 119
carcinogenics, 39
Cargill (company), 27–29, 133
Carmen, 129, 135–39
Carolina Mushroom, 20
Carolina Reapers, 34
cattle farming: by Abrego, 122; contract system in, 9; by Halley family, 10; process of, 122; rescued animals from, 96, 98–101, 103–4. *See also* dairy industry; slaughterhouses
CBD, 15, 18
centennial farm, 53
Center for Economic and Policy Research, 135
Centers for Disease Control and Prevention, 18, 135–37
cesspools. *See* waste from hog farming
chicken farming, xi–xii; of Boles family, 41–42; contract-based, xix; COVID-19 and, xvi; debt of, xx; of Halley family, 3–5, 6–7, 10, 11–14; humane laws on, 71; industry statistics of, 8, 24–25; by Lim family, 149–55; rescued animals from, 6, 62–71; statistics on, 147; suffering and, 62; volume of,

10–11; work-related injuries from, 12. *See also* egg production industry; industrial animal agriculture, overview; slaughterhouses
child labor, 12, 14, 133–34
Chiquita (company), 137
chronic disease epidemics, xvi
citizenship, 139, 144. *See also* undocumented workers
Civil Eats, xvii
Clarkson, Georgia, 143–44
cleaning services in industrial animal work, 133–34, 137
climate change, xvi, xxi, 51
cockfighting, 94
complex, as term, 11
consumption and price relationship, 38–41
contract labor systems, xix, 8–9, 27–28, 41–42, 56, 110, 133, 144. *See also* cattle farming; chicken farming; hog farming; slaughterhouses
corn earworm, 16
corn farming, 31, 32, 46, 50
COVID-19 pandemic, xv–xvi, xxi, 9, 40–41, 62, 135–37, 153
cows. *See* cattle farming; dairy industry; Norma (cow)
coyotes (smugglers), 131, 133, 134
cucumber farming, 23, 24, 35, 36, 43, 108

Dairy Farmers of Canada, 97
dairy industry, 97–98, 99, 102. *See also* cattle farming
Danone (company), 98
Dead Zone, 51
Deany, Ashby, 16
Deany, Devvie, 3–5, 6–7
Deany, Evan, 3–4, 11, 12–13, 14, 16, 17, 18
Deany, Morgan, 16, 17
debt: of Boles family, 41–42; of Butler family, 56; factory farming industry and, xx, 21, 23; of Halley family, 3, 7, 13; of Watts, 22–23, 147, 158. *See also* poverty

Defense Production Act, 136
deforestation, xiii–xiv, xvi
DeLauro, Rosa, xx
Delmarva Peninsula, 94
Denison, Iowa, 122, 125, 127–28, 135, 139, 141
diarrheal diseases, 72–73
diet, 38–41, 47
disease: bacteria-related, 12, 39, 66, 72–73, 80, 102, 110, 123; cancers, 44, 119; in chickens, 13; COVID-19 and pandemics, xv–xvi, 135–37; in cows, 103; due to hog CAFOs, 112–14; from meat consumption, 39; in pigs, 40; respiratory-related, xvii, 68, 70, 113, 118, 119, 141. *See also* suffering; work-related injuries
disposability of workers, 126–29, 141. *See also* work-related injuries
dog rescue and rehabilitation, 3, 11, 18–19
Donaldson, Sue, 93
donkey sanctuary, 19
Dove, Rick, 145–46
downer cow syndrome, 103
duck, 95
dysentery, 72

Eastern Shore Sanctuary, 94. *See also* animal sanctuaries
ecofeminism, 93, 94–95
Economic Policy Institute (EPI), 144
economic recessions, 40
egg production industry, 38, 39, 94, 137, 162, 164, 165, 168. *See also* chicken farming
El Salvador, 121, 133, 139
environmental impacts, overview, xiii–xiv, xvi, 166–67. *See also* air pollution; waste from hog farming; water pollution
environmental racism, xvii–xviii, 107–20
Environmental Working Group (EWG), 41
Environment Programme (United Nations), xx

Equity Commission (USDA), 170
Eritrean refugees, 144. *See also* refugee workforce

Faaborg, Tanner, 46, 47–52, 58, 159, 161
Faaborg family, 45–49, 57–58
factory farming. *See* chicken farming; hog farming; industrial animal agriculture, overview
Fair and Equitable Tobacco Reform Act, 38, 39
Farm Action, 25, 169
Farm Bill, 160, 167
"Farmed Animal Sanctuaries: The Heart of the Movement?" (Donaldson and Kymlicka), 93
farming alternatives, overview, xiv–xv, 21–25. *See also* hemp farming; mushroom farming
Farm System Reform Act (proposed), xix–xx, 21–22, 39, 167
farrowing crates, 86
Felix (pig), 86, 87–91
feminism, 93, 94–95
fertilizer, 50, 109, 111. *See also* waste from hog farming
FFH (Future Farmers of America), 100
fibromyalgia, 138
Finland, 99
flip-over syndrome, 42, 76–77
Food and Agriculture Organization (United Nations), xv
foodborne illness, 39, 72–73. *See also* bacteria; disease
Food Not Feed Summit, 160
food poisoning, 39
Food Safety and Inspection Service, 164
Food & Water Watch, 47
4-H, 49, 100–101
Frasier, Kevin, 25–26
Fudge, Marcia L., xx

Gates, Bill, xvi
generational land inheritance, xi, xiii, 53, 56, 115

Georgia, 143–44, 147
gestation crates, 80–81, 83, 86, 90, 134
ghost peppers, 34, 37
Global Animal Partnership certification program, 98, 99
Global Village Project, 144
"going-down," 102–3
Gorsuch, Neil, 83, 90
government subsidies, 21, 22, 38, 40–41, 96–98, 169
Great Migration, 108, 116
greenhouse gas emissions, xiii, 166–67
Gulf of Mexico, 51

Halley, Bo, 3, 7, 12, 13–14, 17, 18
Halley, Sam, 3 , 7, 12, 14, 17
Halley family, 3–5, 6–7, 10–19
Han Farms, 148
harassment, 134, 138–39, 152
Harding, Warren, 8
Haw River Mushrooms, 155, 157
health effects of meat consumption, 39. See also disease
hemp farming, xiv, 4, 12, 14–19, 23, 24, 36, 62
Henrietta (hen), 6, 66–71, 73–78
Herring, Elsie, 115–17, 119, 120, 159, 171
Highland Economics, 23, 34, 35
Hispanic Project, 125–26
Hmong refugees, 151–54. See also refugee workforce
hog farming: of Barrientos, 121–24; by-product of, 54, 58, 80, 109–13, 145; contract-based, xix, 56; of Faaborg family, 45–50, 57–58; in North Carolina, 53–55, 145; pig rescue from, 84–87; process of, 54–55, 86; suffering in, 80–81, 131–32, 134–35; Supreme Court case on, 81–84, 89–91. See also Felix (pig); slaughterhouses
Honduras, 137
House Bill 1325 (2019), 15
Humane Methods of Slaughter Act, 71, 168
Hurricane Florence, 79–80, 84

Hurricane Floyd, 80, 84
hypoxia, 51

IBISWorld, 38, 171
ICE (Immigration and Customs Enforcement), 126
illness. See disease
immigrant workforce, 121–42. See also refugee workforce
immigration raids, 126–27
Industrial Agriculture Accountability (IAA) Act, 167–68, 169
industrial animal agriculture, overview, xii–xv, xvi–xvii, 6–9, 38, 46, 126–27. See also cattle farming; chicken farming; hog farming
infant mortality, 113
injuries. See work-related injuries
insanity, 81
institutional racism, xvii–xviii
Iowa, 47, 50–51. See also Denison, Iowa
Iowa Select, 45
Iraqi refugees, 144. See also refugee workforce
Ireland, 99

Jackson, Ketanji Brown, 83, 90
JBS (company), 8, 24, 133
Jernigan, Katherine, 57, 154
Jewel, Jesse, 6
jones, pattrice, 93–96, 101, 102

Kagan, Elena, 82, 83, 90
Kavanaugh, Brett, 83
Khmer refugees, 149–55. See also refugee workforce
King, Martin Luther, Jr., 120
King, Steve, 128
Klein, Ezra, xix
Kneedler, Edwin S., 82
Koch Foods, 138–39
Ku Klux Klan, 109
Kymlicka, Will, 93

labor standards, 163–66
labor union organization, 125, 127

lagoons, 54, 58, 80, 110–13, 145–47.
    See also waste from hog farming
land inheritance, xi, xiii, 53, 56, 115
The Latehomecomer (Yang), 151–52
Latinx immigrant workers, 121–27.
    See also immigrant workforce
lavada work, 133–34
Leshko, Isa, 93
Leticia, 129, 130–32
Licolli, Magaly, 141
Lim, Tom, 149–55, 159
lion's mane mushrooms, 23, 26. *See
    also* mushroom farming
livestock production tax, 166
Lovato, Erika, 84–88
low-income rural communities,
    xvii–xviii
lung ailments, xvii. *See also* disease
Luter, Joseph, III, 110

manufacturing of consent, xx
Maple Leaf (company), 133
Marisol, 129, 133–35
mastitis, 101, 102, 103
Maxwell, Joe, 25
McGovern, Jim, 167
McKitterick, Will, 38
meat consumption and price relation-
    ship, 38–41
Meatonomics (Simon), 38–39
meatpacking. *See* industrial an-
    imal agriculture, overview;
    slaughterhouses
meat taxes, 39, 166–67
Mekki, Doha, 29
Mercy For Animals, xviii–xix, 14, 46,
    159. *See also* Transfarmation Proj-
    ect (Mercy For Animals)
microgreen production, 23, 24, 34–35,
    36, 43, 171
migra, 131
migration stories, 121–22, 130–31,
    133, 137, 151–52. *See also* immi-
    grant workforce
Miller, René, 113–17, 119, 159, 160
Ming Farms, 148
Miriam, 94–95

Mississippi, 125–26
monoculture, 46
moral injury, 135
morality, 81–83, 89–91
moratorium on factory farming,
    170–72
Mountaire (company), 146, 148
Murphy, Wendell H., 110–11, 145
Murphy's of Iowa, 49–50
Muscovy duck, 95
mushroom farming: by Butler family,
    56–57, 58; by Morgan Deany, 16;
    economic profit statistics from,
    36; by Faaborg family, 52, 58; by
    Tom Lim, 154–55; specialty types,
    defined, 23; by Craig Watts, 20,
    23–27, 30–31, 156–58, 171
Muyuan Foodstuff Co., Ltd., 54

NAFTA, 97
National Antimicrobial Resistance
    Monitoring System (NARMS), 73
National Chicken Council, 24
National Pork Producers Council,
    81–84
National Pork Producers Council v. Ross,
    81–84
National Rural Health Association, 98
Native Americans, 53
nesting, 54, 80–81, 86–87
New Swine Inspection System, 164
New Zealand, 166
Nina (cow), 100, 101, 103, 104
Nineteenth Amendment, 22
nitrates, 50, 51
Nixon administration, 110
Norma (cow), 96, 98–101, 103–4
North Carolina, xvii, xix, 38, 79–80,
    112–13, 147. *See also* Black
    communities
Norway, 99

Obama administration, 10
Open Philanthropy, 162
*Open Philanthropy Farm Animal Welfare
    Newsletter*, 90
organic certification, 34

Oxfam, 144
oyster mushrooms, 23. *See also* mushroom farming

Packers and Stockyards Act (1921), 8, 165
Packers Sanitation Services, Inc., 133
pancreatic cancer, 119
pandemic, xv–xvi, xvi
Parker family, 107–8
Pella (company), 135
Perdue (company), xi, 8
PETA (People for the Ethical Treatment of Animals), 97
phosphorus, 51
physical abuse, 134
pig behavior, 86–87, 88–89
pigs. *See* Felix (pig); hog farming
pig sanctuary, 84–87, 88–91. *See also* animal sanctuaries
Pilgrim, Aubrey and Bo, 5–6
Pilgrim's Pride (company), 3, 5–6, 7, 10, 24, 143–44
pollution. *See* air pollution; waste from hog farming; water pollution
pork. *See* hog farming
poverty, 21, 152. *See also* debt
product bans, 82
Proposition 12 (California), 81–84, 89–90, 163
PTSD (post-traumatic stress disorder), 135. *See also* suffering; trauma
Purington, Joseph, 84–88

racial inequity, xvi, xvii–xviii
racial integration, 108–9
Reagan administration, 9
refugee workforce, xviii, 143–55. *See also* immigrant workforce
reishi mushrooms, 23. *See also* mushroom farming
reproductive freedom, 95–96
respiratory ailments, xvii, 68, 70, 113, 118, 119, 141
Roberts, John, 83
Roecker, Randy, 98

rooster rehabilitation, 94
Rose (cow), 102
Rural Empowerment Association for Community Help (REACH), 114
rural renewal trend, 52–53

Safe Line Speeds in COVID-19 Act (proposed), xx
sanctuaries. *See* animal sanctuaries
Sanders, Bernie, xx, 21
Sanderson Farms (company), 8, 24, 27–29, 146, 148
Sandra, 139
Saura, 53
school integration, 108–9
Scottish immigrants, 53
selective breeding practices, 55
sexual abuse, 134, 138–39. *See also* abuse
Shakira (chicken), 66–71, 75, 78
sharecropping, 108
shiitake mushrooms, 20, 23, 156. *See also* mushroom farming
Shuanghui International Holdings, 111
Simon, David Robinson, 38
sinusitis, 113
Sisu Refuge, 84–87, 88–91. *See also* animal sanctuaries
slaughterhouses, xvi–xviii, 10–11; Abrego's advocacy work against, 140–42; noncitizens and, 126–27, 144; worker recruitment techniques for, 125–26, 143–44; working conditions in, 27–29, 41, 122–24, 126–39, 141, 164. *See also* cattle farming; chicken farming; hog farming; industrial animal agriculture, overview
slavery, 82, 107–8, 115, 143
The Smell of Money (film), 115, 117–18
Smithfield Foods, xvi, 49, 54, 85, 111, 116–17, 136, 138
Socially Responsible Agriculture Project (SRAP), 23
soda tax, 39, 166, 167
Sokchea, 149, 150

solar power, 51–52
Somalian refugees, 144. *See also* refugee workforce
Sotomayor, Sonia, 82, 83, 90
specialty mushrooms. *See* mushroom farming
Stalling, Immanuel, 115
Stalling, Marshall, 115
strawberry farming, 23, 24, 35, 108
Stuesse, Angela, 125
subsidies, 21, 22, 38, 40–41, 96–98, 169
Sudanese refugees, 144. *See also* refugee workforce
suffering: of chickens, 62–64, 68–71; of pigs, 57–58, 80–81, 86–87; of slaughterhouse workers, 121–24, 131–35, 138. *See also* abuse; disease; trauma; work-related injuries
suffrage, 22, 128–29
suicide, 18, 98, 134
Supreme Court cases, 81–84, 89–91, 108
Sweden, 99
Sweet Farms, 148

taxation, 39, 166–67
Teachey, Emily Stalling, 115–16
Texas Department of Agriculture, 15
THC, 15
Thomas, Clarence, 83, 90
Thompson, Bennie, xx
thyroid ailments, 139
tobacco, 37–38, 54, 108, 167, 171
Tobacco Master Settlement Agreement, 37
Tobacco Transition Payment Program, 38, 171
Tom, 149–55
tomato farming, 23, 24, 33, 34, 35, 36, 43, 69
transfarmation, overview, xi–xii, viii–xxi
Transfarmation Hubs, 159
Transfarmation Project (Mercy For Animals), xviii–xix, 4, 21, 23, 32, 43, 61, 152, 158–61

trauma, 134–35. *See also* abuse; slaughterhouses; suffering; work-related injuries
Trump administration, 136, 163
Tuscarora, 53
Twenty-Eight Hour Law, 71
Tyson Foods (company), 8–9, 10–11, 24, 41–42, 133, 165

undocumented workers, 126–28, 131, 133–34. *See also* citizenship
union organization, 125, 127
United Food and Commercial Workers, 127, 164
United Kingdom, 99
United Nations, xv, xvi, xx
US Bureau of Labor Statistics, 127
US Census Bureau, 124
US Department of Agriculture (USDA), 23, 27, 41, 110, 162, 170
US Department of Justice, 9, 10, 25, 27
US Department of Labor, 133

veganism, xix, 3, 56, 72, 93, 135, 140
Venceremos, 141
Vermont, 92, 97
Vermont Law School, 96
vertical integration, 6
Victors' Village Farms, 31
Vietnam War, 151
Vilsack, Tom, 10
VINE Sanctuary, 93–96, 100. *See also* animal sanctuaries
voting rights, 22, 128–29

Warnock, Raphael, 170
Warren, Elizabeth, xx, 21
waste from hog farming, 50–51, 54, 57, 58, 80, 109–13, 145–47. *See also* water pollution
Wastelands (Addison), 110
Waterkeeper Alliance, 145, 148
water pollution, 50–51, 58, 80, 112. *See also* waste from hog farming
Watts, Craig: author's partnership with, xi–xii, xiii, 158; chicken farming by,

xi–xii, 20, 21, 31; debt of, 22–23,
147, 158; mushroom farming of,
20, 23–27, 30–31, 156–58, 171;
2016 video of, xii, 3, 14, 23, 32
Wayne Farms, 24, 27–29
Weaver, Mike, xiv, 3–4, 14
Wens Group, 54
WH Group, 111
white supremacy, 116, 128. *See also*
environmental racism; slavery
Whitley, Tyler, 32–33, 36, 52, 148–49,
150–52, 154, 159
Whittaker, William, 125, 126
wildlife extinction, xiv
William Frantz Elementary School,
108–9
Winders, Delcianna, 96–98
Wing, Steve, 111, 112

women's suffrage, 22
worker recruitment techniques,
125–26, 143–44
worker's compensation, 27, 123–24,
136, 168
Working Lands program, 98
work-related injuries, 12, 13, 122–24,
131–32, 138. *See also* disease; disposability of workers; suffering
World Health Organization, 39
World Trade Organization, 97
Wylie, Cheryl, 100

Yang, Kao Kalia, 151–52
Yang Farms, 148

zinnia flower farming, 33, 34
zoonotic diseases, 39, 40

ABOUT THE AUTHOR

LEAH GARCÉS is a dedicated and influential advocate for animal rights and sustainable food systems. She is the CEO and president of Mercy For Animals and author of *Grilled: Turning Adversaries into Allies to Change the Chicken Industry*, with over twenty years of leadership experience in the animal protection movement. She has partnered with corporations, communities, and governments on her mission to build a better food system.

Garcés is the founder of the Transfarmation Project, an initiative working to transition factory farmers away from industrial animal agriculture and into alternative means of income such as mushroom and microgreen production. She oversaw international campaigns in fourteen countries at the World Society for the Protection of Animals and launched the US branch of Compassion in World Farming. Her work has been featured in many national and international media outlets, and she has presented at global forums including TED, RIO+10, and the World Health Organization's Global Forum for Health Research. Garcés was proud to be named in the "Vox's Future Perfect 50" list in 2022, alongside scientists, activists, scholars, and writers working to build a better future for us all. She lives in Decatur, Georgia, with her spouse, three kids, cat, and two ferrets.